PRAISE FOR *THE WELL-SPOKEN WOMAN*

"From the time when women speakers were pummeled with rotten tomatoes up until today, relatively few women have succeeded in the public sphere. *The Well-Spoken Woman*, cleverly and brilliantly, helps women find their own out-front voice. Jahnke has provided women a great service."

—Joan Wages, president and CEO,
National Women's History Museum

D0249919

THE
WELL-SPOKEN
WOMAN

THE
WELL-SPOKEN
WOMAN

Your Guide to Looking and Sounding Your Best

CHRISTINE K. JAHNKE

 Prometheus Books

59 John Glenn Drive
Amherst, New York 14228-2119

Published 2011 by Prometheus Books

The Well-Spoken Woman: Your Guide to Looking and Sounding Your Best. Copyright © 2011 by Christine K. Jahnke. All rights reserved. No part of this publication may be reproduced, stored in a retrieval system, or transmitted in any form or by any means, digital, electronic, mechanical, photocopying, recording, or otherwise, or conveyed via the Internet or a website without prior written permission of the publisher, except in the case of brief quotations embodied in critical articles and reviews.

Trademarks: In an effort to acknowledge trademarked names of products mentioned in this work, we have placed ® or ™ after the product name in the first instance of its use in each chapter. Subsequent mentions of the name within a given chapter appear without the symbol.

Cover design by Grace M. Conti-Zilsberger
Cover illustration © Kersti Frigell

Inquiries should be addressed to
Prometheus Books
59 John Glenn Drive
Amherst, New York 14228–2119
VOICE: 716–691–0133
FAX: 716–691–0137
WWW.PROMETHEUSBOOKS.COM

15 14   5

Library of Congress Cataloging-in-Publication Data

Jahnke, Christine K., 1963–
    The well-spoken woman : your guide to looking and sounding your best / by Christine K. Jahnke.
        p. cm.
    Includes bibliographical references and index.
    ISBN 978–1–61614–462–3 (pbk. : alk. paper)
    ISBN 978–1–61614–463–0 (ebook)
    1. Public speaking for women. I. Title.

PN4192.W65J35 2011
808.5'1082—dc23

2011019049

Printed in the United States of America on acid-free paper

For Madam President

CONTENTS

PART 4: THE FINISHING TOUCHES

FOREWORD

by Barbara Lee

Growing up, I was the shy girl who wouldn't raise her hand in school—even to ask permission to use the bathroom. Whenever I was called on to speak in class I felt overwhelmed. Flustered, I would feel my face turning warm and redness creeping into my cheeks. I was always relieved when the experience was over.

Decades later, in 2000, I took the stage at the historic Million Mom March in Washington, DC, to stand up against gun violence and advocate for safer communities for America's children. The crowd was passionate, energetic—and enormous. But this experience wasn't overwhelming. It was exhilarating.

What made it possible for a once timid girl to speak to a million people? Certainly, maturity and confidence had something to do with it. But at the core of that speech—and my own journey to becoming a well-spoken woman—was hard work, determination, and the expert guidance of Chris Jahnke.

I first met Chris in the late 1990s after co-founding the White House Project with Laura Liswood and Marie Wilson. Chris worked to prepare us for the public launch of our project. I spoke at the kickoff press conference at the National Press Club in Washington, DC, and I clearly remember Chris's encouraging nods from the audience as I delivered my remarks. It was the first time I had spoken to a group of people outside my own home.

Soon after, I founded the Barbara Lee Family Foundation with the goal of advancing women's equality and representation in two areas that are my passions: American politics and contemporary art. As I prepared to launch my second major project, Chris continued to help me develop my voice, craft my message, refine my style, and ultimately become more effective in communicating the mission of my work.

Chris gave me two critical pieces of advice when we began working together. First, she explained that while some people are born public speakers—like the great Governor Ann Richards, profiled in this book—most of us are not. But, she said, *anyone* can make significant improvement—as much as 85 percent. Second, Chris told me that improving as a public speaker takes work, and lots of it. As you'll learn in this book, preparation is key for everyone—even Governor Richards.

Chris is truly passionate about helping women convey their most confident selves in person and in front of the camera. Her passion comes from her understanding of a phenomenon that my foundation has researched for more than a decade: Men's voices and opinions dominate our news, our policy debates, and our political discourse.

Of course, we all know of women who excel as communicators and who make their voices heard. The women featured in this book are unbeatable examples of verbal style, presence, and skill. But my foundation's research on women's gubernatorial campaigns shows that, overall, women candidates struggle to appear comfortable and confident when speaking in public. What's more, voters and the media evaluate women on the campaign trail differently than they evaluate men on dozens of measures, from debate performance, to image, to competence. Women are simply held to a different standard.

Debates are a particular challenge. Women candidates often view political debates as "high-risk" events rather than opportunities to communicate and score points with voters. Debates can become a focal point for anxiety, requiring hours of preparation time and coaching, and meticulous policy papers and briefing books. The overall effect is that while some women candidates perform well, conveying competence and confidence in debates, they often do not project enough likeability or warmth. This is a serious liability for women in campaigns, since debates continue to be an important source of information for voters. And communicating confidence is key to demonstrating leadership.

In today's culture of reality television, it is also more important than ever for women to hone their public image. My research shows that nowadays voters expect candidates not only to be qualified for public office but also to entertain and perform. This is potentially dangerous territory for women who have to work harder to prove themselves as "serious" candidates in the first place. Of course, voters usually assume that male candidates are both serious *and* qualified.

Women candidates must develop an additional skill set to meet these challenges. But in a world in which men dominate public discourse, these challenges aren't specific to candidates and campaigns. *All* women need the skills to communicate with confidence and poise. That is the focus of *The Well-Spoken Woman*. Using examples and advice from women of power, toughness, and plain old-fashioned audacity, Chris Jahnke provides a comprehensive, hands-on guide for women who want to make their voices heard.

I hope this book inspires you as Chris continues to inspire me.

Barbara Lee
Founder and President
The Barbara Lee Family Foundation

INTRODUCTION

Does this speech make my butt look fat? Endless zany obsessions can race through your mind before a presentation. The answer to that specific question is no, a speech will not make your butt look fat. However, on-camera appearances are another matter. What you have likely heard is true. A TV camera can add as many as fifteen pounds.

Whatever may be on your mind—your appearance or something else—this book is about traversing the minefield of questions, worries, and dilemmas that can prevent you from delivering your best in person and on camera. Everyone has a nightmare story about the fear of speaking in public. Have you felt the sensation that your ankles are going to shatter as you shakily make your way to the podium? At one time or another, we have all felt vulnerable standing in front of an audience. This book is meant to help you stop second-guessing, undervaluing, or falling short with your speaking abilities.

The well-spoken women profiled here faced similar obstacles on the path to becoming masterful presenters. You will learn from women who have been there and learned how to pick themselves up and brush themselves off. By examining their stories of trial and triumph we will answer the questions "How did she do it?" and "What can I learn from her?" You will gain the skills and knowledge to earn a standing ovation.

Now, you may be wondering: "Who are these women?" Sarah Palin is an entertaining presenter who speaks with candor and humor. Is she well-spoken? What about the widely respected CEO of PepsiCo, Indra Nooyi? The outspoken Nooyi gave "the finger" to graduates and their well-wishers during a commencement address at Columbia University. Does giving the finger disqualify her? Perhaps personal finance guru Suze Orman fits the bill. Millions trust her money management advice. Former member of Congress Barbara Jordan is remembered as the "voice of God." Certainly, she must meet the criteria.

The well-spoken women featured in this book are a cross section of Americans who have used their voices to enrich and expand our national dialogue. They speak to express ideas, create change, ignite imaginations, coach teams to victory, and argue against injustice. They aren't professional communicators schooled in broadcast journalism or drama and didn't dream of becoming celebrities like Oprah Winfrey or Meryl Streep. Yet, they have much to teach us about using the old-fashioned art of public speaking to excel in a wired world. As communications channels continue to expand, these women demonstrate core skills you can use to engage audiences near and far.

ISO MORE WOMEN SPEAKERS

This book is a heartfelt effort to help more women find and use their voices. My aim is to share what I've learned from twenty years of prepping women speakers from every walk of life. As an adviser to Hillary Clinton's presidential campaign, I witnessed how some women with the audacity to venture into the public square are not well received. In the historic 2008 campaign, Clinton and Palin represented the full spectrum of women's views. Their philosophies and speaking styles could not have been more dissimilar. Both, however, were disparaged with sexist labels and demeaning stereotypes.

A recent study about the speaking challenges faced by women law school students serves as another wake-up call. At Yale Law School, women revealed that they are much less likely to speak up in class than their male counterparts. Nearly 90 percent of female survey respondents agreed with the following: "Male students tend to have more confidence in themselves as public speakers and feel more comfortable speaking in large classes, even when the point they are making is minor."[1]

This hesitation and uncertainty is not confined to students. Nor is sexism directed only at women in politics. In corporate suites, women don't move up if they've "screwed" up. Often, the trickiest business is figuring out what constitutes a screwup. Leaders take charge, but a woman with a dominant style can be viewed as too abrasive or pushy. The glass ceiling is cracked, yet women still wage battles against sexism, outdated notions of leadership, low self-esteem, and stage fright. These age-old challenges were dealt with by the women who first dared to buck convention. Susan B. Anthony was not deterred by the officials—all men—who scoffed at her demands for the vote. In fact, the open condescension she endured inspired the suffragist to organize a sisterhood of action.

IT'S A GIRL THING

By focusing on women, I have no intent to exclude men. They can gain from the book, and I invite you to share the tips with family and friends, male and female. But the male voice still dominates the public square. As long as women remain a vocal minority in corporate boardrooms, on TV talk shows, and in the halls of Congress, we pay the price of being voiceless. The world needs well-spoken women to state opinions in every venue from PTA meetings to presidential debates. It is not that a woman's perspective is better. What matters is that it is different.

As a speech coach I try to help women articulate their unique perspective. For some, this comes more naturally; for others, it is easier said than done. Think about your last presentation. How much of yourself did you bring to it? Or did you psych yourself out with negative self-talk before you opened your mouth? Even the most accomplished have white-knuckled their way through presentations before unfamiliar crowds. How much thought have you given to how you might improve? Do you focus on the professional development of colleagues, leaving yourself out? Maybe you are skilled but are coasting on your ability to get by.

YES, YOU CAN!

The ten well-spoken women whom I have selected as role models provide guidance on every aspect of looking and sounding good. The practical advice in this book will help you successfully navigate difficult audiences and excel in a new media environment. Public speaking is no longer limited to standing behind a lectern or next to a PowerPoint® screen. This book shows the way to achieve excellence before Internet, TV, and live audiences. The "what to do" strategies will be contrasted with "what not to" examples of the biggest blunders. Each chapter features a well-spoken woman who has mastered a particular technique or practice. You will learn from the best of the best.

THE TALENTS OF WELL-SPOKEN WOMEN

Chapter 1: Ann Richards—Your Best Self

Governor Ann Richards had it all—Texas-sized hair, a quick wit, and deep conviction. Her bigger-than-life personality embodied the well-spoken woman's Power Persona, a persona that helped her deliver her best. The Power Persona is made up of the enduring traits shared by the speakers who consistently deliver outstanding performances. These traits are the foundation on which you can build a distinctive style.

Chapter 2: Indra Nooyi—Take-Charge Confidence

PepsiCo's Indra Nooyi didn't reach the top echelons of corporate America by second-guessing her decisions and keeping mum about her accomplishments. Nooyi is a remarkably candid CEO who isn't afraid to speak her mind. An immigrant who graduated from the Yale Management School without the cash to buy an interview suit, Nooyi solved the clothing dilemma by embracing her East Indian culture. Nooyi demonstrates how you can assert your authentic self to slay the imposter dragons.

Chapter 3: Barbara Jordan—Voice of Authority

Do you speak with the power of Minnie Mouse? If so, your voice is the weak link in your presentation style. Projecting well doesn't require the resonance of cable TV host Rachel Maddow or the range of Mariah Carey. But, to be a contender, you must sound like an authority. Barbara Jordan's speaking ability was unparalleled. When Jordan spoke, audiences reported it was if the gates of heaven had opened. As the voice of moral authority, she stirred our nation to higher ideals during the Watergate hearings. With this chapter's practice exercises, you will be able to voice your ideas with eloquence and power.

Chapter 4: Pat Summitt—All the Right Moves

If you've been getting feedback that your delivery style needs work, maybe, just maybe, there is something to the critique. The world's most successful basketball coach has learned over her thirty-year career that her style, which has produced winning teams, can also be too demanding. Without question, Pat Summitt's toughness and discipline have enabled her to excel at the University of Tennessee. However, when the coach turned the practice camera on herself, she didn't like everything she saw. Learn how to project podium presence by developing the body language of a champion.

Chapter 5: Melinda Gates—Strategic Messaging

Melinda Gates takes messaging seriously when it comes to tackling the issue of global health. Through the Bill and Melinda Gates Foundation's Living Proof Project, she is debunking widely held misperceptions about the impact of foreign aid on eradicating disease and saving lives. The most effective advocates understand that a vague sense of vision is not sufficient. They purposefully use strategic messaging to excite an audience and elicit a response. A written strategy will enable you to articulate a plan and achieve goals.

Chapter 6: Elizabeth Dole—Preplanned Spontaneity

Procrastination and last-minute scrambling can create unexpected nervousness or ratchet up an already high level of anxiety. Stop putting yourself in the position of frantically jotting notes in the cab or pulling out last year's presentation the night before. Well-executed performances are not produced by waving a magic wand. A former American Red Cross executive and US senator, Elizabeth Dole is a consummate professional who is always prime-time ready. "Preplanned spontaneity" is an approach that will help you prepare for when things go right—and when they go wrong.

Chapter 7: Maya Angelou—Words Matter

Speech writing may seem like something that's necessary only for ceremonial occasions or formal events. In fact, organizing your thoughts on paper is essential whether you are delivering a keynote address, making a toast, or giving a briefing. If you don't write it first, you won't be able to say it nearly as well. Maya Angelou believes each one of us is born with a spark and we need to let it shine. This evocative performer demonstrates how to incorporate creative writing, music, and dance to breathe new life into a speech's organization and content. With Angelou's inspiration, you will learn how to turn a humdrum presentation into one that will leave a commanding lasting impression.

Chapter 8: Suze Orman—On-Camera Savvy

We are a shoot-and-share camera nation. With the rise of digital media, there is no escaping the need for on-camera delivery skills. With her signature look and no-nonsense advice, the people's financial adviser isn't your typical cable TV host. Suze Orman is an accessible personality who projects her best self on camera and off. This chapter demystifies the camera with specific tips on how to sit, where to look, and what to wear. These techniques put you in the driver's seat so you can present a polished, professional on-screen image.

Chapter 9: Madeleine Albright—Charming Troublemakers

Not every audience is going to take what you say at face value or be satisfied with weak, mumbling responses. Be ready for troublemakers with a hidden agenda who may attempt to sabotage your presentation, and be prepared for news reporters with unexpected or biased questions. Former secretary of state Madeleine Albright provides a how-to on handling indifferent, skeptical, or even hostile audiences. Learn how Albright went toe-to-toe with foreign leaders, charming them with her wit and firm resolve.

Chapter 10: Hillary Clinton—Podium Presence

Hillary Clinton has evolved from a so-so presenter to a leader with an international podium presence. The great ones don't get there alone. Behind every strong woman is a ready and able support team. The women who are generous acknowledge the backstage team that helped them to soar. The final chapter offers insights on what each of us can do to lend a hand to our sisters, daughters, mothers, colleagues, and friends so they can be well-spoken, too.

ALL HAIL THE WELL-SPOKEN

Along with providing skill-building tips, this book celebrates the speaking achievements of amazing women. It is time to acknowledge that America's well-spoken women have earned a place in history. What would be more fitting than a monument to recognize great women speakers? I suggest something with the scale and magnificence of Mount Rushmore. Since we have not yet elected a woman to the White House, Mount Rushmore II could immortalize women whose powerful voices have achieved greatness. Women like Margaret Chase Smith, who was the lone woman serving in the US Senate when she denounced McCarthyism. The humanitarian Eleanor Roosevelt, who step-by-step overcame the fear of speaking in public. Special Olympics founder Eunice Kennedy Shriver, who opened the first World Games in 1968 with this message to the athletes and their parents: "Let me win, but if I cannot win, let me be brave in the attempt."

The conversation about whose likeness should be carved in mountain granite would certainly be a lively one. Whom would you choose? Narrowing the list to just a few would be a difficult task, so perhaps a national referendum should be held to select from the many possible candidates.

The list of ten well-spoken women featured in this book could easily have been multiplied by a hundred.

Read on to learn how to carry yourself like a leader and present your ideas with clarity.

The Well-Spoken Woman can be you.

PART 1

THE WHOLE YOU

1

THE WELL-SPOKEN \
PERSONA

> If you give us a chance, we can perform. After all, Ginger Rogers did every-
> thing that Fred Astaire did. She just did it backwards and in high heels.
> —Ann Richards
> Democratic National Convention, 1988 Keynote Address

The sassiness of the Ginger Rogers line was laugh-out-loud funny. It was a heads-up to the audience to fasten their seat belts, for what lay ahead wasn't going to be a typical political speech. Never before had a woman of a certain age addressed the country with such bravado, panache, and heartfelt conviction on live TV. The appearance set a new standard for outstanding performances and propelled the speaker from obscurity into the national limelight. Ann Richards was an overnight sensation, forty years in the making. It was a grand introduction, yet quintessential Ann.

This is a book about women who became great speakers, and it is a guide for you. You may not picture yourself standing before a multitude, but we are all asked at some point to stand up and say a few words. With this guidebook, the next time doesn't have to put you in a cold sweat. You will know what you need to do to prepare for a speaking opportunity, whether it is a staff meeting, panel discussion, local TV interview, or mentor's retirement ceremony. Notice the word *opportunity* is used to describe these events. With the right preparation and practice, you will acquire the techniques to master every in-person or on-camera appearance. When you believe in your ability to say what you want to say, then the occasion becomes a positive experience. You will be able to look back on a pleasant memory and congratulate yourself on a job well done!

Read this book if you would like to learn about the following:

- projecting your best self in person and on TV
- building confidence and controlling nervous anxiety
- delivering advocacy messages with impact
- asserting yourself more proactively
- dealing with hecklers and sexist comments
- preparing for news media interviews and in-studio appearances
- amazing women who've moved audiences with their words

IT'S A PERFORMANCE

While every speaking situation is unique, the road to becoming well-spoken starts with you being you. Richards was celebrated for her wit. The Tina Fey of her day, she delivered zingers with an all-knowing twinkle in her eye. Both Fey and Richards are reknowned for boldly skewering the well-known and self-important from a woman's perspective. Their willingness and desire to "talk like ladies" produced unparalleled observations on our culture. Although from different worlds—comedy and public service—both have shown what it takes to be successful on stage. The best speakers are performers who know that you capture an audience's attention when you put your best self forward.

Public speaking is a performance. This does not mean that the speaking is done for show or that the effort is frivolous. Rather, the concept of performance refers to the effort it takes to walk out there and deliver, whether the audience is eager to hear you or not. Well-spoken women, like accomplished stage actors, learn their lines and practice their movements well in advance of opening night. The vital distinction between skilled acting and good speechmaking is that the most admired public speakers do prepare but they don't play a role. Some people resist working on technique because they have confused the work of skill building with playacting. Did your mother have a telephone voice she could effect on a dime? One moment she was yelling in exasperation for you to clean up your room. The next she was feigning sweetness into the receiver: "It is so nice to hear from you." Playacting is faking your way through a performance. Richards would call it putting on airs.

Becoming well-spoken isn't about being someone else or changing who you are to fit into a preconceived mold. Suze Orman puts it like this: "Don't try to be anyone other than who you are," and she practices what she preaches.[1] Orman was headed to tape an appearance on Oprah Winfrey's new network when I caught up with her to talk about her television experience. On the phone she sounds exactly like she does on her TV show—intense, direct, and brimming with helpful advice. The irony of speech coaching is that it teaches you how to be you—on purpose and on command. It isn't about a massive makeover. Eliza Doolittle transformations only work in the movies. The ability to be you while communicating effectively in front of any audience is fundamentally what it means to be a well-spoken woman. Richards put it this way: "I spent hours of time rehearsing versions of the [convention] speech. It had to sound casual, conversational, but that took work."[2]

WELL-SPOKEN STYLE

The big city and bright lights beckoned Dorothy Ann Richards from an early age. She evolved from a precocious small-town Texas girl to a woman who was nationally admired for her storytelling and stamina. Richards was an only child bursting with so much energy that her father described her as a "perpetual motion machine" squirming like "a worm in hot ashes." Unlike most of us, Richards was not filled with dread at the thought of speaking to her classmates. She would earnestly learn poems and ditties to be the center of atten-

Governor Ann Richards

tion. While women of her generation often stifled their personalities, Richards was never forced into the pigeonhole of being a "good girl," that is, seen and not heard. "I was encouraged to say outrageous things," she said. "My parents actually clapped for me if I spoke out."[3]

In high school, Richards dropped the Dorothy and went with her middle name Ann because she thought it sounded sophisticated and she wanted to be popular. The way into the cool crowd was to do what she did best—talk. Richards figured out that people liked you if you told stories, especially funny stories. Storytelling was valued in the Richards' household, with both her father and grandfather being infamous for their yarn spinning. The outgoing personality led to her selection to participate in Girls State, a program that introduced young women to politics and government. The skinny girl with the mouth got a chance to mingle with the "cream of the crop" of Texas girls and meet important people. Richards found herself enthralled with the "speechifying" and decided that there could be no higher calling than public service.

The speaking abilities of this "natural" were tested in tenth grade when she joined the debate club. Sparring with partners and outwitting opponents taught her to think and speak logically. Not surprisingly, Richards was a standout on the team that brought home the state championship trophy in her senior year. The prize winning continued at Baylor University, where she and her partner were considered "big guns" who were sharp enough to whip a prominent men's team. The debate training and family tradition of storytelling laid the groundwork for the skills and habits that led to Richards's later professional achievements. The family support and guidance of her coaches helped to instill and nurture Richards's strong sense of self. This understanding of who she was allowed Richards to "own" her speaking power.

WELL-SPOKEN WOMAN'S POWER PERSONA

People often ask: "What does it take to be well-spoken?" They are not quite sure how the speakers they admire do what they do so well. The specific qualities and techniques are a bit of a mystery. Look around your office, school, community center, or church. Who are the women who seem to have the ability to express themselves effortlessly? Who can project the confidence of Rosie the Riveter? Remember Rosie from the World War II poster with the patriotic slogan "We can do it"? With her rolled-up sleeves, knowing look, and polka-dot kerchief, Rosie reassured us America would keep working.

Thousands of Rosies took on new jobs and different roles to contribute to the war effort. The willingness to leave the comfort and security of what they knew for something unfamiliar provided many women with valuable skills and revealed talents they didn't know they possessed. Rosie's spirit can help you become a better presenter. If you are willing to try new techniques to stretch beyond your comfort zone, you may be surprised at how good you can be. After twenty years of working with thousands of speakers and watching thousands of hours of speeches, it is clear to me that all well-spoken speakers share a few characterstics.

These characteristics make up the well-spoken woman's Power Persona. The Power Persona is a combination of feminine rapport, masculine strength, and savvy know-how. It is not the type of power that controls people by talking *at* them. It is not about dictating, lecturing, or suppressing ideas. Those styles do not fly in a social media world. Creative expression and engagement are hot; stoicism and pontificating are not. The feminine attributes of engaging in dialogue, listening, disclosing, being animated, and showing empathy—traditionally considered signs of weakness—are now valued and expected. When those characterstics are combined with steady confidence and a bit of a swagger, the sum is a compelling persona. The Power Persona is a trifecta of style, substance, and self-esteem.

Power Persona Trifecta

Signature style—an engaging presence
Synchronized message—relevant and purposeful
Self-assured manner—ready to handle anything

The Power Persona is not a mask you put on in front of an audience. It is not a cape like Wonder Woman's that will help you leap tall buildings. The trifecta is a set of underlying, enduring traits that contribute to long-term success. The attributes are fundamental principles that good speakers have developed and honed through practice and real-life experience. For example, the specific techniques a speaker uses to project assuredness may vary, but the underlying need for assuredness is timeless and essential. Ann Richards was a confident speaker, but the way she communicated her confidence is different from the way Maya Angelou, Hillary Clinton, or Suze Orman do it. All these women are self-assured; each communicates this quality with a distinct personality and speaking style. The Power Persona empowers you to demonstrate that you know who you are and what you are talking about. Like Rosie the Riveter, you will be able to project inner strength.

POWER PERSONA PRINCIPLE: SIGNATURE STYLE

Public speaking can feel like a striptease, except that you are much more exposed. The body feels bare, and people are judging your looks and ideas. There is no escaping the fact that women seeking to initiate a dialogue or contribute an idea are scrutinized from hair to hemline to heel height. Have you considered how your look is impacting your ability to be heard and taken seriously? By *look*, I am referring to everything that comprises your overall appearance, including clothing, hair, makeup, accessories, mannerisms, and idiosyncrasies. Do the components add up to a total package that projects confidence and capability? Or is there an attribute that is missing or an element that is holding you back?

Let's tackle head-on the issue of physical appearance and attire so we can deal with it and then move on. Like it or not, it is what people notice first, and it is the basis for snap judgments that may impede others' ability to hear what you say. *60 Minutes* correspondent Leslie Stahl reports that a good chunk of viewer mail over the past twenty years has critiqued her earrings. "People write, 'We love them,' or, 'Never wear that pair again.'"[4] The journalist who covered the Gulf War, a presidential assassination attempt, and world economic summits gets more feedback on dangling jewelry than her reporting. The chatter about the superficial is exasperating and demeaning, but ignoring it would be a mistake. You may discount the importance of appearance, but audiences do not. Caring about how you look isn't about vanity but rather about awareness of the message you telegraph through appearance.

Step 1: Recognize That Appearance Counts

If the dress is dowdy and the hair last-century, the woman and her opinion can be dismissed as outdated. Do your suits look like the wardrobe from the movie *Working Girl* with big shoulders in somber charcoal gray? If so, it's time to hang up the body armor. This doesn't mean you have to follow fashion's latest trends or spend exorbitant sums on designer clothes. Melinda Gates can afford to wear anything, but she doesn't flaunt showy labels that might be off-putting. Her every-woman outfits ensure that clothing is a nonissue.

My heart goes out to younger generations who are bombarded with pop culture images pushing sexy and provocative attire. The fashion industry focuses on glam and seasonal trends, which can result in disastrous consequences. Young women often end up dressed inappropriately for professional settings. A vice president for corporate communications says she has assistants who show up looking like an unmade bed. They can't sit without clutching at a skirt hem that is too short and too tight. They can't walk in four-inch heels. And they can't reach for a glass of water without exposing cleavage. Some women in some settings have the attitude to pull that look off—and more power to them. But they are the exception, as most of us want attention focused on our abilities.

Dr. Dorothy Height, godmother of the civil rights movement, was always impeccably turned out and never left the house without a signature hat. Height said she would not be seen without the appropriate headwear, and for her that meant a piece spectacularly adorned with feathers, bows, and flowers. Height's attention to her public image sent a deeper message: "Too many people in my generation fought for the right for us to be dressed up and not put down."[5] Dr. Height put her appearance on the agenda in such a way that she controlled it and could have pride in it.

Step 2: Take Charge of Your Look

It is not possible to change our culture's obsession with the external, but you can take control of how you want to be perceived. There are at least two ways to take charge of your appearance. One option is to neutralize it so that it becomes a nonissue. This would be the anti–Dolly Parton approach. Another tack is to purposefully accent a distinguishing feature à la Parton. The country-western singer has said her look is a country girl's idea of glamour: "It takes a whole lot of money to look this cheap."[6] Don't let the self-deprecating humor fool you. Dolly presents her style with a conspiratorial wink. As she has said: "I'm not offended by all the dumb blonde jokes because I know I am not dumb. And, I know I am not blonde."[7]

The point is to be purposeful, whether you prefer a neutral look or one that will guarantee that you are noticed. Establishing that look can be especially tricky terrain for women who are considered either very attractive or very plain. For them, the focus on appearance by others can be all-consuming and a serious distraction. When an audience gets stuck on the exterior, they seem blind to the individual. The person inside disappears or is discounted.

Former Michigan governor Jennifer Granholm is a Phi Beta Kappa scholar with a degree from Harvard Law School and movie-star good looks. Talk with her, and you discover she is a down-to-earth person with a hearty laugh. It took a while, but the governor, with the help of advisers, strategically adopted a look that was authentic to her and ensured her beauty didn't sabotage the agenda. The blonde hair was cut short, and she wore tailored business suits with feminine touches and a simple cross necklace. Although tall, she kept her three-inch pumps because she liked to wear them. Because Granholm downplayed her packaging, the pundits had to pass judgment on her record, not on what she wore to a groundbreaking ceremony. In a state rocked by the near collapse of the auto industry, voters gave Granholm a vote of confidence, twice.

Singing sensation Susan Boyle with her never-been-kissed image entered our psyche with an incredible debut on a TV competition. Emerging from nowheresville, Scotland, Boyle was besieged by paparazzi and a public that openly snickered about her frumpy dress and heavy brows. The onslaught of unflattering photos and snarky comments nearly prevented her from being able to perform. With a modest makeover, Boyle was able to put the attention back on her rich, angelic voice. The point is that minor steps and small changes can ensure that appearance becomes a secondary consideration.

If you haven't purchased a suit in years or have gotten feedback about your waist-length hair, you need help figuring out how to get back in style. On the TLC program *What Not to Wear*, the hosts surreptitiously videotape the poorly dressed who are in desperate need of a style intervention. It is a humbling tactic, but the video does the trick. The pictures provide a blunt assessment of the unsuspecting subjects' inability to present themselves well on sales calls and at meetings. Some of the fashion victims lack an interest in shopping or self-awareness of body type. If a day at the mall sounds like spending time in a torture chamber, enlist a stylish friend or personal shopper so you can invest in the right clothes. The adage about dressing for the job you want applies. You want to meet the audience's expectations by looking as though you have something to say that is worth hearing.

Step 3: Dress to Impress Strategically

Ann Richards was never seeking to blend in with the crowd. Everything about her persona made a statement, and she used her silver hair and silver tongue to her advantage. The Texas-sized, dairy-whip hairdo defied nature and flouted the stereotypical image of leadership. Men with gray hair are "distinguished," whereas women with white hair are "old." Barbara Bush, the formidable wife of President George H. W. Bush, was often mistaken for his mother because her hair had turned white prematurely. What could have been a huge liability for Richards was turned into an asset. To paraphrase Emerson, strength often grows out of a perceived weakness. Richards's bouffant do became a prop when she mailed postcards with photos of it being styled in a beauty shop, and as governor she declared an official Texas Big Hair Day in 1993. She often quipped: "I get a lot of cracks about my hair, mostly from men who don't have any."[8]

The hair wasn't the only feature of Richards's appearance that was tactically and deliberately deployed. Dressed to impress could mean black leather and hunting camouflage. The tough imagery burnished her good ol' boy bona fides in a state where macho rules. At the age of sixty, the governor posed in biker regalia astride a Harley-Davidson® to promote road safety. In the fall, she would suit up in camo to lead excursions for game birds. The hunting trips weren't stunts orchestrated for the press cameras. Richards's father had taught her how to shoot straight and cast a fishing line. By defying conventional stereotyping, Richards purposefully molded her image to avoid the traps that often limit women seeking executive positions in government and business.

A unique accessory can set you apart, but it need not be on the scale of Lady Gaga's raw meat dress. Gaga said she wore the slabs of meat draped around her otherwise nude self to signify that she is not a piece of meat.[9] Draw a distinction between a costume that opens you up to ridicule and an accessory that can set you apart. A forerunner of designer Donna Karan, Amelia Bloomer attempted to fashion a look for the busy woman on the go. In the 1850s, the rage in women's fashion was multiple layers of floor-length petticoats, which became mud-encrusted from walking on

*Richards Driving the
Art of Image Control*

unpaved roads. Long before Spandex, women wore painfully confining corsets that made breathing difficult. Bloomer's practical idea, an outfit of shorter skirts with long pants underneath, was considered outrageous. The "bloomers" were a bit goofy, but women could breathe and move in them. Fans of the new style eventually abandoned the pants when they felt the outfit was distracting from the fight for the right to vote.

A statement piece can be something simple. Women's rights activist Bella Abzug had her own collection of hats, although they were more conservative in style than those worn by Dr. Height. As a young attorney, Abzug wore a hat so she would be taken more seriously by her predominately male counterparts. Sarah Palin looks smart in her rimless eyeglasses, a style that is an update of Gloria Steinem's thick hair and aviator glasses from the 1970s. Congressional powerhouse Nancy Pelosi doesn't leave the house without a strand of oversized pearls or chunky beads. The necklaces frame her face in much the way a tie frames a man's.

Step 4: Package the Entire Package

Projecting a well-groomed persona isn't limited to the clothes on your back. The audience is also observing your physical movements, gestures, and vocal expressions. They are taking in the whole package. TV cook and talk show host Rachael Ray dresses like the girl next door and projects a friendly sensibility. Ray unleashes a jovial laugh whenever she burns the toast or adds extra dollops of whipped cream. In her signature crisp white shirt, Diane Sawyer speaks in a husky voice that is authoritative and reassuring as she delivers the daily digest of calamity and recovery. An arched eyebrow was all it took for Amanda Priestly to instigate a frantic scramble among her underlings as they tried to satisfy her every command in the movie *The Devil Wears Prada*. The conversation on the power of dressing was summed up in a cartoon that appeared in the *New Yorker* magazine. A shopper and sales clerk are standing in front of a dressing room mirror. The sales clerk says in a reassuring manner: "Madeleine Albright kicked butt in that suit."

A signature style encompasses how you look, sound, and move. Develop your own style with the body language, voice enhancement, and appearance suggestions outlined in chapters 3 and 4. The fundamentals of effective delivery technique provide a platform on which you can develop a distinctive style. Once you know the essentials of voice and body language, you will be able to showcase your personality. With thoughtful attention to appearance and attire, you need not worry about fashion faux pas and wardrobe malfunctions. Chapter 8 provides guidelines on what looks best on television and discusses special delivery techniques and wardrobe suggestions for the on-camera appearance.

POWER PERSONA PRINCIPLE: SYNCHRONIZED MESSAGE

Music is what guides the underwater choreography performed by a team of synchronized swimmers. With each swimmer following the rhythm, the team is able to execute a routine in seamless unison. Just as the swimmers coordinate their movements with the beat, an audience is looking to the presenter to set the pace. Audiences will follow the tempo of the speaker, who takes the lead with an interactive style that creates a bond. This bond is one that Bette Midler's character in the movie *Beaches* didn't comprehend. In conversation with her best friend after a long absence, she says: "Enough about me, let's talk about you. What do you think about me?" No one wants to listen to a diva unless she can really sing. If the speech is all about you and not about them, it will likely fail. As the presenter, it is your job to find the point where your topic intersects with what the audience cares about. Accomplish that, and they will be eager to follow your lead.

Shoveling out reams of data or delivering a stream-of-consciousness monologue will not engage them. If you don't purposefully connect with the audience, it doesn't matter if you have something to say and can say it well. At a popular, independent bookstore in Washington, DC, two broadcast journalists were discussing their book about the financial leverage women should exercise in the workplace. The broadcasters were articulate and the topic was provoking, yet when they finished, there were few questions. The pros fell into the trap of relying on the one-way style of broadcasting; that is, let us read the news to you. They talked at the audience for thirty minutes when a two-way dialogue would have been better suited to the setting. The broadcasters hadn't thought about how to engage the live audience and, as a result, came across as somewhat self-absorbed.

Step 1: Connection Is the Goal

Successful engagement is a balancing act. It is a three-legged stool with the speaker, the audience, and the topic each representing one leg. Together, all three legs keep the stool balanced. If one of the legs is shorter or missing, the stool will wobble or topple over. Don't give short shrift to any of the three legs. They all require attention as you prepare for an event and draft what you will say.

Presenters caught up in "What am I going to say?" neglect to consider the topic from the audience's perspective. Instead, ask yourself, "What do they need to hear?" This is an area where an aim-to-please mentality can serve you well. If you tend to put others first, this habit will serve you well in public speaking.

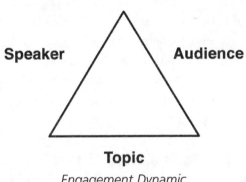

Engagement Dynamic

It will prevent you from being a disconnected speaker who alienates the audience by not establishing rapport. Soviet leader Nikita Kruschev, who famously pounded a table with his shoe, was a pontificator. Fidel Castro once delivered a four-hour-and-twenty-nine-minute harangue at the United Nations. But US president William Henry Harrison earned the distinction of "death by public speaking." Oblivious to the weather, Harrison gave a two-hour inaugural address as planned in the pouring rain. The president caught a cold and died a month later. The connectors listed below are qualities that draw the audience in. The qualities in the disconnected column turn off the audience.

Connectors	Disconnected
Approachable	Isolated or self-absorbed
Unpretentious	Overrehearsed
Sincere	Playacting
Having a sense of humor	Dry or overly technical
Engaged	Giving a didactic lecture
Risk taking	Insecure or boring

Ann Richards connected with audiences by using a narrative that employed well-honed stories and down-home humor to express shared hopes, fears, and dreams. Richards acquired the knack of speaking simple truths at the knee of her storytelling father. "I would lie in bed as a child and listen to my father and his friends talk well into the night, telling stories of plain people. Basic, gentle, and optimistic stories, forever taking aim at the self-important and dishonest."[10] The Richards narrative was based on real life: she humanized issues by relating them to a common situation. The aim was always "to speak so that my Mama understood what I was talking about."[11]

Step 2: Paint a Word Picture

Messages crafted with her mother in mind ensured Richards didn't talk down to people. Rather she conveyed that she understood what caused them to lay awake at night. She often accomplished this through the use of vivid imagery. Painting a picture with descriptive words greatly enhances the audience's ability to remember what you want them to remember. The address she gave at the convention shared tiny slices of life that transported the audience to another place and time.

I was born during the Depression in a little community just outside Waco, and I grew up listening to Franklin Roosevelt on the radio. Well, it was back then that I came to understand the small truths and the hardships that bind neighbors together. Those were real people with real problems and they had real dreams about getting out of the Depression.

I can remember summer nights when we'd put down what we called a Baptist pallet, and we listened to the grown-ups talk. I can still hear the sound of the dominoes clickin' on the marble slab my daddy had found for a tabletop. I can still hear the laughter of the men telling jokes you weren't supposed to hear, talkin' about how big that ol' buck deer was, laughin' about mama puttin' Clorox in the well the day the frog fell in.

They talked about war and Washington and what this country needed. They talked straight talk and it came from people who were living their lives as best they could.[12]

The syntax captures a commonality of experience. Words were chosen to encompass sound and texture: Roosevelt on the radio, dominoes clickin' on the marble slab, and puttin' Clorox in the well. Not only do you see the dominoes, you hear them clicking on that marble slab. Simple descriptors and phrases ring true: *Baptist pallet, small truths, grown-ups,* and *my daddy.* With the right words, the ordinary and the everyday are seen in living color and heard in stereo sound.

Even the most technical, dry subjects can be made relevant with well-chosen language. Shortly after she was elected governor, Richards rounded up a bunch of women politicos from across the country for networking and barbeque at the Texas governor's mansion in Austin. During the opening remarks, the others and I who gathered on the stately mansion lawn were held in sway by her unique way with words. Richards had the ability to take what could be the dullest of dull subjects—the role of government—and breathe energy into it:

Government is the most pervasive influence in our lives. It is the institution that determines the price you pay at the grocery, what happens when you flip the light switch and the electricity comes on or doesn't, whether your environment is clean, whether or not the garbage is picked up in the morning, all the way to the questions of life and death, and whether or not we will give our children in war. That's how pervasive government is.[13]

Step 3: Give Them Something to Chuckle About

Former speechwriter to President Lyndon Johnson and a buddy of Ann Richards, Liz Carpenter, wrote that the three basic rules for any speech are these: "Start with a laugh, put the meat in the middle, and wave the flag at the end."[14] At the beginning, humor can be a connector that closes the gap between you and the audience. It signals that you don't take yourself or the subject too seriously, and they can relax, knowing the talk is not going to be nearly as bad as they thought it would be. Humor doesn't require joke telling. In fact, trying to tell a joke can be a prescription for failure. The most effective humor is drawn from daily life. Self-deprecating humor can create an instant bond. You can comment on "insider humor," something everyone is talking about. And, if a story goes over well, don't hesitate to recycle it. Sarah Palin made hay talking about her "mamma grizzlies."

Richards's unsurpassed brand of Texas wit ranks her with some of America's most beloved humorists. She is to the one-liner what Mark Twain was to satire. Richards had the ability to make just about anyone laugh until they cried and was once described as an "unabashed feminist who could make unrepentant chauvinists laugh out loud." Audiences came to expect belly laughs, and she delivered on those high expectations with humor that was distinctive for its edge. Critics sometimes accused her of going too far. Yet, the line most identified with her was the poke she took at Vice President George H. W. Bush.

Richards was quick to point out that the chance to deliver such a line doesn't come along every day. All the pieces fell into place—the right speaker, right place, right time, and right subject. Richards later said she couldn't resist: "It was a great line . . . and you have to go with a great line." Bush to his credit harbored no ill feelings about the laugh at his expense and later presented Richards with a silver-foot pin. Richards appreciated the gesture, saying she "always wears a gentleman's jewelry when he comes to call."[15]

The nuts and bolts of coming up with something funny are covered in chapter 5 in the section on memorable sound bites. Chapter 5 also introduces the Message Map approach to developing strategic messages to advance positions on policy, legislation, and public debate. How to prepare for different types of forums and events is covered in chapter 6, which explains step-by-step how to prepare to take charge of a room and prepare tools such as notes and visual aids. Chapter 7 is

> ### All-Time Great Line
>
> Poor George, he can't help it. He was born with a silver foot in his mouth.
> —Ann Richards

all about speechwriting, with tips on how to open and close with a bang and how to organize the speech content and flow.

POWER PERSONA PRINCIPLE: SELF-ASSURED

> How many cares one loses when one decides not to be something but to be someone.
>
> —Coco Chanel

A former telephone operator was the first person in the US Senate to speak out against Joseph McCarthy and his anticommunist crusade in the 1950s. While the men remained silent, the lone woman in the chamber delivered a "declaration of conscience." Senator Margaret Chase Smith put aside concerns that she would be labeled a communist sympathizer to address a vacuum in leadership that she felt could result in "national suicide" if McCarthy pursued his witch hunt unfettered. Speaking as a "woman" and "senator," she said: "I don't like the way the Senate has been made a rendezvous for vilification, for selfish political gain at the sacrifice of individual reputations and national unity. I am not proud of the way we smear outsiders from the floor of the Senate and hide behind the cloak of congressional immunity and still place ourselves beyond criticism on the floor of the Senate."[16]

Well-spoken women have often had to go it alone. Six of Smith's colleagues signed onto the declaration, but she was the only member with the courage to publicly stand by her principles. Smith entered politics as a secretary to her husband and won election to his House seat after he died in 1940; she then served thirty-two years in Congress. She had the distinction of being the first woman to serve in both the House and the Senate and later had presidential aspirations. In a 1964 speech to the Women's Press Club, Smith laid out the reasons why she should not consider seeking the presidency. The list included severe limitations on money, organization, and time and the contention that as a woman she would "not have the physical stamina and strength to run." Smith then announced: "So, because of these very impelling reasons against my running, I have decided that I shall."[17]

Step 1: Quash the Illusions of Assuredness

One doubts that Smith dreamed of running for president while she answered phones for the Maine Telephone Company. She was an ordinary person who went on to do extraordinary things by working hard, always striving to improve, and being willing to take a risk. The decision to speak out against a Republican colleague was not one she made lightly, nor was it a ploy for publicity. Unlike McCarthy, Smith was not a camera hog showboating for the press. She stepped into the role of moral leader when she felt such leadership was lacking.

Smith knew who she was, and she brought that sense of self-assuredness to her public pronouncements. The tough stance wasn't affected but was grounded in the values that guided her life, values such as directness, self-reliance, and integrity. For Smith, remaining silent was simply not an option, for she was compelled to take issue with anyone she felt was abusing power. Self-assured speakers command our attention with their conviction, not their arrogance. They speak to higher principles and for the greater good but do so in a genuinely humble manner. Projecting self-assuredness is not about positioning yourself as "the" expert, meeting perfectionist standards, or allowing the ego to run wild. Arrogance, flawlessness, and dogmatism are merely illusions of self-assuredness.

The Expert Illusion: You Must Know Everything

Being self-assured does not mean you have to be an expert on a topic to speak about it. Don't allow a belief that you need to be an expert throw you into a tizzy that causes you to miss opportunities. Stop turning down invitations because you know something but not everything about the subject matter. Men are often more willing than women to fake it and learn as they go. Also, don't attempt to compensate for perceived knowledge gaps by cramming before a presentation. It is not possible to know the answer to every single question that could arise. Forget about memorizing endless factoids and data. There is nothing wrong about telling a questioner you will get back to her with the specific information she seeks. Last-minute cramming makes you more self-conscious and more anxious. Moreover, plenty of experts come across like pompous jerks. You just need enough material to credibly fill the seven minutes on a panel or twenty minutes at lunch.

The Perfectionist Illusion: You Must Perform Flawlessly

Like Girl Scouts, well-spoken women are prepared, but they don't attempt to project like a Stepford wife. Striving for perfection on the scale of the "early" Martha Stewart is a misplaced goal. As we came to learn, Martha didn't bake all those cakes and pies herself. She had loads of helpers in the wings. Neither was her household so "hospital-corner" perfect. Once we knew she had limitations, as we all do, Martha was eminently more likable. Space scientists at NASA need to be technically accurate. But forcing yourself to memorize a presentation will result in a lifeless, stilted performance. Forget the unobtainable and focus on making the connection.

The Egotist Illusion: You Can Do No Wrong

Then there are the presenters who have loads of experience and rarely feel nervous. Don't allow a high skill level to allow you to become complacent or overly confident. And, recognize that as you move up the ladder of success, audiences expect more from you. A false sense of greatness can lead to a public-speaking purgatory I call the land of the "almost famous." Some talented, intelligent people think they are better than they are, so they don't spend much time preparing or any time practicing. The mindset is "Why rehearse when I'm already good?" The skills of these presenters tend to plateau at slightly above average. Their overconfidence breeds an arrogance that limits their ability to improve. These speakers often find watching video of themselves to be a humbling experience.

Step 2: Workhorses Become Show Horses

Before she was a superstar, Ann Richards was a mom with a résumé that had big gaps. As much as she loved the tussle of debates in college, she left the team in her junior year. At the age of nineteen, she didn't think twice about putting aside her professional ambitions for love and marriage. For the next several years, debating and politicking would take a backseat to husband David and raising their four children. Richards was a stay-at-home mom who volunteered on local campaigns, answering telephones and licking stamps. It was her lawyer husband who seemed destined to be the politician in the family. However, when a local seat opened up, Ann was asked to run. In 1976, she was elected the first woman to serve as Travis County commissioner.

The victory was not universally applauded or welcomed by a large swath of the county employees who found themselves under her domain. By defeating a longtime incumbent, she had alienated the all-male road crew who maintained county highways. The men were less than thrilled about their new boss, expecting her first order of business would be to replace them with women and minorities. So, Richards carefully prepared a little pep talk to reassure them during her initial foray into their world—that of the maintenance shop.

Arriving on the appointed day, Richards was greeted outside the shop by "the ugliest looking mutt" and learned it was the crew's mascot. Talking about the dog seemed like a good way to break the ice, so she asked the men about the dog's name. The room fell silent until a defiant voice yelled from the back: "The dog's name is Ann Richards." A young man seated up front quickly added: "But, we call her Miss Ann." Richards's response was a belly laugh that broke the ice. It was a shaky start, but over time the men got used to working for a woman, and Richards says they eventually became friends.

Any woman maneuvering in a man's world has to prove herself. Orit Gadiesh was a management consultant at Bain & Company when she delivered a speech that became the basis of a Harvard Business School study on leadership and that propelled her to the top of her industry. At the company's annual convention in 1992, Gadiesh's aim was to rally her colleagues with an approach that was unconventional for the buttoned-down, data-driven, Boston-based firm. Bain, which had been hammered by years of turmoil and poor revenues, had recently completed a successful turnaround. Although Gadiesh agonized about it for weeks, she decided "to give a personal 'no numbers' speech to her colleagues."[18]

The message about collective pride and holding firm to founding principles brought Gadiesh's colleagues to their feet cheering, and within a year she was appointed company chair. Those in attendance said the speech worked only because Gadiesh gave it. Gadiesh is a Diane von Furstenberg look-alike who dresses with flair in bold accessories and strong colors. If that wasn't enough to set her apart from the Brooks Brothers suits, she had also trained in military intelligence with the Israeli army. Gadiesh worried that a personal speech would not be well received in the rarified air of management consulting. But she meant what she said, and her colleagues believed her and supported her agenda.

Step 3: Risk Taking Yields Rewards

Putting yourself out there is not for the faint of heart, as any woman who has broken or cracked a glass ceiling will tell you. If you challenge a conventional norm, push an unpopular agenda, or reach for the golden ring, you can expect judgment, pushback, and condemnation. Taking a risk often means hesitation and second-guessing, but if you proceed, you'll get the tremendous satisfaction of knowing you had the guts to put your ideas on the line. It is an unparalleled thrill to move an audience and empower them to take a course of action. When you articulate a shared passion, suddenly anything is possible.

When Richards's children were grown, she divorced and battled alcoholism. As governor on prison visits, she would introduce herself: "My name is Ann, and I'm an alcoholic." Molly Ivins wrote that "anyone who ever heard her speak at an AA® convention knows how close laughter and tears can be."[19] Her willingness to speak freely about her struggles made her an inspiration to thousands. Through the ups and downs of public life she never lost her sense of where she came from. This is evident in a story about preparing for a royal visit. Just weeks after being elected governor and still wet behind the ears, she was informed that the queen of England was coming to Texas.

> You can imagine what it's like, there's a great deal of turmoil going on, the legislature was already in session, the issues were already hot and heavy, I was trying to assemble a staff, plan an inauguration with all of the attendant balls and marches and such.... I don't know how many of you have entertained the Queen but it's a very complicated deal. We all had to go to school to learn, not to touch the elbow and things like that. I had to go have a dress made—one of those sort of suitable, queenly-looking outfits with the silk pleated skirt and the raw silk jacket in a bright color.
>
> After all of this preparation, obviously we were nervous and we wanted the visit to go very well. I was running across the Rotunda of the Capitol building to wait there on the front steps for the Queen and racing through my mind came my mother's voice just as clear as a bell, saying, 'Where do you think you're going... to see the Queen of England?' Here, some 40 years later I was![20]

Consider what about your life experience sets you apart. Your story doesn't have to be deeply personal, but audiences do want to get to know you. The more you can share, the more likely the presentation will generate a positive buzz that can create a competitive advantage. At a prestigious New York City law firm, a senior partner named Judy had recently spoken about intellectual property at an American Bar Association conference. The conference was a potentially lucrative rainmaking opportunity, but Judy knew it hadn't gone as well as she would have liked. As she related some of the speech, it was clear she had articulated her expertise, but there was nothing memorable about what she had said. Judy had come across like a cog whose marketing abilities were unlikely to turn prospective clients into billable hours.

When Judy finished, a colleague remarked that the abstract nature of the topic made it difficult for potential clients to understand the nuances of the law. It was suggested that she might want to draw upon her talents as an artist to render a more relevant talk. Judy had a mini-lightbulb moment as she realized she could stay within her comfort zone while adding depth and color to her legal expertise by using visual metaphors to simplify complex points. Judy's hobby sets her apart from other lawyers in navy-blue suits. When you let your hair down, you will step beyond the realm of the commonplace.

Self-assuredness comes from confidence, which is a habit all speakers can adopt. Chapter 2 lays out the techniques you can use to develop a balanced level of confidence that will ensure the audience takes you seriously. You can take a number of proactive steps to overcome fears so you can stay focused on accomplishing objectives. In some situations, a difficult audience can derail you. In chapter 9, guidance is provided on how to handle troublemakers and difficult questions, including hostile interviews. There is no reason to cope with the challenges of public speaking alone; chapter 10 has suggestions on how you can tap into a sisterhood of support to help yourself and the other women in your life.

STANDING OVATION POINT: WELL-SPOKEN WOMEN PROJECT THEIR BEST

Ann Richards embodied the well-spoken woman's Power Persona. Her signature style, synchronized message, and self-assured manner broke the mold. With straight talk, unbendable hair, and good humor, she packed more personality and charm into one appearance than most manage in years. After leaving politics, Richards continued to share her passion for service and hard-earned wisdom. An invitation that was always accepted was the annual request to return to the Texas Girls State conference. A story she liked to share with the newest crop of young dynamos was from the *Cinderella Complex* by Colette Dowling: "If Prince Charming shows up, he isn't going to be on a white horse; he's going to be on a Honda and expect you to make the payments."[21] Part of her legacy is the encouragement she gave to the next generation of women leaders. She wanted them to learn how to take care of themselves and to take responsibility for their own lives.

Richards was outspoken from an early age, but many well-spoken women never envision themselves becoming a big deal. Plenty of women, like Senator Margaret Chase Smith, speak out only when they realize no one else can or will. Candy Lightner was a heartbroken mom who touched a nerve with the story of losing her daughter to a repeat drunk driver. Lightner turned her family's loss into Mothers Against Drunk Driving—the organization that makes nearly every American think twice about getting behind the wheel after a few drinks.

Another mom who didn't envision herself as a nationally recognized advocate was Patty Wetterling. Her quiet life in a small Minnesota town was shattered the night a masked gunman kidnapped her eleven-year-old son. Five years after Wetterling created a foundation to protect children from exploitation, Congress passed the Jacob Wetterling Act, which requires states to create sex offender registries.

When I first met Patty Murray, she was a suburban mom juggling the demands of kids, marriage, and aging parents. Murray experienced a defining moment when a state legislator dismissed her concerns about cuts to a parent-child education program by saying: "You can't do anything. You are just a mom in tennis shoes." The slight was a slap to many women (and men) trying to do their best for their families. The unassuming Murray turned the dismissal into a rallying cry to mobilize the constituency that carried her to the US Senate.

Lightner, Wetterling, and Murray show us that not all leaders wear wing tips. These "moms in tennis shoes" turned their anguish and outrage into movements that touched millions. Women often enter the public arena not for power and prestige but to achieve something for their families and communities. They are motivated by a deep sense of justice, and some have risked personal harm to say their piece. They are compelled to make a difference by circumstances bigger than themselves. In each of the following chapters, you will meet extraordinary and ordinary women who used their speaking talents to create change.

Applause Principles: Bring Your Best Self

- The Power Persona Trifecta is a set of underlying, timeless principles possessed by the most accomplished speakers.
- Recognize the myth of "overnight success." It takes time and effort to develop a signature speaking style.
- Paying attention to appearance is an integral part of the credibility equation.
- Savvy messaging starts with connecting the audience's interests with yours.
- Self-assuredness comes to those who are willing to take a public stand.

2

THE CONFIDENCE CONUNDRUM

There is no more liberating, no more exhilarating experience than to determine one's position, state it bravely and then act boldly.
—Eleanor Roosevelt, *Eleanor Roosevelt: Volume One 1884–1933*

How confident are you in your speaking abilities? How do you react when you are asked to make a presentation? Do you beg off, believing others can do a better job? Do you fret that a mistake will reveal vulnerability? Do you hesitate to ask for help because you believe your senior position means you are supposed to have all the answers? Does your apprehension result in procrastination that leaves you once again white-knuckling it or faking your way through? As Deborah Sampson could attest, faking it only takes you so far.

Sampson was a patriot with an adventurous spirit who pulled off not one but two masquerades. At the age of twenty-two, the unmarried part-time weaver devised a scheme to enlist in George Washington's army. The former indentured servant had few prospects and may have been enticed by the bounty money paid to new recruits. Clad in a man's suit and posing as her deceased brother, Sampson successfully enlisted with the Massachusetts Fourth Regiment without raising suspicion about her gender. It helped that no physical exam was required.

For two years, Sampson kept her true identity hidden, and she might never have been found out if not for a wound sustained during a skirmish. Since she was handy with a needle, she removed the musket balls lodged in her thigh. However, she subsequently fell ill, and the jig was up when a doctor discovered the injured soldier was a woman. It was illegal for women to serve in the army, and Sampson could have been charged with defrauding the government and impersonating a man. The newspaper accounts of her predicament stated she had comported herself with "great activity, courage, and valor," and she escaped punishment with an honorable discharge.

Upon returning home, Sampson did something no other soldier in the Continental Army could do. She married and gave birth to four children and most likely would have lived out her life more conventionally if her family hadn't struggled financially. Denied a military pension, Sampson decided to take the story of her wartime adventure to the stage with a professional speaking tour. The decision to become a public lecturer was as unprecedented as the one to enlist. No other American woman had done such a thing. The act was frowned upon by the likes of Thomas Jefferson, who stated that if women were allowed to engage in the public meetings of men, doing so would result in a "depravation of morals."[1]

Despite or perhaps because of the peculiar nature of her presentation, Sampson brought the house down at the Federal Street Theatre in Boston on a March evening in 1802. The portion of the talk performed in drag was a real crowd pleaser. In full uniform, she executed the soldier's manual exercise of arms, twirling her musket with precision and confidence. The talk was a rousing star-spangled address that included an apology. The expression of regret was likely an attempt to secure public acceptance so she could win back wages and a pension. Although the performance earned positive reviews, Sampson's speaking career was short-lived due to ongoing illnesses, which were likely related to her injury. She spent the last thirty years of her life fighting for benefits, and she enlisted the help of neighbor Paul Revere to secure a small retirement income. When she died, there was little public notice, and there is no record of a memorial service to honor her service. Despite astonishing achievements, one of America's most unconventional soldiers and public speakers has nearly been lost to history.

No More Masquerades

Sampson is a role model for anyone who questions whether she has the right stuff for the public arena. When Sampson marched on the battlefield and took to the stage, she courageously defied what was considered appropriate behavior for women. By breaking through gender barriers, she led an independent life and provided for her family. Consider how far she might have gone had she not been constricted by societal norms. Don't allow a lack of confidence or skills to hold you back. Think about how you can seize opportunities when they come your way. Otherwise you can find yourself caught in a catch-22 situation. After all, you can't improve if you don't practice. The more you procrastinate, the more you agonize, the more likely what was an opportunity becomes an obligation that causes you to effect a pose as you suffer your way through it.

Most presenters who pretend at the podium are not trying to put one over on the audience. An affected or stilted performance is a coping technique, but it has the serious downside of masking the speaker's true potential. Internal psych-outs such as nagging self-doubt and stage fright stymie progress. Those negative states of mind can be alleviated and even eliminated with specific strategies to face down fears. Knowing how to psych yourself up allows you to get past fear to achieve personal and professional goals.

SLAY THE IMPOSTER DRAGON

Studies have shown that some high-achieving women feel like frauds before an audience. They convince themselves that they do not belong and do not deserve what they have earned. Both women and men experience the "imposter syndrome," but with a gender twist. Women tend to blame themselves more for perceived shortcomings. Men are likely to place the blame on external factors such as bad luck. Men are also less likely to feel like frauds because they convince themselves they would have done better if they had prepared. From my coaching experience, men tend to view themselves as being better than they are, while women think they are worse than they are.

At the age of forty, Tina Fey was the youngest comedian to be honored with the prestigious Mark Twain Prize for American humor. In her acceptance speech, the self-deprecating Fey said she never expected the honor but thought she might qualify for "the Judy Blume Prize for awkward puberty or the Harper Lee Prize for small bodies of work."[2] When asked how she felt about her achievements, Fey replied: "The beauty of self-doubt is that you vacillate between extreme egomania and feeling like I'm a fraud. You just try to ride the egomania and then slide through the imposter syndrome."[3]

Self-imposed feelings of being an imposter are sometimes reinforced by others. A diverse group of young women physicians shared some of the labels and stereotyping they encountered in their ob-gyn practices from both patients and colleagues. A Latina doctor said patients look at her and think she's the cleaning lady, even after she has consulted with them. An African American doctor added: "And, I'm the nurse." A question the physicians commonly faced was "How long have you been practicing medicine?" which the women agreed is code for "How old are you?" These professional women are constantly asked to establish their bona fides because they do not fit the traditional doctor model.

Step 1: Recognize Speech Mode

The first step to slaying the imposter dragon is to recognize that both external and internal challenges to competence can trigger self-doubt. The head of a national philanthropic organization couldn't believe eight hundred people had showed up for her address: "Do they really want to hear what I have to say?" This type of negative framing causes many presenters to lapse into "speech mode." The telltale signs of speech mode are weak eye contact, stiff body language, and a rapid speaking pace. Presenters caught in the grip of speech mode are suffering physically and emotionally. The speaking event becomes an exhausting exercise in survival.

When I first met Nikki, a leader in the local branch of an international labor union, I was immediately drawn to her personal warmth and quiet sense of competence. With her relaxed, engaged style, it was not surprising to learn she had earned the distinction of being the first African American woman to achieve a top leadership position in the union. But, as soon as the camera rolled for speech practice, Nikki morphed into a frozen lump with no facial expression and a choppy speaking cadence. When we watched the video playback, Nikki's eyes teared up as she realized her personality changed because she was trying to project what she thought a labor leader should look and sound like. She was taken aback by her tough-guy posturing. Nikki saw that she was trapped in speech mode. By adopting a persona that wasn't true to herself, she was impeding her ability to improve. Nikki had been masking her true self out of fear she wouldn't be accepted by the boys. With the awareness that she would be better off being herself, Nikki was freed to develop her leadership skills.

Step 2: Eliminate Telltale Body Blunders

The most revealing outward sign of speech mode is a look of dread in the eyes. The eyes truly are the window to the soul. No facial expression or vocal inflection can mask distress in the eyes. Neither is it possible to genuinely convey passion or enthusiasm if it isn't visible in the eyes. Another dead giveaway of speech mode is poor posture. Is the body ramrod straight? People suffering from anxiety forget how to use their arms. Sud-

---

To Wink or Not to Wink?

Twisted leg twine—knees and ankles intertwined while seated or standing

Adoring eyes—chin down and eyes uplifted in the Nancy Reagan gaze

Bobble head—constant nodding that signals you agree with whatever is being said

Laced fingers—clenched hands that telegraph fear; fidgeting that spells boredom

Hair touching—preening, flipping, and patting that are oh so junior high

Limp wrists—flapping wrists that look weak, like Tweety Bird

The clutch—grabbing the table, lectern, chair, pencil, or laser pointer for dear life

---

denly, the appendages that have been hanging from your shoulders all your life feel wooden.

Sometimes I catch women trying to position themselves behind furniture in an awkward attempt to hide real or imagined figure flaws. Others have never learned how to move their bodies effectively. Be wary of expressions, gestures, and postures that can be misread, leaving the audience questioning your intention. Sarah Palin's trademark wink is endearing to some, while others are annoyed by what they perceive as her nonchalance and lack of decorum. The intent of a wink is unclear. It can be interpreted as flirtation or affable conspiracy. Eliminate the gender-centric mannerisms that signal you are out of your comfort zone.

Step 3: Put Mistakes into Context

Sometimes you can be your own worst enemy with bad body language or a big blooper. We all have memories that make us wince. PepsiCo CEO Indra Nooyi lit up the blogosphere with her best-known speech, which is also the one she would probably most like to forget. Nooyi's trademark outspokenness was on display during a commencement address to the 2005 graduates of Columbia University's Business School. During the speech, she gave the audience "the finger." Nooyi used a middle-finger analogy to describe America's place in the world, comparing the five major continents to the five fingers on her hand with the United States occupying the middle-finger spot.

> Each of us in the U.S., the long middle finger, must be careful that we extend our arm in either a business or political sense, we take pains to assure we are giving a hand...not the finger. Unfortunately, I think this is how the rest of the world looks at the U.S. right now. (Middle finger pointing up.) Not as part of the hand giving strength and purpose to the rest of the fingers...but instead scratching our nose and sending a different signal.[4]

Not your typical feel-good commencement address. Many of the graduates and their family members were offended by her unbefitting gesture, which detracted from the ceremonial nature of the event. When *Today Show* anchor Ann Curry delivered a commencement address at Wheaton College, she gave a shout-out to a list of distinguished alumni, mentioning among others Reverend Billy Graham; movie director Wes Craven; and Todd Beamer, a passenger on downed United Flight 93. The problem was, everyone Curry named had attended Wheaton College in Illinois, not Massachusetts.

The graduates and school administrators knew Curry had misspoken but gave her a standing ovation anyway. Curry was mortified and sent letters of apology to both schools. Later, on a late-night talk show, she said the incident taught her to "never Google drunk."[5] It is unlikely you will be able to save face with a national television appearance, but a sincere apology is always in order for major missteps. A light touch of self-deprecating humor can make the contrition less awkward for everyone. In her atonement, Nooyi reaffirmed her gratefulness to her adopted country, calling America "the promised land she loves."[6] The erroneous alumni list and errant finger were high-profile embarrassments, but genuine, good-natured responses ensured they weren't blown out of proportion.

PROJECT YOUR AUTHENTIC SELF

Indra Nooyi

The Indian woman is a remarkable species.... The ability of the Indian woman to multitask and to put up with a lot of crap is just amazing.

—Indra Nooyi,
CEO, PepsiCo

Conventional is not a word that comes to mind upon hearing Nooyi speak. How did a woman who was born in India, was raised Hindu but sent to Catholic schools, played guitar in an all-girl rock 'n' roll band, was raised by a mother who said she would fast until she died if her daughter left the country—how did she become a titan of American business?

Apparently, she learned how to deal with a whole lot of crap.

Corporate-speak is not a part of Nooyi's DNA. The executive of a company that would be the thirty-seventh largest republic in the world if it were a country speaks freely about the exhilaration of being in charge. In the next breath, she will openly discuss the resulting guilt that she isn't doing enough for her children. Sacrifices come with the privileges of a big job, and there is no sugarcoating with Nooyi. She is a frank storyteller with a sharp sense of humor who draws upon her Indian heritage to articulate her worldview. As a woman of color, Nooyi is the rarest of rare birds in the corporate suite. Minority women hold less than 2 percent of all corporate officer positions in Fortune 500 companies. Nooyi says she learned early to embrace rather than hide her differences, and she believes PepsiCo hired her because she is a woman, is foreign born, and is willing to speak her mind.

Authenticity Is Positively Revealing

Nooyi says you must bring your whole self to projects every day. It doesn't work to create a persona for the workplace that is different from the one that left the house in the morning. The other roles—mother, daughter, wife—can't be checked at the office door. She believes people perform better on the job if they can be themselves. Practicing what she preaches, Nooyi has brought influences from Indian culture into the workplace with unique employee retention and recruitment practices. The outreach was a by-product of a trip to India to visit with her mother shortly after being promoted to CEO. Friends and neighbors stopped by the house, theoretically to offer Nooyi congratulations. It soon became clear the guests were there to acknowledge her mother's success, saying: "So this is the daughter. You are wonderful. You gave birth to this child. How did you bring her up? What did you feed her?"[7]

After witnessing this outpouring of appreciation, it occurred to Nooyi that she should reach out to the parents of her executive committee members. When she returned to the United States, she hand wrote twenty-seven letters telling the parents of her top management team how much she valued the contributions of their children and invited them to communicate with her. One parent wrote back saying how delighted she was to receive a report card on her child as it had been decades since the last one. Another said her son was thinking about leaving PepsiCo, and she had advised him it would be crazy to take another job.

The Journey

Nooyi says there is no line that can be drawn from where she started to where she ended up. In the conservative, middle-class household where she grew up, her parents and grandparents kept close watch over her. At the same time as she was encouraged to dream big about becoming a prime minister or an astronaut, her mother anticipated that her arranged marriage would take place by her eighteenth birthday. After earning an MBA, Nooyi decided graduate school in the United States would help her achieve her career goals. Her parents allowed her to apply only because they didn't think she would be accepted. And, if she did get in, they couldn't afford the tuition. Nooyi says her acceptance and full scholarship to the Yale School of Management was unheard for someone like herself. Her mother's great concern about her daughter's continuing education was that it "would make her an absolutely unmarriageable commodity."

When she arrived in the United States in 1978, Nooyi compared her communications style to a character in a funny television commercial. She reminded herself of the delivery man in a FedEx® ad who spoke so quickly no one could understand a word he said. Her approach was that of a bomb thrower—someone who was willing to say anything. At Yale she began to tackle her speaking weaknesses, and she credits the university for teaching her "how to speak." All graduate students were required to take an effective communications class. Nooyi barely squeaked by, but recognizing its importance, she challenged herself by taking the class again.

While a graduate student, Nooyi lived on a tight budget, financing her studies with odd jobs such as night desk clerk at a college dormitory. When it came time to interview for a real job, she fretted about how to dress professionally. With $50 to her name, she headed to Wal-Mart® to buy a serious suit. In the dressing room, panic set in: she realized she wouldn't be able to try on the clothes. By custom, Indian women do not expose their ankles in public, and the dressing room curtains were so short, her legs would have been visible. Unable to buy a traditional suit, she found herself sitting in the waiting room at the Boston Consulting Group in a brightly colored sari. In a sea of conservative navy pinstripes, she felt like a "freak." The interview was a good lesson in the competitive advantages of self-expression. She got the job.

JUST SAY NO TO PUBLIC FREAKING

> The centipede was happy quite, until a toad in fun
> Said, "Pray which leg goes after which?"
> That worked her mind to such a pitch,
> She lay distracted in a ditch, considering how to run.
> —Mrs. Edward Craster, *Speech: A Text with Adapted Readings*, 1871

The befuddled mind-set of the centipede resembles the mental gymnastics some speakers experience prior to interviews, panel discussions, meeting presentations, and other public-speaking situations. Many concerns—from doubts about appearance to anxiety about what to say—can inhibit your ability to be you. It is not possible to be yourself, much less project your best self, when you feel overwhelmed. When the mere thought of being the center of attention sets off an onslaught of negative mind chatter, you can find yourself slipping into speech mode.

Worry is often exacerbated by a memory of a previous bad experience. Who hasn't . . . gone blank and turned red? brought the wrong PowerPoint® to the panel discussion? been intimidated by someone in the room? mishandled a question? worn mismatched shoes to the important client meeting? It is difficult to get back on the horse after you've been bucked off, but you have to do it. Any feelings of dread and apprehension must be dealt with; otherwise, they can become paralyzing.

Arsenal of a Warrior Princess

Whether you need to slay a dragon or beat back destructive thoughts, it's good to be armed with a shield of confidence and some martial arts moves. Xena, Warrior Princess—the heroine of ancient times—kickboxed her way past the demons and bad guys with steely aplomb. Xena's wardrobe of breastplate and knee-high boots may not suit all occasions. But calling up your inner warrior princess will help you develop self-assurance for the stage. Any worries that flood your mind can be alleviated. You can develop practices that will unlock the mystery surrounding confidence. Three sure-fire habits will help you conquer the confidence conundrum.

Unmask Your Well-Spoken Persona

- Set rational expectations.
- Calm the fight-or-flight response.
- Practice with purpose.

Step 1: Set Rational Expectations

Not all speaking occasions are created equal—some are more important than others. Actress Sally Field gushed with exuberance during her Oscar acceptance speech: "I can't deny the fact that you like me. Right now! You like me!" Winning an Academy Award is a big deal, and Field was obviously deeply moved by the experience. There's nothing wrong with relishing well-deserved recognition, but most events are not earth shattering, and it is a mistake to view them that way. Most audiences are not expecting you to usher in a day of new reckoning. This isn't meant to undermine a talk but rather to help you keep it in perspective. Don't allow yourself to get so caught up in the headiness of giving a speech that you overemphasize a meeting or discussion or overestimate the audience's expectations.

The problem of having unrealistic audience expectations is common among some law students. When I met with the Yale Law Women student group, I was stunned to learn that these otherwise dynamic women were afraid they might misspeak in class. Several said their anxiety prevented them from responding to questions because they did not want to be judged by classmates who send text messages while someone is speaking. A second-year student described how she spent an entire semester changing her classroom seat so the professor could never call on her.

These stories echoed the findings of a 2006 study, which showed that the behavior of male students at Yale was different. The men exhibited more confidence in the classroom and were much less hesitant to speak up. Thus, the women's excessive worry was preventing them from honing the skills of articulating arguments and defending positions. The self-imposed gag order was negatively impacting their classroom experience and could put them at a competitive disadvantage in the job market and the courtroom.

Setting unrealistic expectations for the audience and for your own performance will result in a correspondingly high level of anxiety. This anxiety can be managed with an exercise that will help you keep the speaking situation in perspective and not blow it out of proportion. Develop a list of everything you dread. What could go wrong while you are talking? Start by identifying your most pressing worries so you can assess the consequences should those things actually happen. Here's a sample list:

- My voice will crack, and I'll be embarrassed.
- My mind will go blank.
- My face will turn bright red.
- I will make a mistake.
- Someone will ask me something I don't know.
- People will laugh when I'm not trying to be funny.
- The audience will be bored.

Now let's manage these concerns by considering the result if any of these things happened. What is the worst possible reaction of the audience? Put yourself in the place of the audience. How do you react when you notice a presenter is nervous? Would you ridicule her or empathize with her situation? You can also take comfort in the fact that most audience members are not hanging on your every word. Don't allow self-absorption to blind you from the reality that while they are listening, they are also thinking about lunch, glancing at notes, and checking e-mail. If you don't draw unnecessary attention to your discomfort, it likely will go unnoticed.

My Mind Will Go Blank

This is the number-one concern of presenters who suffer stage fright. Prepare by bringing notes with you. When the brain freezes, you can simply pause, look down, and gather up the next point. No one in the audience knows what you were planning to say, so they are often unaware if you skip something.

My Voice Will Crack

This common problem at the beginning of presentations can be prevented by properly warming up the voice and relaxing the vocal chords. The next section lays out breathing and relaxation exercises that improve vocal quality.

My Face Will Turn Bright Red

It is impossible to stop blushing on command. While a hot face feels uncomfortable, it may not be apparent to the audience, particularly if they are several feet away. The degree of redness can be reduced with proper breathing techniques. Blushing is exacerbated if you hold your breath or take shallow, rapid breaths.

I Will Make a Mistake

If your goal is to be perfect, you will never achieve it. Comfort yourself with the knowledge that you can correct mistakes later during the question-and-answer period. If the error is simply a misspoken word, continue on. If you have stated something inaccurately, go back and restate the point to lessen confusion. It is possible to make a minor mistake and still do well.

Someone Will Ask Me Something I Don't Know

Don't try to fake your way through an answer. The better technique is to say: "I haven't seen that, but I can tell you this...." Or, "I don't know, but I will find out for you. Right now, I can tell you this...." Chapter 9 covers how to handle difficult or tricky questions in more detail.

People Will Laugh at Me

Most audiences are well behaved, but seeing a segment of your audience snickering is no barrel of monkeys. Don't belabor the situation. Put on a smile, nod as if you are in on it, and keep talking.

They Will Be Bored

No one is expecting you to be as entertaining as comedian Kathy Griffin. If you prepare your material in advance and rehearse, you will be able to deliver. Chapters 5 and 7 cover everything you need to know about developing a compelling message tailored to the audience's interests.

Step 2: Calm the Fight-or-Flight Response

The body's reaction to stage fright is similar to the body's reaction to a sudden threat: this is what is known as the fight-or-flight response. When confronted with a physical danger, such as the sudden appearance of a wild animal, the body responds by instinctively readying to protect itself. The same physical reaction is felt by many speakers at the prospect of public speaking. A rush of adrenalin makes the heart beat faster, circulating more blood to the brain and muscles. The racing heart causes the muscles to tense and the flow of perspiration to increase. As the heart continues to race, more oxygen is needed, which can cause breathing to become shallow and rapid.

For some, the physical reaction is extreme because they actually perceive the speaking event as threatening. Since you shouldn't flee or pick a fight, you need other outlets for the excess nervous energy. While it can be channeled so it doesn't reach an extreme level, it shouldn't be completely alleviated. An initial surge of adrenalin provides the needed oomph to fire up the brain. If properly harnessed, nervous energy can provide momentum to power through to the end. Some speakers become so physically exhausted that they run out of gas before reaching the conclusion. Everyone gets the butterflies—the well-spoken woman trains them to fly in formation.

Simple relaxation exercises can abate the physical trauma of the fight-or-flight response. These exercises can be performed beforehand to calm nerves and focus the mind. Some can be done onstage if you go blank during the presentation. They all have a tranquilizing effect and are recommended over the use of any mood-altering substances. Liquid courage may be tempting, but it can result in a sense of false courage, impaired articulation, and scrambled ideas. A more reliable approach is having a routine that will allow you to take control before and exercise control throughout.

Beforehand: Offstage Exercises

- **Deep breathing:** Rapid, shallow breathing focused in the upper chest accelerates a racing heartbeat. More effective breathing starts with the diaphragm. Take a deep breath in through the nose, using the diaphragm to raise and lift the chest. Hold the breath for two or three seconds and then audibly exhale. Deep breath in, hold it, and audibly exhale. Repeat slowly as many times as needed. A yoga class or exercise tape will help internalize the breathing so it feels like second nature.
- **Walk it off:** If your hands and legs feel jittery, release some of the excess energy by walking. Purposefully walk down a hallway while slowly swinging your arms back and forth across your chest. Take long, even strides.
- **Neck and shoulder rolls:** An enormous amount of stress can center in the neck and shoulders. Release it with loose, relaxed rolls. Drop your chin to your chest and slowly roll your head from shoulder to shoulder. Avoid rolling your head in a circle because this movement may strain the neck. Roll the head—slowly—back and forth 180 degrees. Then roll your shoulders back slowly. This movement will open and expand the chest while also releasing tension in the neck and shoulders. Repeat the rolls several times.
- **Face squeeze:** The face squeeze looks strange, so do this one in the restroom or in your office with the door closed. Scrunch up the muscles in your face, squeezing them into the middle around your nose.

Hold for second and then slowly relax. Open your eyes wide, hold, and release. Work the muscles in your jaw: slowly open your mouth wide, hold, and relax and then move the lower jaw side to side. This exercise also helps warm up the vocal cords and improve the sound of your voice.

Prior to Talking: Onstage Exercises

Often you are seated onstage prior to a presentation or panel discussion. While you are waiting in front of the audience, tension can build up in your body, even though you did the above-mentioned exercises. With some moderation, it is possible to do some of the same exercises without anyone noticing.

- **Deep breathing:** Use a slightly less exaggerated form of the breathing exercise. Take the breath in and release it slowly. Just be careful not to exhale into a microphone.
- **Body movement:** While seated in a chair, it is possible to relax nearly every muscle in your body. Push your chair back from the table a couple of inches. Lean forward from the waist slightly to stretch your back. Slowly cross and uncross your legs. While you are uncrossing your legs, shift all your body weight from one side to another. When you have finished crossing your legs, you can release more tension with simple ankle turns. Slowly, deliberately turn your ankle five times in one direction and then five times in the other direction. Then you can cross and uncross your legs again. This movement will ensure that your body stays loose.
- **Neck and shoulders:** Don't rest your elbows on the chair's armrest because the position causes shoulders to crunch up. Rather, allow both arms to hang loose from the shoulders at your sides. This will prevent the buildup of tension. When you drop your arms, sit up slightly and pull the shoulders down and back for more of a stretch.

Exercises during the Presentation

It happens to all of us. The mind goes blank while you are talking. The best remedy is to take a deep breath. It only takes three to four seconds to take a breath in, hold it, and exhale. A couple of seconds may seem like a lifetime, but it is nothing to the audience. They will think you are pausing to collect your thoughts. When you take the breath in, pause and lower your head so you can look at your notes. Find your place in the notes, then exhale, look up, and begin. Voilà—it works like magic!

Here's a secret no one tells you. "All audiences are stupid." No, I'm not referring to the average intelligence of the group but rather to the fact that they do not know the order of your presentation or what you were planning to say next. They do not know that you have skipped the most important part or that you have lost your place—unless you telegraph it by freaking out. So take that breath, glance at your notes, let the breath out, and then continue. If you realize you have forgotten something important, don't panic. You can circle back to it during the conclusion or the question-and-answer period.

Step 3: Practice with Purpose

It is imperative that you rehearse by practicing aloud. It is not enough to have a speech written on paper, nor is it sufficient to run through it in your head. Often you will discover that what looks right on paper sounds very different when you try to articulate it. However, the goal of rehearsal is not to memorize the entire speech word for word. Memorization is not a good way to prep because you risk coming across as robotic and overly scripted. Instead, rehearse to become familiar with the flow and order of the presentation so you can anticipate what is coming next.

Practice Positivity

Positive visualization is a form of positive thinking that combines productive mental imagery with constructive affirmations. It will build prespeech confidence by helping you focus on core strengths. World-class athletes

---

Time-Efficient Rehearsal

1. Read through the speech aloud. This will give you a sense of the flow and whether rewriting is necessary.
2. Read through again to time yourself. You may discover you are way over or under the allotted time.
3. Now that you are familiar with the content, practice aloud and tape yourself. Videotape is best so you can focus on body language and vocal techniques.
4. Review the tape. What needs to be adjusted—pacing, hand gestures, eye contact?
5. Do another taped practice session and review.
6. Now you are close to being ready. Decide if you want to keep the full speech text or condense the script into bullet points or a PowerPoint presentation.
7. Another run-through will seal the deal.

---

use the technique to enhance their mental toughness by repeatedly visualizing themselves overcoming obstacles and competing successfully. Runners envision themselves executing the strides that put them at the head of the pack. A figure skater completes the perfect double-axel jump in her mind. A softball player experiences the thrill of hitting a home run and rounding the bases.

Visualization works by giving you a process to negate worry by refocusing it. Worry is negative visualization that reinforces fears about profuse sweating, a technical glitch, or a challenging audience. If you allow worry to take over, it can lead to a constant swirl of negative self-talk in your head. If you constantly picture bad outcomes, you are going to experience corresponding bad feelings. Positive visualization helps you develop a mental blueprint of how you want the experience to play out. The technique will be most effective if you invest the time needed to foster the good habit.

For a high level of anxiety, begin several weeks before the scheduled presentation. If you are less anxious, a few days in advance or the night before may be soon enough. A good time to use the technique is at night before you fall asleep. While lying in bed, envision yourself in front of the audience. Look around the room and notice how everything is in place because you arrived early and the equipment is set up just as you need it to be. Think about the outfit you have on and how good it looks. Take a deep breath and exhale. Practice the opening aloud. Work your way through your main points, saying this here, telling that there, and sharing a funny story that gets a chuckle. As you conclude, pause and smile to acknowledge the audience's applause. With all visualizations, it is important to end on a high note. Bask in the glow you feel from the ovation.

Practice the visualization again, this time from the perspective of an audience member. From a chair in the audience, watch yourself calmly and confidently approach the lectern. Take in the smile on your face and laugh at the humor in the opener. Nod in agreement on the key points. Make a mental note about a question you would like to ask later. Clap your hands to demonstrate your appreciation for a job well done. The more you practice the internal and external visualizations, the more effective the technique will be. Reinforcing the positive experience by repeating the exercise strengthens its benefit.

Game-Day Routine

Most top-level athletes develop a set routine they follow religiously prior to walking out on the court or field. They eat the same pregame meals. Wear the same lucky socks. Run through the same warm-up drills. The consistency of the ritual helps to eliminate last-minute distractions and allows them to focus on their game-day strategy.

Develop a routine of your own. Before facing the audience, arrange to be in a room or another space that is separated from the noise of the crowd where you can be alone with your thoughts. Close your eyes and play out the positive visualization. As you think through what you will say and how you will say it, warm up your voice and body with the relaxation and breathing exercises. If you are not able to find a quiet space, try listening to music to block out noise and interruptions. Alternatively, record a motivational tape with inspirational quotes, simple meditations, and reminders about what you want to do.

After an event, athletes watch game tapes to further refine technique and identify weak spots. Be sure to include a post-speech review in your visualization routine. Watch a tape of your appearance and give yourself at least three positive comments about what worked and what the audience responded to. Limit yourself to two corrective comments on areas that need to be strengthened. Make a note to work on these areas during your next rehearsal session. This constructive analysis will speed your rate of improvement.

HOLISTIC APPROACH

When Nooyi told her mother she had been promoted to CEO at PepsiCo, her mother asked two questions: "Are you sure you can do it?" and "Why do you need more publicity?" Nooyi says she has inherited her mother's tendency to worry and finds herself feeling anxious about how her decisions impact her children and the PepsiCo family. Few CEOs share candid stories about how they manage the juggling act of trying to find that elusive balance between home and the office. Half jokingly, Nooyi says part of the solution was to make sure her daughters never saw her in the role of a "good stay-at-home mom" but only as a "career mom." When one daughter complained that she never attended the Wednesday morning coffee with all the other moms of her classmates, Nooyi's reaction was to ask: "Wednesday, 9 a.m. coffee—what is this? A plot against working women?"[8]

Well-Spoken Myth Busters

Nooyi has put a new face on corporate leadership, and her story illustrates that you can be accepted and admired for who you are. Further, her corporate leadership demonstrates that a woman's style with all its differences can be rewarded. Meet other well-spoken women like Nooyi and Deborah Sampson who have defied norms and laughed at conventions. These myth busters shattered stereotypes and blazed trails by refusing to back down or be intimidated. When faced with abuse, discrimination, sexism, or tokenism, these women unleashed their inner warrior princess. Nothing kept them from their calling.

Myth 1: Only Founding Fathers Rocked the Vote

Lucy Stone is another brave American you may never have heard of. Stone was the rock star of her generation who could fill lecture halls with fans and curious onlookers who wanted to catch a glimpse of the girl speaker. If alive today, she would host a cable talk show and have millions of Facebook® fans. Stone was the first woman to travel the country advocating for a woman's right to vote. At the height of her career in the mid-1850s, she was raking in as much as $1,000 per week—quite an accomplishment, given admission tickets were priced at just 12½ cents.

Some of those ticket buyers showed up to see a woman they considered an oddity. Stone's parents worried for her soul because she was violating the biblical injunction against women preaching. She braved audience insults and became adept at dodging the rotten apples and frying pans hurled her way. Those who came to listen said she "possessed a great personal magnetism and a remarkable speaking voice."[9] With her intellect, calm demeanor, and sense of humor, she turned hostile mobs into receptive crowds. She was said to have the "voice of angel."

Stone road-tripped across the country, often on horseback or in a horse-drawn buggy through snow and mud, to encounter skeptical crowds and sketchy lodgings. With her unrelenting will and remarkable talents, she broadened the public discourse in this country. Stone never lived to cast a ballot, but she ensured that her daughter, Alice, and succeeding generations of women would enjoy the rights of citizenship.

Myth 2: All Amazons Are Tall

If César Chávez was the hero of the farm workers' movement, then Dolores Huerta is its "unheralded heroine." Together, Huerta and Chávez founded the National Farm Workers Association (now the United Farm

Workers of America) to fight on behalf of migrant workers. Huerta's five-foot-two-inch frame packs a powerful punch. Known as *la Pasionaria*, "the passionate one," for her toughness and outspoken personality, she has won major victories on behalf of thousands of poor working families. Over six decades, this woman warrior has brought hope with the enduring social justice refrain "Si, se puede!" or "Yes, it can be done!"

In 1988, Huerta, the mother of eleven, suffered a vicious beating at the hands of San Francisco police officers while leading a peaceful protest. Huerta was hospitalized after sustaining life-threatening injuries, and doctors operated to remove her spleen. Speaking about the dangerous nature of her organizing efforts, Huerta said: "When you choose the path of the warrior, you can get beaten or shot at or even killed—that comes with the work."[10]

Myth 3: Just Another Pretty Face

What would you do if someone surreptitiously taped you through a peephole while you dressed in your hotel room and then uploaded the video to the Internet? How would you handle the mortification of such an extreme invasion of privacy? Would you show your face in public? ESPN-TV sportscaster Erin Andrews was one of the victims of a creepy voyeur who was jailed for his crimes. Determined not to let a slimebag silence her, within months Andrews was back on the job, covering college football games and speaking out about the assault.

Andrews shared the difficulties she encountered as she worked to get her life back. "I need to find my smile again. . . . I had the wind knocked out of my sails. I didn't get a choice about it at all." Andrews knows her appearance is a double-edged sword. "I'm a person that kind of overprepares just because I know the stereotypes out there for someone like me; I know the stereotypes for women."[11] For every woman who has been judged on looks alone, Andrews's fighting spirit is a testament to never let them get you down. She refused to allow her TV career to be derailed by a malicious act that was beyond her control. Her willingness to talk about the incident is helping people understand the seriousness of a crime that affects primarily women.

Myth 4: She's Just a Girl

The declaration by an American president that the Soviet Union was an "evil empire" caused a schoolgirl in Maine to worry that a nuclear war would "wreck the Earth and destroy the atmosphere." Another war seemed "so dumb" to Samantha Smith that she decided to send this letter to Soviet president Yuri Andropov.

> Dear Mr. Andropov,
>
> My name is Samantha Smith. I am ten years old. Congratulations on your new job. I have been worrying about Russia and the United States getting into a nuclear war. Are you going to vote to have a war or not? If you aren't please tell me how you are going to help to not have a war. This question you do not have to answer, but I would like to know why you want to conquer the world or at least our country. God made the world for us to live together in peace and not to fight.
>
> Sincerely,
>
> Samantha Smith[12]

President Andropov responded personally with an invitation for Smith and her family to visit Moscow. When the press arrived, Smith, a girl who was too shy to try out for a school play, demonstrated poise beyond her years. Soon she was known as "America's youngest ambassador," and she made many public appearances, including giving a speech at a children's symposium in Japan. At the event she proposed an "international granddaughter exchange" so the children of world leaders could spend time with the families of leaders in other countries.

Today a bronze statue of Smith honors her as an international symbol for peace near the Maine State Museum in Augusta. In 1985, three years after she wrote the letter, Smith and her father were killed in an airplane crash. They were returning home after filming a television program.

Myth 5: A Woman's Voice Should Be Soft and Low

Shirley Chisholm declared herself to be "unbought and unbossed" when she became the first African American woman elected to the US Congress.

During the turbulent 1960s, Chisholm never, ever hesitated to speak her mind. She opposed the Vietnam War; fought for women, minorities, and the poor; and ruffled the political establishment's feathers. With deep, heartfelt conviction, she entered the presidential campaign in 1972 confident in her ability to lead the country in a new direction. Her entry into the race was again history in the making. A revolutionary spirit and true patriot, Chisholm was the first African American to compete in a presidential primary, forty years before Barack Obama.

This excerpt from her announcement speech reflects her lifelong crusade on behalf of others:

> I stand before you today as a candidate for the Democratic nomination for the presidency of the United States. I am not the candidate of Black America, although I am Black and proud. I am not the candidate of the women's movement of this country, although I am a woman, and I am equally proud of that. I am not the candidate of any political bosses or special interests. I am the candidate of the people.[13]

Myth 6: A Woman's Place Is in the House

The above statement is true when she holds the title Speaker of the House. In 2007, Representative Nancy Pelosi became one of the most powerful women in the world when she was elected the first woman Speaker of the US House of Representatives. The Speaker is second in the line of presidential succession after the vice president. Not too shabby for a mother of five and grandmother of six.

Three years after picking up the speaker's gavel, Pelosi delivered on a promise that was forty years in the making. Her steady hand guided the passage of historic healthcare legislation. According to the *Washington Post*, Pelosi transformed herself from someone who was known as a millionaire, West Coast liberal in Armani suits into a towering figure who rules the House with an iron fist. Pelosi says there is a lot at stake: "You're in the arena. And, when you're in the arena, you know that someone's going to throw a punch. And, if you decide to throw a punch, you'd better be ready to take one, too."[14]

Myth 7: Tokenism Ensures Silence

Brooksley Born had something to say to the financial bigwigs in charge of US monetary policy, but none of them would listen. In 1996, Born was running the Commodity Futures Trading Commission when she proposed regulating the derivative markets that would contribute to upheaval in the markets a decade later. As the only senior woman in the room, she was isolated and ignored by Federal Reserve chair Alan Greenspan, Securities and Exchange commissioner Arthur Levitt, Treasury secretary Robert Rubin, and his deputy Larry Summers (the same Summers who was ousted from the presidency at Harvard University in part for declaring that women can't compete with men in math and science). The *Wall Street Journal* summed up the situation: "The nation's top financial regulators wish Brooksley Born would just shut up."[15]

In 2009, the John F. Kennedy Profile in Courage award was presented to Born for her attempts to sound the alarm that could have helped forestall economic crisis. If action had been taken on her accurate predictions, thousands may have well been spared monetary ruin. Accepting the honor, Born spoke out again against what Warren Buffett has dubbed "financial weapons of mass destruction."[16] Though vindicated, she is far from satisfied and refuses to remain silent as long as the problems remain unfixed.

STANDING OVATION POINT: WELL-SPOKEN WOMEN SHOW THEIR TRUE COLORS

Indra Nooyi says she dutifully attempts to follow her mother's advice "to be an Indian woman first." By being herself, taking risks, and learning from mistakes, Nooyi has earned respect and admiration as the leader of a successful multinational corporation. One gets the sense from Nooyi that she enjoys brandishing her dragon-slaying sword. When she hears complaints that her agenda sounds "so woman," her response is "That's me running the company so live with it."[17]

Allow your inner warrior princess to shine, and the dread of speaking in public speaking can be turned into anticipation for an opportunity. Getting a handle on anxiety with proactive practices and habits allows you to quash feelings of inadequacy. With practice, the scary nervousness will become a fun nervousness—the kind of nervousness that gives you the energy to deliver your best self, the energy that drives a well-spoken woman's Power Persona.

Applause Principles: Conveying Confidence

- Confidence is a habit developed through positive thinking, physical readiness, and purposeful practice.
- Feelings of inadequacy and negative self-perceptions will trap you in speech mode.
- Everybody makes mistakes, so there is no need to blow them out of proportion.
- Authenticity is not an act.
- Nothing is more appealing than the presenter who maximizes her unique talents and life experience.

PART 2

MAXIMIZE BODY PARTS

3

THE VOICE: YOUR WEAKEST LINK?

You know, I think, really, um, this is sort of a unique moment, both in our, you know, in our country's history and in, you know, my own life, and, um, you know, we are facing, you know, unbelievable challenges.

—Senate candidate Caroline Kennedy, December 2008

Did a vocal tic hinder Caroline Kennedy's efforts to become a US senator? Is it possible that the repeated use of the phrase "you know" contributed to the derailment of her bid to fill the seat that was once held by her uncle Robert F. Kennedy? Did the sloppiness of her sound drown out her ability to communicate the passion she would have brought to the job? At a minimum, the "you knows" were vocal chatter that inhibited her ability to express her desire to serve and caused her to appear uncertain. This chapter is a wake-up call about the enormous impact your voice has on the overall impression you make. Did you ever wonder if some aspect of how you sound is holding you back from the job, promotion, or recognition you seek?

The genesis of Kennedy's saga was an interview conducted by the *New York Times*. The entire interview transcript was released verbatim online, and that's when the "you know" count began to pile up. Subsequently, Kennedy made appearances where she seemed unable to articulate a complete thought without saying "you know." Soon, the "you knows" went viral, becoming fodder for late-night comedians and mocking videos.

Months later, Kennedy referenced what she called her "adventures in public speaking"[1] at the memorial service for her uncle, Senator Ted Kennedy. Caroline said it was Uncle Teddy who had often called with his notion of a great idea: "How would she like to introduce him at a political event?" She said those introductions were kind of a part-time job that was "unbelievably stressful." Given the stress she experienced, Caroline would have been well advised to have assessed her speaking style before seeking a high-profile position. Had the campaign team taken the time to rehearse and review practice tapes, the vocal tic would surely have been identified. Who knows what the outcome would have been had she been better prepared?

Kennedy is not the first woman to have the quality of her voice be judged so harshly. The female voice has long been deemed inferior to that of a male's. A high pitch can grate. And, outspoken women have been ridiculed or silenced for stepping out of traditional roles. In colonial America, women were publicly punished for talking too much and talking too loudly. Scolds and nags were bound to a dunking stool and submerged in tanks of water in the village square. A loquacious woman could choose between silence and drowning: "If she repentantly promised to control her speech, the dunkings would cease."[2] In 1847, Lucy Stone was one of the first women to earn a bachelor's degree and the near-unanimous choice of her classmates to give the commencement address. But the administration at Oberlin College would not permit her to deliver it "as it was deemed a breach of propriety to have young men and women together on the speakers' platform."[3] As a compromise, college officials said she could write the speech but not give it. Stone refused.

Even women in positions of authority cannot be certain that they will be allowed to be heard. Senator Kirsten Gillibrand was cut off before she had finished introducing Sonia Sotomayer at the Supreme Court nominee's confirmation hearings.[4] The New York senator was extolling the virtues of her sister New Yorker and ran long, as had some of her male colleagues. Yet she was the only senator to get the gavel from the committee chair. Gillibrand, who had been appointed to the seat Caroline Kennedy had sought, has also been criticized for how she sounds. Early in her tenure, critics tried to dismiss her as a blonde with a "baby doll voice" and a "tendency to ramble."[5] As you rise up the ladder, expect that every aspect of your speaking persona will face more intense scrutiny.

BUILDING VOCAL GRAVITAS

Many presenters who agonize over what they are going to say and how they look don't pay enough attention to the quality of their voice. They will endlessly futz with PowerPoint® slides and worry about their outfit without giving a thought to how they sound. Speakers who don't maximize their vocal potential will not realize their full effectiveness. The size of your voice can add more to your stature than any pair of high-heeled designer shoes. There is no need for the Jimmy Choos once you know how to use your voice to heighten your presence. Of all the delivery techniques, the voice is the most underused and overlooked tool. Let's repeat: "The voice is the most underused and overlooked tool."

What does your voice project? Is the tone warm and confident? Or could it etch glass? Julia Child was as well-known for her distinctive trill as for her French cooking. The voice is more likely to be a weak link for women than it is for men, but not because we have a genetic tendency to mumble or say "you know." Female vocal cords are generally shorter than male cords. As a result, a woman's voice tends to be thinner, higher pitched, or more breathy. Traditionally, the deep, low tones of a baritone are preferred over the soprano. It was Shakespeare who wrote of King Lear's daughter Cordelia: "Her voice was ever soft, gentle and low; an excellent thing in woman."

ELIMINATE THE HOWLS, HOOTS, AND HISSES

Maximizing your vocal potential starts with the recognition that the voice is an instrument that can be misused. "Howls, hoots, and hisses" limit effectiveness because the audience tunes the speaker out. These gaffes detract from vocal power because they put attention on how the speaker sounds instead of on what is being said. The "you knows" lead the list of worst vocal meltdowns.

- **Filler noise:** Phrases like "you know" and words like "um" and "ahh" are extraneous noise filling what should be silence. Conjunctions like "so" and "and" can also be mindlessly repeated. Listeners will tolerate the filler sounds up to a point. One or two per minute will likely go unnoticed, but more than six or seven will distract the audience. Pausing is the corrective measure. Record yourself practicing aloud, then play back and listen for if, and when, you use superfluous words or sounds. Is it at the beginning of a sentence, the end, or midsentence? Identifying when you add unneeded noise will help you stop.

- **"One-two-three, one-two-three, one-two-three, and so on"**: A repetitive dance pattern can help you learn a new dance step. A repetitive speech pattern means you are stuck in a vocal rut. Does your voice lose volume at the end of sentences? Are all your sentences the same length—either too choppy or too long? Do you drone on at one monotonous pace? Audiences soon notice these patterns and begin to anticipate the next tic rather than focusing on content.

- **"I pledge allegiance to the flag..."**: Memorization is a recipe for disaster. Memorizing an entire presentation word for word increases the likelihood that you will project like a second grader reciting the Pledge of Allegiance. Rote memorization sucks the life blood out of subject matter, leaving the delivery robotic and indifferent. If you focus too much energy on getting the right words in the right order, the words will lose their meaning.

- **The girly-girl**: A grown woman who speaks with the voice of an eight-year-old is communicating "Don't expect too much from me" or "Don't hurt me." Princess Diana's high, thin voice contributed to the mystique surrounding her fairy-tale royal wedding. Later, when she served as an international ambassador for the anti-landmine campaign, the girlishness was gone. It had been replaced with a voice that sounded steady and was reassuring to those who had been affected by the deadly weapons of war.

- **"Please pass a tissue"**: A nasal voice makes the speaker sound as though she is suffering from a permanent head cold. Nasality is due to a lack of resonance in the chest. When breathing is centered in the nose, the air resonates in the nasal cavity. The nasal quality is often exacerbated by nervous tension, especially in the jaw and tongue. Unclench the jaw and avoid pushing your tongue against the roof of your mouth. Instead, open up the voice by yawning and feel your throat muscles widen and relax.

- **"Fu-gge-tt about it"**: A regional accent can spice up a presentation style and reveal something about the speaker. Most people enjoy the distinctive flavorings of Boston, Brooklyn, New Delhi, or Paris. However, some regional sounds may be disconcerting if they over-power your style by conjuring up negative stereotypes, such as all New Yorkers are rude, Southerners slow, and Brits pompous. A strong accent may also be more difficult to understand. If your accent is pronounced, consult a professional voice coach to gain tips on diction, pronunciation, and pacing.

- **Inappropriate giggles and titters**: Lisa Loopner and her geeky friend Todd of *Saturday Night Live* fame were two social misfits with a plethora of grating habits. The character Lisa, played by the brilliant comedian Gilda Radner, would emit a snorting laugh anytime she was embarrassed. Todd's junior-high antics, particularly his "noogies," were certain to set it off. Lisa's laugh was a hilarious reminder of how awkward it was to be a geeky teen, but laughter can be too much of a good thing when a speaker repeatedly uses it as punctuation at the end of sentences. A repetitive giggle for no reason signals discomfort and anxiety. It is another variation of extraneous noise used to fill what should be a pause.

THE THREE Vs OF COMMUNICATION

The voice is one of three components that enable a presenter to connect with an audience. Well-spoken women use all of the three Vs of communication: vocal, visual, and verbal. *Vocal* refers to the quality of sound. *Visual* includes what the audience sees: eye contact, body language, visual aids, and appearance and attire. *Verbal* is the content of the message, that is, what is said.

Most people believe the verbal component is the one audiences remember best. That is not the case. More impact is created with the vocal and visual elements. Psychologist Albert Mehrabian studied the way in which audiences zero in on how something is said. His classic research is known as the 7-38-55 percent rule. According to Mehrabian, the audience's initial impression of the speaker is drawn most prominently from what they hear and see rather than from the words used. Just 7 percent of the initial impact comes from the content. The voice is much more powerful, accounting for 38 percent of the audience's reaction. Visual information is strongest at 55 percent.[6]

Three Vs of Communication

Visual—55 percent body language and appearance
Vocal—38 percent voice quality
Verbal—7 percent message

Audience members listen to the timbre of the voice and watch body language to form an impression. In fact, the audience can be so preoccupied with nonverbal messages that, while they do "hear" the words, they rely on tone and actions to interpret what is being said. Mehrabian wrote: "Our silent messages may contradict what we say in words; in either event, they are more potent in communication than the words we speak," and "others weigh our actions more than our words as they try to understand what we feel."[7]

Enunciate Your Intention

Audiences interpret what is said according to how it is said and how it sounds. The voice is capable of providing many clues regarding a presenter's feelings about a topic. The way you choose to stress words or inflect your voice can change the meaning of a sentence. Raising your pitch at the end of a sentence makes it sound like a question. Increasing volume and slowing the pace can communicate anger. Here is a simple exercise to illustrate the point. Try this yourself: it's easy and just takes a minute. Read the following sentence out loud:

"I didn't say she stole my purse."

Good, now repeat the sentence seven times out loud. Each time, emphasize a different word in the sentence. So, read it again and stress the word "I." Then read it stressing the word "didn't."

"*I* didn't say she stole my purse."

"I *didn't* say she stole my purse."

Do you notice how the meaning of the sentence changes depending on which word is emphasized? When "I" is stressed, you communicate that you didn't accuse her, but someone else may have. When "didn't" is stressed, you convey the point that you never raised the allegation.

Sentence	Meaning
"I didn't *say* she stole my purse."	You didn't say it, but it was implied in the e-mail message.
"I didn't say *she* stole my purse."	It wasn't her—it was him.
"I didn't say she *stole* my purse."	But she took it without asking permission.
"I didn't say she stole *my* purse."	It was my friend's purse.
"I didn't say she stole my *purse.*"	It was my laptop bag, and I want it back.

THE GIFT OF VOICE

A well-spoken woman who epitomizes how to command an audience with the voice is former Representative Barbara Jordan. The enormity of Jordan's vocal gift was summed up by humorist Molly Ivins when she quipped if a casting call went out for the role of Great God Almighty, Jordan would have no competition for the part. Jordan is remembered as having booming pipes that seemed heaven-sent. The power of Jordan's voice was in the clarity of her diction and the deep resonance of her sound. Her unique vocalization was coupled with enduring insights into what it means to be an American. In Congress, Jordan became known as the conscience of the nation for the leadership she displayed during the Watergate hearings. Audiences didn't just listen to Jordan; her words could pierce your soul.

Her commanding vocal quality could have been overwhelming if Jordan hadn't possessed a lively sense of humor. She took herself very seriously but wasn't above joking about herself. In a 1977 commencement address at Harvard University, she told the graduates she viewed a Harvard education as "the unexcelled badge of intellectual achievement, if not superiority. My appearance here may not honor you, but it certainly honors me. One reason I attended Boston University Law School was so I could be close." She then went on to reminisce about the day her undergraduate alma mater, the Texas State University for Negroes, took on the Harvard debate team. Jordan was a standout member of the team and was pleased when the contest was judged a tie. But upon reflection, she thought the judges got it wrong: "It now occurs to me that if Harvard students were as superior as everyone thought, they should have won. Since the score was tied, we must have won."

A Nurtured Gift

Barbara Jordan knew she had the gift of voice as a teenager. Good Hope Missionary Baptist Church was the center of the Jordan family, and it was where Barbara heard and assimilated the rhythmic cadences of Baptist sermons. Her parents, Ben and Arlyne, raised three daughters in Houston's fifth ward, a racially segregated community. Ben was a Tuskegee man who worked

Barbara Jordan

as a warehouse clerk and part-time minister. From her father, Jordan learned the importance of precise diction. Her mother was an orator in her own right who spoke at church revivals and missionary meetings.

Born and raised in Texas, Jordan had a voice with a decidedly New England, Kennedyesque quality. This may have been due in part to her law school years in Boston and her time as a volunteer for John F. Kennedy's presidential campaign. Her distinctive voice contributed to her sense of being exceptional, which had been reinforced by her grandfather, John Patton. He encouraged her to think of herself as smarter than other kids, telling her that "she could do better, she could be better." She strived to exceed his expectations and in high school decided she must be named "Girl of the Year." Her strategy to secure the honor focused on maximizing her vocal talents and minimizing what she lacked. Jordan was not born with many of the things that mattered to other teenagers—the right clothes, "the right light color," and the right hair.[8] So, she set out to become the best public speaker at Phillis Wheatley High School by winning debates and oratorical contests.

What Jordan might ultimately do with her speaking ability was made clear during a school assembly in 1950. A guest speaker named Edith Spurlock Sampson, a trailblazing African American attorney, knocked Jordan's socks off with her poised, assured demeanor. Sampson told the students they should consider the law as a career. Jordan remembered Sampson as an incredible presence: "I didn't know what I was talking about, but I declared in the tenth grade I will become a lawyer."[9] It wasn't until 1949 that law schools began to admit African American students, but Jordan's mind was made up. After being selected "Girl of the Year" in her senior year, she was on her way.

A Talker Who Walks the Walk

Jordan liked to remind people that she graduated from Texas State University (TSU), a school that was created to keep black students out of the University of Texas. At TSU, Jordan was a speaking champion, yearbook editor, sorority sister, and student council member. When she applied to law school, Jordan chose Boston University because it was one of only two schools in the country that had always been integrated. In Massachusetts, Jordan felt isolated in an unfamiliar community and outmatched by her peers. Her class of over six hundred students included only two black women, and the competition was rigorous. She was up against equally ambitious students, some of whom had the advantage of degrees from top schools. For the first time, she questioned whether she would be able to compete.

> I realized, starkly, that the best training available in an all-black, instant university was not equal. Separate was not equal, no matter what face you put on it. It came to me that you couldn't just say something was so, because somebody brighter, smarter, more thoughtful would come out and tell you it wasn't so. Then, if you still thought it was, you had to prove it. I really can't describe what that did to my insides and to my head. I said I'm being educated, finally. I'm doing sixteen years of remedial work in thinking.[10]

In her first year, Jordan feared the remedial work she needed would cause her to fail, so she studied in private, not wanting her classmates to see her struggle. There was no money to travel home for the holidays, and she spent her first Christmas alone at the movies. Later, Jordan commented that those trying years taught her to always be ready. She would go so far as to prepare for conversations with other students so they would never perceive any shortcomings. The discipline she gained is evident in the texts of her speeches—every word is purposefully chosen. Unlike the speakers of much of today's overblown political rhetoric, Jordan made sure she knew what she was talking about.

With law degree in hand, Jordan returned to Houston and set up shop as an attorney, but her law career was short-lived. In 1960, she volunteered for Kennedy's presidential campaign and traveled extensively, rallying African American business and community leaders and speaking in black churches. Her popularity as a speaker led to her decision to run for a state legislative seat, for which she campaigned twice and lost. In 1964, the Civil Rights Act passed, and Texas was ordered to reapportion a number of legislative districts. Two years later, Jordan ran and won in a predominately minority district in Houston, becoming the first African American elected to the state senate since 1883. She served her constituents for eight years and in 1972 was elected to the US House of Representatives, becoming the first African American Texan to serve in Congress.

In Washington, DC, Jordan was soon heralded as a forceful voice for change, as someone who championed the rights of the oppressed and spoke out against bigotry, hatred, and ignorance. She gained national recognition as a member of the House Judiciary Committee when she spoke at the impeachment hearing of President Nixon. Millions of television viewers watched her impassioned speech on the fundamentals of democracy.

> Earlier today, we heard the beginning of the Preamble to the Constitution of the United States: "We, the people." It's a very eloquent beginning. But when that document was completed on the seventeenth of September in 1787, I was not included in that "We, the people." I felt somehow for many years that George Washington and Alexander Hamilton just left me out by mistake. But through the process of amendment, interpretation, and court decision, I have finally been included in "We, the people."[11]

In her distinctive cadence, Jordan explained how the president had put himself above the rule of law and why his misdeeds were crimes. The discipline she developed in law school was on full display as she logically laid out a convincing argument for impeachment while articulating her patriotism and love for country. When she finished, committee members had tears in their eyes, and within days Americans were calling for Barbara Jordan to be president. Jordan was no longer just 1 of 535 members of Congress. She was an inspirational leader who would speak for justice and equality for all.

All-Time Great Line

My faith in the Constitution is whole; it is complete; it is total. And I am not going to sit here and be an idle spectator to the diminution, the subversion, the destruction, of the Constitution.
—Representative Jordan, 1974 Watergate hearings

FIVE Ps OF A VIBRANT VOICE

Some clients are reluctant to work on their voice because it brings them too close to the feeling that I'm trying to "change who they are." Those concerns are valid because the voice is an important part of individual personality. But consider the fact that you may not be using the full range of what is available. Small changes can help you discover the fullness of your sound and help you project more of your personality. This section introduces five essential ways to develop the voice as a power tool. The five Ps of a vibrant voice help you control the voice and use it more purposefully.

Step 1: Pleasing Pitch

What is your natural pitch? Is it high or low on the musical scale? There are two general pitch ranges: chest voice and head voice. The chest voice resonates in the top part of your chest. The head voice vibrates behind your eyes and in your nose. Men tend to use more chest voice, which produces lower tones. Lower tones can be advantageous because they are associated with qualities like authority, control, confidence, and expertise. Imagine the booming bass of James Earl Jones in the role of Darth Vader: "You don't know the power of the dark side."

Women who tend to speak with more head voice will have a slightly higher pitch. High notes are often associated with shrillness or stridency. The stress of nervous anxiety can compound the problem by causing the voice to rise or break into a falsetto. Volume can also raise pitch. If you speak loudly in order to be heard above the noise of a crowd or to fill a vacuum in a large room, you may sound nervous or overly excited. A higher-pitched sound can also convey energy and enthusiasm, however. Political pundit Mary Matalin's voice is unusual with its sharp, nasal quality. Matalin knows how to control her sound and uses it to break through cacophony on cable talk shows.

The ideal voice mixes high and low tones. Variety in pitch and inflection will keep listeners engaged. A voice that lacks any change in pitch is a monotone. A dull, flat sound is easy to tune out, particularly after a heavy meal or during a long meeting. Make your voice come alive by using inflection, raising and lowering pitch purposefully. The most captivating voices utilize a full range of notes on the musical scale.

Step 2: Pick Up the Pace

The ideal speaking pace is a conversational rate. This rate is pleasing to the listeners, and it provides the speaker with the time to think and breathe properly. A moderate rate of speech is approximately 140 to 170 words per minute. The first two paragraphs of this section on pace contain 152 words. Read the two paragraphs out loud and time yourself with a stopwatch. Stop reading when you reach one minute. (If you finish the second paragraph before time is up, start over with the first paragraph again.) Then go back and count the number of words you used during the minute. Does your voice fall within the conversational rate range?

If you use more than 170 words in a minute, you need to slow your overall pace. For fast talkers, this requires serious concentration and practice, plus the use of pauses. If you are below 130 words, you need to quicken your overall pace. Your normal rate is too slow and will sound like it is dragging.

(Did you time yourself reading the last two paragraphs out loud? If not, do so now so you can get a sense of your rate of speech.)

Within the range of conversational speech, your speaking style will be much more dynamic if your speed changes from time to time. Varying the speed prevents you from falling into a sluggish or predictable tempo. A change of pace can also signal to the audience that a change of mood or a transition in subject is taking place. Slowing the pace makes what you are talking about sound more important. A slower rate gives more weight or puts more emphasis on the meaning of the words. The audience will feel as if they should pay closer attention to what is being said. Conversely, picking up the pace will sound more energetic. Changing the pace literally sounds like you are changing gears.

Step 3: Purposeful Pauses

The pause is the most underused of the vibrant voice techniques. When presenters do pause, they generally do so too seldom and too briefly. The pause is extremely helpful to you, and it is necessary for the audience. There are three reasons to pause.

1. Pause to dramatically highlight key words and phrases. Set up important lines such as "I have a dream." The pause serves as a verbal signal to the audience to pay attention because what is coming next is worth listening to.
2. Pauses are opportunities to breathe. Getting oxygen to the brain helps you relax and is vital to your ability to control your vocal quality. While you take a breath, you can think about what you are going to say next so the words don't just rumble, tumble out of your mouth.
3. Finally, pauses make excellent transitions from main idea to main idea. The pause signals that you are moving on to another topic.

The audience uses the pause to take in what is being said. The silence gives the listeners a moment to do more than just hear the words. During a two- to three-second pause, they have a chance to synthesize and absorb the meaning. Pausing also allows the audience to keep pace with you. It can be tempting to hurry through a presentation, particularly if you have given it before or are nervous. Bear in mind that most of the information is brand-new to the audience. Pauses allow the audience time to hear and remember.

Step 4: Pronounced Pronunciation

It has been said, when in doubt, mumble. But don't risk sounding like your mouth is filled with marbles. Mumblers—people who speak softly and with poor diction—are more likely to be regarded as less decisive, less intelligent, and poorly informed. Speakers who use crisp consonants and round, open vowel sounds are listened to more seriously. Muttering is the vocal equivalent of not looking someone in the eye.

Another good reason to use a moderate rate of speech is that a slower pace allows for clear enunciation of each word and syllable. If your speech is rushed, it is easy to drop the hard consonants like *t* and *d* at the ends of words, creating a slurred sound. Slow it down, articulate the syllables, and then you will be clearly heard and understood.

Step 5: Project to Be Heard

The voice has a wide volume range from barely audible to ear piercing. Prolonged whispering and screaming can damage the vocal cords, but less dramatic changes in volume are another way to add interest. Resist the temptation to always speak louder when you want the audience to pay close attention. It can be more effective to drop the volume a notch or two. You create the sense that people need to lean in and listen hard to what's being said. Here again, variability is the secret. Purposefully vary volume level throughout a presentation. Changing the volume keeps the audience more attuned.

If you have trouble projecting at a normal conversational level, improper breathing may be the cause. You will not be able to fully project unless you breathe using the diaphragm. See the section on relaxation techniques in chapter 2 for more details on how to take a deep breath that will sustain your voice. If you are soft-spoken, consider using a microphone before groups larger than twenty-five people or when speaking outside.

PRACTICING THE VIBRANT VOICE

Here's a great exercise that will help you activate the five Ps of a vibrant voice. It gives you a chance to explore the range of your voice by purposefully varying pace, pitch, and projection. Be sure to interject good, healthy pauses, all the while using crisp, clear pronunciation. Begin by reading the following lines from a poem by Emily Brontë called "High Waving Heather 'neath Stormy Blasts Bending." This poem was chosen because the dated language and unfamiliar phrasing is difficult to read quickly. Deliver the first stanza aloud once to acquaint yourself with the words and cadence.

> High waving heather 'neath stormy blasts bending,
> Midnight and moonlight and bright shining stars,
> Darkness and glory rejoicingly blending,
> Earth rising to heaven and heaven descending,
> Man's spirit away from its drear dungeon sending,
> Bursting the fetters and breaking the bars.[12]

Notice how the unusual words and distinctive phrasing force you to slow down and think about each word as you pronounce it aloud. The next step is to use a highlighter to select one or two words from each line to emphasize. For example, you could select the words as I have illustrated below. Now, read the poem aloud again, this time stressing the highlighted words.

> High waving *heather* 'neath stormy *blasts* bending,
> Midnight *and* moonlight and bright *shining* stars,
> Darkness and glory *rejoicingly* blending,
> Earth rising *to heaven* and heaven *descending*,
> Man's spirit away from its *drear dungeon* sending,
> Bursting the fetters *and* breaking the *bars*.

I bet what you just read sounds infinitely more interesting. I would also wager that it was much more fun to vocalize. You are now close to sounding like a voice-over professional. Mark up the full poem below and recite it for a friend. There is no right or wrong way to do this. The point is to make the poem come alive through your vocalization.

> High waving heather 'neath stormy blasts bending,
> Midnight and moonlight and bright shining stars,
> Darkness and glory rejoicingly blending,
> Earth rising to heaven and heaven descending,
> Man's spirit away from its drear dungeon sending,
> Bursting the fetters and breaking the bars.

All down the mountain sides wild forests lending
One mighty voice to the life-giving wind,
Rivers their banks in their jubilee rending,
Fast through the valleys a reckless course wending,
Wider and deeper their waters extending,
Leaving a desolate desert behind.

Shining and lowering and swelling and dying,
Changing forever from midnight to noon;
Roaring like thunder, like soft music sighing,
Shadows on shadows advancing and flying,
Lightning-bright flashes the deep gloom defying,
Coming as swiftly and fading as soon.

No longer are you just reading words on a page. The inflection and tempo changes help you sound passionate and engaged. Try it with a favorite poem or another reading. Next time you prepare for a presentation, do the same thing with your speech text. Mark it up just as you did the poem and read it aloud in its entirety so you can plan pauses, pace changes, and inflections.

The following are additional exercises to maximize vocal range and quality. Experiment with the techniques to explore your full potential. You can do the exercises in the car, while you're loading the dishwasher, or anytime you have a few minutes to spare.

- **Bedtime stories:** Vocalize all the characters and animals in a favorite like *Winnie-the-Pooh*.
- **Tongue-twisters:** Pick one and say it quickly, out loud, several times. "She sells sea shells by the sea shore." But don't go so fast that you are not able to articulate every word.
- **Sing a song:** Sing a favorite song or imitate an admired performer. Try letting loose with Aretha Franklin's "Respect." Do it just a little bit and find out what it means to free the creative left brain to express ideas with freshness and emotion.
- **Join the *Mad Men:*** Join the team at the fictional advertising agency Sterling Cooper Draper Pryce. Be Peggy Olson or Don Draper and

voice the attitude depicted in the words and pictures in a favorite magazine. Ad copy is concise; each word has meaning. Vocalize the emotion.

- **Be an impersonator:** Mimic the people you encounter throughout the day. The ultimate impressionist, Anna Deavere Smith, created a new theatrical genre combining interviews with her ability to "walk in [the] words" of her subjects. A sampling of memorable characters includes a Korean shopkeeper, urban homeboys, a Jewish mother, and a fiery preacher.

THUNDEROUS SPECIAL EFFECTS

Barbara Jordan didn't wave her arms around like a used car salesperson. She didn't roam the stage like a motivational speaker. Neither did she preach the fire and brimstone of an evangelical. She didn't need wild theatrics to hold her audience. Her technically superior voice projected what she wanted to express. Toward the end of her life, Jordan was diagnosed with multiple sclerosis and eventually was unable to walk. While her body may have let her down, the physical ailments couldn't rob her voice of its force.

Once you have mastered the five Ps of a vibrant voice, you will be ready to attempt some special vocal effects. "Who Then Will Speak for the Common Good?" was the speech Jordan gave at the 1972 Democratic National Convention. Listen online, and you will hear a range of vocal techniques. As you take in Jordan's majestic sound, note how she used the techniques outlined below.

Step 1: Extreme Confidence

Any self-doubt Jordan may have experienced was never conveyed in public. Onstage, Jordan's confidence reverberated in her tone, pacing, inflection, and grand pauses. It is also evident in how she talked about her specialness. At the Watergate hearings, she referred specifically to how race and gender had been originally excluded from the Constitution. In the convention address, she noted that 144 years after the Democrats first met, they finally invited a woman to give the keynote.

But there is something different about tonight. There is something special about tonight. What is different? What is special?

I, Barbara Jordan, am a keynote speaker.

A lot of years passed since 1832, and during that time it would have been most unusual for any national political party to ask a Barbara Jordan to deliver a keynote address. But tonight here I am. And I feel that notwithstanding the past that my presence here is one additional bit of evidence that the American Dream need not forever be deferred.[13]

Step 2: Purposeful Repetition

The total running time of the speech is approximately twenty minutes without applause. In that brief span, Jordan repeatedly hits on the theme and refers to the "common good" seventeen times. She drives home her message with the use of four related phrases: *common good, common spirit, common destiny,* and *national community.* Key words are also repeated. Jordan uses the word *share* five times. The *concept of governing* is repeated four times.

Step 3: Exaggerated Pronunciation

We are a people in search of a (pause) *na-tion-al* (pause) *co-mmun-i-ty.*
We are a *hete-ro-gen-e-ous* party....
It is *hy-po-cri-ti-cal* for the public official....
Our concept of *go-vern-ing....*

Step 4: Dramatic Volume Drops

Jordan's voice uses volume in unexpected ways. Some speakers fall into the trap of repeatedly lowering or raising volume at the ends of sentences. Jordan, on the other hand, would mix things up by raising the volume in the middle of the sentence, as is shown in the first two sentences below. (As the font size increases, so does the volume.)

We are attempting to fulfill our national purpose; **to create and sustain a society** in which all of us [pause, drop pitch] are equal.

Let's all understand that these guiding principles cannot be **discarded for short-term political gains**. They represent what this country is all about. They are indigenous to the American idea. And these are principles which are not [pause] negotiable.

In addition to varying the volume within a sentence, Jordan was very effective at using volume to build to a crescendo. In the sentence below, the volume slowly and deliberately rises as she reaches her big point.

We have a positive vision of the future founded on the belief that the gap between the promise and **reality of America can one day be finally closed. We believe that**.

Step 5: Clipped Sentences Used as Punctuation

Now what are these beliefs?
Let everyone come.
We believe that.
They must have that.
It can be done.
We must be.
We have to do that.
Strike a balance.

THE CARE AND FEEDING OF THE VOICE

Now that you've done all the work to add inflection and interest to your voice, don't sap it of its new vigor and vitality. In junior high school, I played the trumpet in the marching band. It was my responsibility to keep my instrument in good working order, so I faithfully oiled the valves and cleaned the mouthpiece. Your voice is an instrument that needs regular maintenance to keep it in good working order. Follow the care and feeding guidelines to ensure your voice stays in top form.

Good for the Voice

- **Warm-up exercises:** Slowly roll your shoulders back. Feel the chest open and expand. Slowly open and close your mouth. Feel your facial and neck muscles relax.
- **Talk to yourself:** Practice aloud using the five Ps of a vibrant voice.
- **Yoga breath:** Breathe in deeply through the nose, hold for a count or two, and slowly exhale through your mouth. Repeat as often as needed.
- **Water:** Hydrate as much as possible because water keeps the vocal cords lubricated. Avoid ice water because the cold constricts the vocal cords. Warm tea or room-temperature water is better.
- **Throat lozenges:** Add a little extra moisture to prevent cotton mouth.
- **Humidifiers:** Dry air aggravates the vocal cords.

Bad for the Voice

- Milk products and chocolate coat the inside of your mouth.
- Carbonated drinks may make you burp.
- Alcohol will slur your speech.
- Caffeine acts as a diuretic and flushes water from your system.
- Smoking and secondhand smoke can damage the vocal cords.
- Frequent throat clearing can be distracting; use honey to soothe or lemon to clear away phlegm.
- Yelling causes strain.

The following warning signs may indicate trouble with the voice. If you experience any of these symptoms for more than a few days, be sure to consult with a medical professional:

- Your voice feels sore or tired.
- You are hoarse.
- You have to strain to speak.
- You lose your voice intermittently.

Many professional singers and broadcasters work with a vocal coach. Voice lessons are not about belting it out like Christina Aguilera. Rather, they help you learn how to control an extreme nasal quality, a high pitch, breathiness, or other vocal issues. With a qualified instructor, you will learn how the voice works so you can avoid damaging it and maximize its full potential.

STANDING OVATION POINT: WELL-SPOKEN WOMEN RESONATE LOUD AND CLEAR

In 1984, Barbara Jordan received one of her many honors when she was named the "World's Greatest Living Orator." Another fitting tribute to the size and scale of her contribution to American life would be her likeness carved on the Mount Rushmore of Well-Spoken Women. Imagine hearing her crisp, deep voice echo against the granite wall. It would carry for miles across the South Dakota plains. Jordan was an extraordinary American whose vocal abilities made her even more special.

Applause Principles: Be the Voice of Authority

- The voice, visual, and vocal components are the three integral ways to connect with an audience.
- Strengthen your voice to get the respect you deserve.
- Record your regular speaking voice to assess strengths and weaknesses.
- Use practice exercises to expand your vocal range and capabilities.
- Vocal variability is sweet music to the ears.

4

STAND UP STRAIGHT—
LIKE YOUR MOTHER
ALWAYS SAID

> So I learned how to throw a ball—and a right cross—as well as any boy
> in my neighborhood.
>
> —First Lady Michelle Obama,
> International Olympic Committee Address, October 2009

Michelle Obama says she shared the gift of sports with her father, who taught her how to compete with all the kids in the South Shore neighborhood of Chicago. With Fraser Robinson's guiding hand, she learned "self-confidence, teamwork, and how to compete as an equal."[1] Obama has brought that athletic sensibility to the White House as she works to keep herself, her family, and America's children physically fit. This interest and active participation in sports motivates others to exercise and contributes to her success as a public speaker.

The love of sports was the topic of Michelle Obama's first international address as First Lady. The announcement that the First Couple would join the US Olympic Committee in Denmark to support the bid for the 2016 games in Chicago generated serious buzz in the sporting community and beyond. The world was caught up in the excitement of the new Obama presidency. At the Team USA headquarters hotel in Copenhagen, euphoria broke out with the news that the president and the First Lady would both speak to the International Olympic Committee. Many felt that their presence would be the crowning touch that would secure America's victory against the other finalist countries. Although it did not work out that way in the end, it was an exhilarating experience for all.

As a member of the speech-coaching team that had been prepping the Olympic athletes and officials for their remarks, I was thrilled to learn I would rehearse with the First Lady. The initial coaching session was scheduled to take place just hours after Air Force One touched down. Due to tight security, we could not work in the specially designed training center equipped with digital cameras and big-screen playback. Arrangements were made to meet in the hotel where many foreign dignitaries were staying and where Secret Service could better control access. The practice space was an ordinary hotel room—not the presidential suite—with the bed removed to make way for a speaker's lectern and the teleprompter. As often is the case when working with high-profile clients, the catered food was better than usual, but the accommodations were spontaneously thrown together.

Olympic Workout

The First Lady arrived for the first session slightly out of breath, having just completed a series of one-on-one meetings with voting members of the Olympic committee. If she was suffering from jet lag, the only sign she gave was kicking off her heels to give her feet a break. Otherwise, she looked stunning in a signature designer dress and seemed ready to get to work immediately. The initial run-through was the first chance Obama had to review the remarks, which were a loving tribute to her father. She reminisced about watching former Olympic stars "Nadia and Olga" while nestled in his lap. She also recalled the time he spent with his children on the ball field even after his multiple sclerosis forced him to use crutches. The narrative of the speech captured "the sense of unbridled possibility" that Obama's

First Lady Michelle Obama

father had instilled in her and the lasting effect of watching Olympians excel in competition.

After a few practice runs, I noticed that the First Lady's posture appeared a bit slumped in the shoulders. She explained that she had been previously instructed to "settle in" when standing at a lectern and demonstrated how she was leaning on it by placing her hands and forearms on top. This was a bad suggestion for a woman who stands nearly six feet tall in her stocking feet because it caused her shoulders to hunch forward. I quickly showed her how she could maximize her stature by using the "champion stance." She graciously accepted the feedback and immediately felt the improvement. It worked well for her, and I think she was pleased with that advice. The champion stance is the fix for all posture issues because it helps everyone project a strong presence; the stance works for First Ladies as well as for women of all heights. You'll find more details on how you can use it in the "Well-Spoken Woman's Body Language Playbook" section of this chapter.

Despite a Herculean effort by the First Lady and the president, the international committee awarded the games to Brazil. However, the news media coverage of the US delegation described the First Lady's remarks as the presentation's emotional core. In a shimmering yellow dress, "the First Lady stood out like a star in front of a backup chorus."[2] According to CNN, Obama stole the show, taking home a "gold medal" with her personal story of people like her father "who face seemingly insurmountable challenges, but never give up."[3] Moreover, she carried herself like a winner.

IMPRESSION MANAGEMENT

Well-spoken women get their bodies into the act, and who knows better than athletes how to move with dexterity and strength. Giving it your all on court or onstage is physically exhausting. The initial rush of adrenalin causes the heart to race and palms to sweat. The firing of brain cells provides mental alertness and the ability to concentrate. The vocal cords get a workout projecting to the back of the room. After a twenty-minute talk, it can feel as if you have just run a brisk mile. The best speakers, like the best athletes, strive for every physical advantage to achieve peak performance.

Do you know what your body language is communicating? Are you sending accurate signals about competence and readiness? Do distracting mannerisms mask your true potential? Is your posture submissive? Hand gestures aggressive? Eye contact nonexistent? This chapter takes up the second of the three Vs of communication—the visual. How you look has the strongest overall impact on your audience. It is more memorable than what you say. Many presenters do not realize the impact of body language. When TV's Mary Richards joyfully tosses her hat in the air, we feel her exuberance and root for her to "make it after all." Gestures large and small speak volumes. If you haven't considered your physicality, you might be surprised to learn what you are communicating while you are talking.

The Disconnect of Cognitive Dissonance

Cognitive dissonance refers to a disconnect that exists between what you think you did and how you actually came across. With cognitive dissonance, your self-image is blurred. For example, you thought it went well, but the audience was distracted by your constant finger tapping and couldn't pay attention to what you said. Or you felt you bombed because of your shaky hands and quivering voice; meanwhile, the audience never noticed because they were being blown away by your creative PowerPoint® presentation. For an accurate sense of what you project, you need to watch yourself in action. Verbal feedback from a colleague likely isn't sufficient to help you accurately process the performance.

At the suggestion of her boss, a lobbyist for an education group came in for a public speaking training session. She had been told that her rushed, jumbled presentation style was causing others to question her competence. When we met, the first thing out of her mouth was "People tell me I talk fast." She repeated this several times, very quickly: "I know I talk fast, I have always talked fast. I can't stop talking so fast." Despite her acknowledgment of the feedback, it hadn't sunk in that she needed to change if she was going to improve. When we played back the training tape, she experienced a revelatory flash. "Boy, I really *do* talk fast!" The rushed words were accompanied by jerky hand movements and darting eyes. She finally saw how her frenetic style came across to others. Reviewing practice tapes can help you break through the cloud of misperception that can be created by cognitive dissonance.

The Coaches' Coach

No one is better positioned to focus on the fundamentals of body language than the world's most successful basketball coach. Pat Summitt was named head coach of the University of Tennessee Lady Volunteers at the age of twenty-two, and thirty years later the school named the court for her—The Summitt. She has won more college basketball games than any other coach, male or female. Coach Summitt preaches the gospel of "winners communicate." This core belief in the necessity of communication has made the Lady Vol players winners on the court and off. Great coaches, like great speakers, learn lessons from wins and losses, and Summitt is no exception.

During NCAA tournament play, a photograph of the coach grabbing a player by the uniform and screaming at her was plastered on the front page of *USA Today*. Summitt lost her cool when the player celebrated a three-point shot late in the game rather than hustling down the court to play defense. The misstep resulted in an easy score for the opposing team. In the heat of the game, Summitt was upset with her player's lack of discipline—but not nearly as upset as she was when she saw the photo. Immediately she called the player's mother to reassure her: "I'm not abusing your child, I promise."[4]

While the Kodak moment of her "General Patton" style made instant headlines, Summitt isn't a

Coach Pat Summitt

coach who throws chairs or punches. She is best known for telegraphing her legendary toughness with intense eye contact, otherwise known as "the stare." The fierce look has been described as cold enough to freeze time. When her son Tyler sees the glare, he asks his mother to please put her sunglasses on. Given Coach Summitt's proclivity for the stare, it is not surprising that eye contact is the first technique the Lady Vol players must master. Summitt equates eye contact with self-respect and mutual respect: "It demonstrates that you are confident enough to look at the person who is speaking and that you will give her your full attention."[5]

THE WELL-SPOKEN WOMAN'S BODY LANGUAGE PLAYBOOK

No visual technique is more important than establishing and maintaining eye contact with the audience. It is a sign of respect and it provides you with valuable feedback. How to make good eye contact is detailed here in the "Well-Spoken Woman's Body Language Playbook." The playbook contains diagrams and descriptions of how to execute the essentials: eye contact, posture, movement, facial expression, and hand gestures. These drills will ensure that you avoid a Kodak moment and are ready with your game face on.

Step 1: Eye Contact

Don't use the Summit glare unless you want to drive people from the room. Staring or an intense gaze can create pressure or tension, whereas solid, steady eye contact can communicate trustworthiness, sincerity, and seriousness. Being able to look at the listeners is essential to establishing your presence and maintaining a connection with them. Poor-quality eye contact can blow your credibility in a matter of seconds. Weak or nonexistent eye contact can leave the impression you are unprepared or ill informed. Avoid the biggest mistakes that cheat you and the audience.

Eye contact is mutually beneficial. It helps the audience connect, and it provides you with feedback to accurately gauge how you doing. What

---

Eye Contact Cheating

- Swinging your head from side to side. You look like you are watching Venus and Serena Williams play tennis on TV.
- Rapid eye darts. The movement will tire out your neck and eyes. Plus, nobody in the room feels like you are looking at them.
- Head buried in notes.
- Searching the ceiling for the answers.
- Turning your back to the audience to read from PowerPoint slides.

---

signals is the audience sending you? Do they appear to be attentive and listening? Do they look like they get it, or are they confused? Have you gone on too long? If they no longer make return eye contact, then they may be bored. The first two plays in the body language playbook are designed to help you keep your eye on the ball. The ball is always the listeners.

"Four-Box" Play

The "four-box" play ensures you look at everyone in the room, no matter the audience size—ten or ten thousand. The four-box play teaches you how to make quality eye contact with individuals by looking in all areas of the room but looking only at one person at a time. Implement the four-box play by mentally drawing a line across the middle of the room horizontally and then vertically, as you see below, to divide the room into four sections or boxes. Envision yourself standing in the rectangle at one end of the room.

Now that the play is diagrammed, here's how it is run. Each box is numbered to represent an area with people in it. Start by looking toward the first box and talking to one person seated in it. Then, move on to box two, again looking at one person. Work your way around the room in a clockwise fashion. When you look at one person, keep your eyes steady on that person until you finish a sentence or a thought. Keep looking at one person until

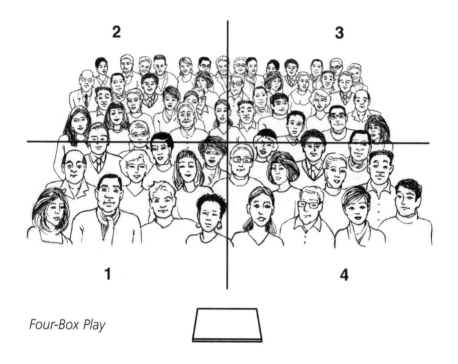

Four-Box Play

you get a whole sentence or idea out. The technique requires that you look at individuals a bit longer than you do in one-on-one conversation.

Initially, it may feel like you are overdoing it by staring. Researchers say we break eye contact every two or three seconds when talking one-on-one. In front of an audience, however, you don't want to cheat by flitting your eyes around the room. Extending the contact projects confidence, especially when you hold your eyes on one person until you finish your sentence. The four-box play gives you a way to practice so you remember to hold eye contact longer than you are accustomed to.

After you've moved around all of the four boxes, go back to the first box. This time, look at a different individual seated in the area. Same thing for box two; look at a different person. You don't want to keep looking at the same people in each of the boxes. Run the drill several times before using it with a live audience. With practice, you get into the swing and will not need the clockwise pattern. Continue using the four boxes to ensure you hit all areas, but no longer move from box one to two to three to four.

Instead, look at someone seated in box two, then at someone in box four or box one. The clockwise movement isn't the key. What is key is to hold eye contact steadily on one person until you complete a thought.

"Sweet-Spot" Play

Use the "sweet-spot" play when you want to make eye contact with everyone at once. First, locate the sweet spot. The sweet spot is the area directly in front of you, slightly above the head of the person seated farthest away. The sweet spot is in the center of the back of the room. When you direct your eye contact to the sweet spot, you appear to be looking at everyone in the room when actually you are looking at no one.

Looking at the sweet spot ensures that your chin is slightly raised. This helps you project to the entire room. Use the sweet spot at the beginning when you greet the audience and at the end to wrap up. Additionally, use the spot anytime during the presentation when you have an important point you want to share with everyone.

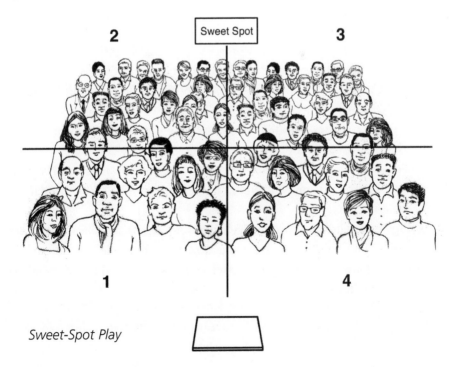

Sweet-Spot Play

Step 2: Posture

On the sidelines, Coach Summitt says she often looks like "a cross between a traffic cop and an orchestra conductor,"[6] getting her whole body into the action. She prefers to stand so she is visible to everyone in the basketball arena. Plus, she feels closer to the game and is in a better position to communicate with her players one-on-one. The coach purposefully uses her posture to convey conviction and strength, especially during stressful stretches of the game. How you stand may be communicating more than you think.

Posture Imperfect

- **The Mae West:** When someone stands with one hand on her hip, with the hip jutting out, don't you expect to hear, "Why don't you come on up and see me sometime?"
- **Crossed ankles:** This is a sign of insecurity and can be dangerous. Speakers with ankles crossed while standing risk falling on their face if they attempt to step forward.
- **Sway:** Tilting like a seesaw makes you look as if you are speaking from the deck of the *Titanic*. Yes, the ship is going down.
- **Superwoman:** Hands on hips, chest puffed out and up, feet shoulder width apart—the stance feels empowering but looks comical, especially if you are petite.
- **Cocked or tilted head:** You may be listening, but you look submissive and remind people of a curious dog.
- **Ten-hut!** No need to snap to attention. If your arms are held rigid, back ramrod straight, and shoulders tense, it will be a long presentation. At ease.
- **Fig leaf:** The position of Eve's daywear is not the place for your hands. The stance provides protection but communicates insecurity.
- **Locked-down arms:** Crossing your arms against the chest makes you look defensive or bored.

Champion-Stance Play

The champion stance is not just for First Ladies. It will help you project confidence with a relaxed yet commanding posture. Try the stance right now. Stand up and place one foot slightly in front of the other. Experiment to figure out which foot you prefer to place in the forward position. Pick whichever one feels more comfortable. Then, stand up straight with your body weight resting slightly on the back leg. Avoid positioning the feet shoulder width apart, which locks the knees in place. The champion stance provides the loose-kneed stance of a tennis player or downhill skier. With the knees loose, you feel more relaxed and look less rigid. If the knees are locked, nervous tension can run up the spine and settle in the neck and shoulders.

Now, with the feet in place and weight on the back leg, position your face forward. Pretend a string is attached to the lower part of your spinal column. The string extends up the spinal cord, through the neck, and out the top of the head. Project the string straight up from the crown of your head into the ceiling. Next, drop your shoulders back slightly. Don't stick your chest out. Just drop your shoulders back with your arms hanging loose at your sides. The shoulder drop-back is the secret to carrying yourself like a world champion.

Champion Stance

1. Position feet, one in front of the other.
2. Place weight on back leg.
3. Face forward.
4. Head up.
5. Shoulders drop back.
6. Weight moves forward.
7. Smile.

At this point, you likely will feel as if you want to move your body weight forward onto the front foot. Forward movement keeps the knees loose and appears interactive because you are moving toward the audience. This stance also prevents you from swaying side-to-side. Try the stance again in front of a mirror.

To Sit or Stand?

Whether courtside, at Carnegie Hall, or in a local community center, you will look and sound better if you adopt the champion stance. Standing posture presents a more dynamic presence and gives you more control. This is particularly true if there will be a question-and-answer session. However, in some forums it is more appropriate to remain seated, such as in a panel discussion. Fortunately, there is a champion stance for seated posture, too, to keep you from slumping in your chair. Don't cross your arms and legs as if you have been stuffed into a small seat on a crowded airplane. Rather, sit up straight with shoulders dropped back and down. Dropping the shoulders is what helps you look like a pro. Then tilt forward from the waist toward the audience keeping your back straight. Don't slouch or hunch your shoulders; just lean forward a couple of inches from the waist.

When seated behind a table or desk, put your hands and forearms on the table

Seated Champion Stance

Seated Champion Stance

1. Sit up straight.
2. Drop back shoulders.
3. Lean forward from the waist. Place hands and forearms on the table in V position.
4. Put one hand on top of the other.

in front of you. Position your forearms so they form a V on top of the table. Don't place your arms parallel to your body, because this position will cause you to hunch your shoulders. With the forearms in the V position, put one hand on top of the other. Avoid interlacing your fingers.

Step 3: Movement

Movement works when it is purposeful, not random. Purposeful movement is interactive, conveys enthusiasm, and keeps the audience attuned. They will shift in their seats to follow you. But you must be aware of how you are moving and where you are going. Otherwise, they will worry that you are going to stumble on an electrical cord, or that you will find yourself wandering in front of the PowerPoint screen and being blinded by the projection light. There are two basic ways to move. Let's start with movement behind a lectern. Then we'll discuss stage movement.

When speaking from a stationary position, many presenters develop tunnel vision as they lapse into speech mode. Grasping the sides of the lectern, they clamp down, and movement is limited to neck turns and eye darts. This is an unnatural stance that appears stiff. Most people do not stand motionless in everyday conversation. Let's revisit the four-box play so we can add a second layer of technique. When you look at someone seated in the box-one area, don't turn your neck. Rather, look at the person by turning from the waist. This is the ultimate secret to appearing engaged and relaxed. When conversing with someone in person, you face that person. Use the same movement in front of an audience.

Waist-Turn Play

To execute the waist turn, twist enough so that your shoulders are squared toward the person you are looking at. Let go of the lectern, and this will be easier to do. Then, when you turn to look at someone in another box, again turn from the waist. The waist turns eliminate excessive neck movement. If you feel your neck turning, that is a signal that you need to get the body moving. The body turns put you face-to-face with individuals, and they feel like you are looking at them because you are.

Three-Star Play

Stage Movement

If you are not using a speaker's lectern, then you need to be careful about how you move across a room or on a stage. Don't pace. Pacing back and forth makes the audience feel as though you've transported them to the National Zoo where they are watching some poor lion trapped in a cage. Use the "three-star" diagram to practice purposeful movement across a stage.

Before the presentation begins, envision the three stars on the floor. At the beginning, position yourself on the center star that is slightly behind the other two stars. If you start in a center-back position, then when you move, the movement will be forward toward the audience. Avoid moving away from the audience, particularly at the beginning, because you will look unsure.

Stay on the center star for a while before walking to one of the other stars. Deliver a couple of sentences or paragraphs of information before you move. When you arrive at the next star, stop and, again, stay a while to prevent pacing. When you walk again, you can go to either of the other stars, being careful not to turn your back to the audience. This requires being prepared to walk a little sideways but, with practice, is easy to do. Don't move too fast, or you will tire yourself and the audience out. Pace yourself so you don't run out of breath.

Step 4: Facial Expression

Coach Summitt says she has yet to see a newspaper photo of herself with her mouth closed. She thinks photographers wait until she yells before they snap away. Facial expressions should match the words coming out of your mouth. Look like you are happy if you say you are happy. This is basic, but people often start presentations by mouthing the words: "I'm so pleased to join you today." Meanwhile, their grim expression is anything but pleased. If you don't appear to be engaged and invested in the subject matter, you are giving the audience a reason not to listen. Some people use a limited range of facial expressions. However, most public-speaking situations are not the time for a poker face. The evolutionary theorist Charles Darwin wrote one of the first books examining facial expressions. Darwin found that monkeys and apes have the same facial muscles as humans and are capable of making many of the expressions we use. If monkeys can be expressive, so can you.

Animated Face Play

Begin with a smile, and you increase the odds the expression will be mirrored back to you. That sure beats looking at a bunch of stone faces. Women are generally more expressive than men, but some women mistakenly believe it is inappropriate to smile in a professional setting. The primary reason to smile is to project confidence. Some expressions don't work. President George W. Bush's closed-mouth smirk made him look contemptuous. A tight-lipped smile can be perceived as an attempt to mask anger or rejection, and a twisted smile may convey sarcasm. Researchers have also found that audiences can easily detect false expressions, so don't try to force a grin if you don't feel like smiling. A true smile is one that is visible in your eyes. Supermodels learn to smile with their eyes to prevent photographs from having a dull or flat expression.

Step 5: Hand Gestures

Not every speaker is a type-A personality like Coach Summitt, who has a tendency to flail her arms dramatically in the air. A low-key style can project steady calm and quiet confidence. But if you lack vocal inflection and are uncomfortable moving your body, you run the risk of being perceived as boring, stiff, or uninterested. Hand gestures can make your delivery more compelling. Hand gestures help the audience connect with your message—

a gesture can be used to underscore a central theme—and they can help you. Moving the hands loosens up the upper body to help you appear more relaxed. Gestures are a great way to externalize excess energy or anxiety. Get rid of nervous tension by letting it go through your arms and hands.

Keep gestures round and smooth. Harsh karate-chop jerks communicate aggression or nervous tension. Gestures should start in either the shoulder or the elbow. Do not flip your wrists around. You will look like Tweety Bird trying to take off. Here are other distracting movements to avoid.

Stop Fidgeting, Fiddling, and Futzing

- Don't get dressed in front of the audience by closing your jacket and smoothing your skirt while you walk to the lectern.
- Avoid tapping a pen or shuffling papers.
- Don't tap the lectern with your fingers or bang bracelets against it.
- No karate chopping or punching.
- Stop twiddling your thumbs.
- Avoid repeating the same gesture over and over.
- Don't do finger push-ups on the table or lectern.

Open-Hands Play

Hand gestures are a welcoming signal. They open you up so you look more accessible to the audience. When someone wants to communicate honesty, she will often raise her hands with palms facing the other person and say, "I mean it," or "I didn't do it." This intuitive gesture expresses openness and honesty.

There are three hand positions that work well with the champion stance.

1. Allow your arms to hang loosely at your sides. This is a neutral position but can feel awkward if you are nervous.
2. Another option is to raise both hands to waist level. Again, avoid interlacing your fingers. You can put one hand on top of the other or lightly brush your knuckles together.

3. Hold one hand at waist level with the other hand hanging at your side. Salespeople and politicians often use the one hand up and one hand down approach. If you have pockets, it is perfectly acceptable to put one hand in a pocket. However, putting both hands in your pockets will look sloppy.

The Body Language Playbook Summary

Four box—ensures quality eye contact.
Sweet spot—use when you need to look at everyone at once.
Champion stance—projects strength whether you are seated or standing.
Waist turns—engages individuals.
Three stars—achieves purposeful stage movement.
Animated face—look like you care.
Open hands—convey welcome and warmth.

THE FIRST IMPRESSION

"You had me at hello."

First impressions matter a great deal. People form an impression in seconds, and it can stick with them for a lifetime. Sometimes it is all they remember. Plan the first impression you will make in advance, especially if you feel anxious. Heads turn your way as soon as the introduction is read: "Please give a warm welcome to our speaker...." Start by greeting the audience visually. When walking into a room, onto a stage, or up to a head table, hold your chin so it is slightly raised. Don't stare at your feet or notes. Avoid rushing, as you may find yourself breathless and scrambling to control a racing heartbeat. Presenters often start talking before they are physically ready to begin.

Open with polish by taking a moment to get set. When you arrive at the spot from which you will be speaking, keep your head down while you arrange notes or cue up the PowerPoint. The bowed head sends a signal that you are not quite ready. Take a couple of seconds to get set and give the audience a moment to get ready to listen. They will adjust their seats, put away the cell phones, and wrap up the chitchat. Next take a deep breath and exhale so your vocal tone is warm. While you exhale, settle into the champion stance. Then, look up with a smile—at the sweet spot. Give them a nod; this is the signal you are about to begin. Take another breath, exhale, and deliver a greeting. All this will take only three or four seconds.

Prepare a written greeting in advance so you have the first two or three lines down pat. It may be as simple as "Hello, everyone. Thank you for inviting me. I'm delighted to join you today." Being prepared reduces the last-second pressure of deciding what to say. It also ensures your mind will not go blank. By taking a moment to get set, you will look prepared and assured. You will begin to develop a rapport with the audience right from the get-go.

Ready, Set, Go: A Winning First Impression

1. Take a second or two to ready yourself.
2. Keep your head down.
3. Use the champion stance.
4. Put on a smile.
5. Look up at the sweet spot.
6. Acknowledge the audience with a head nod.
7. Begin with a prepared greeting.

PODIUM PRESENCE

Coach Summitt is almost as tall as First Lady Obama, and their height gives both a decided advantage at a lectern—you can see them. Most lecterns are designed and built to fit people who are six feet tall, primarily men. Most women stand about five feet four inches, so a lectern often becomes a barrier. When Queen Elizabeth spoke at a press conference in the White House Rose Garden, the occasion was immortalized with photographs of the Queen's "talking hat." White House staff had overlooked the need for a podium, and the result was a pillbox hat bobbing up and down as the queen's face was masked by the press microphones.

Two types of podiums can provide a needed lift: a small box that is placed behind the lectern or a riser

---

All-Time Great Line

It's OK to let down your guard and allow your players to get to know you. They don't care how much you know until they know how much you care.

—Coach Pat Summitt

---

that is built into the floor. Consider purchasing your own box podium if you plan to speak frequently. The technical name for a small podium is an "apple box." Apple boxes are inexpensive, lightweight, portable, and available in varying heights. They can be purchased online. You may also ask the event host to provide one. Most do not think of this detail, so request it in advance.

Now that you can be seen, here are some pointers to ensure you look good up. A lectern is generally used for more formal occasions such as conferences, debates, and keynote addresses. It is furniture that can be employed to hold a microphone, a speech text, or a glass of water. It is not there to hold you up, so don't try to hide behind it. Avoid standing too close to it. Give yourself some wiggle room by backing away about eight inches or so. If you must touch it, rest your fingertips or hands lightly on top.

Lectern Gaffes

The death grip—knuckles turn white from clutching the sides.

The slouch, slump, or sprawl—are you too tired or weak to hold yourself up?

The footballer—men own this position; I've never seen a woman do it. Men will place their hands on top of the lectern near the forward edge with their arms straight. After a moment they start doing push-ups by flexing their elbows.

The barricade—the lectern is not there to hide behind.

The best friend—don't talk to the lectern rather than the audience.

WELL-SPOKEN MEANS WELL-DRESSED

Coach Summitt's courtside uniform is no longer an afterthought, as her clothing was when she was a tomboy growing up on a Tennessee farm. As a global ambassador for women's sports, she now suits up appropriately. Although it isn't easy finding stylish, camera-ready suits in the team color—bright orange—the coach's goal is to dress like a winner. Learning how to dress well took some effort because appearance wasn't always a priority for her.

The Summitt family lived on a dairy and tobacco farm, and by the age of ten, Pat was driving a tractor and baling hay alongside three brothers. On the farm, Summitt said: "A shopping spree was to buy a pair of striped pants at K-Mart."[7] When she headed off to the University of Tennessee–Martin, the transition was rocky. She described herself as a lanky, shy "farm kid with crooked teeth and all the wrong clothes, who said *ain't* and *reckon* and *yonder*."[8] Her suitcase was filled with dresses and jumpers that fell below the knee when miniskirts and knee-high boots were the rage. She began to pay attention to how she presented herself after joining the Chi Omega sorority. Her sorority sisters smoothed out the "ain'ts" and updated the wardrobe.

Unlike members of a basketball team, presenters don't need to be dressed uniformly with matching jerseys, socks, and warm-ups. However, certain clothing options will ensure your garb doesn't stand in the way of a good performance. Making wise choices in advance prevents the discomfort and embarrassment of ill-fitting clothes. Onstage, the entire package is up for review, so follow the basics to ensure your speaking uniform is a good fit.

> When a man gets up to speak, people listen, then look. When a woman
> gets up to speak, people look; then if they like what they see, they listen.
> —Pauline Frederick

Step 1: Avoid Wardrobe Malfunctions

A big presentation is not the time for a wardrobe malfunction. Remember Janet Jackson's Super Bowl halftime performance? When you are onstage, don't allow a popped bra strap or too-short skirt to steal the show. The act of giving the speech is demanding enough without having to worry about whether you can walk in the shoes or whether undergarments will show when you raise your arms. Women are much more likely to suffer a fashion faux pas than men. The guys have three basic uniforms: the formal dark suit, the navy blazer/khaki slacks combo, and the tuxedo for special occasions. These outfits ensure they are literally covered for all public appearances.

For women, our wardrobe choices are infinite, yet finding comfortable and smart-looking suits and shoes is sometimes nearly impossible. The fashion industry seems to conspire against us, pushing trendy, seasonal items. There are many traps: toe-crunching shoes, revealing necklines, clingy knits, and low-waist pants. *Functionality* is not a word generally associated with women's wear. If the industry paid more attention to a woman's needs, there would be more pockets in pants and jackets, and cute shoes would be comfortable.

Test-Drive the Outfit

Plan the speaking outfit in advance so you aren't caught in a bind: "It's the night before, and the dry cleaner is closed." Slacks with a stain or a skirt with a ripped hemline are more apparent when you are standing front and center. The likelihood that you can pick up a blouse in a flattering color that fits the day of the event is slim to none. Never wear a new outfit for the first time on the day of an important presentation. Take it for a test-drive by wearing it to another event when you are not the featured speaker. The "day of" is not the time to discover the pants weren't taken in properly or that the jacket is constricting.

A skirt that is slightly short when you are standing can ride up too far and expose the thighs when you are seated. If you find yourself in this revealing situation, the best recourse is to cross your ankles and pull both feet under the chair. This will reduce the amount of leg that is visible to the audience. Wrap and slit skirts are trouble because they tend to fall apart as soon as you sit down. It is more difficult to make a substantive point when your skirt keeps sliding open. Audiences may also interpret fidgeting with clothes as nervousness.

A petite economist wore a favorite blazer that was at least two sizes too big. She thought the jacket made her appear more authoritative. The opposite was true, she looked shrunken inside the droopy shoulders and too-long sleeves. Also, don't try to hide extra pounds with extra material. Clothes that are too big make you look heavier. If you have recently lost or gained weight, try on everything. Are there items that can be salvaged with tailoring? Purge or donate to charity clothes that are too large and too small. Alternatively, tailoring is an investment that can save money in the long run. You get more mileage out of comfortable clothes because they feel good and you will want to wear them.

Step 2: The Well-Suited Uniform Rules

Stage-ready clothes and accessories don't have to be budget busters, but no suit is worth the price tag if it is too tight, too short, or the wrong color. Since women are targets for endless fads, it is penny-wise to know how and where to invest wardrobe dollars. Follow the well-spoken woman's uniform rules below to avoid blowing your clothing budget on choices that aren't stage ready.

Uniform Rules

- **Clothes must fit:** Well-tailored clothes hide body flaws. If you've put on weight, a well-fitted suit can do wonders to conceal extra pounds. A poor fit can accentuate problem areas.
- **Cover up:** Visible cleavage or thighs send mixed signals.
- **Be audience-appropriate:** Don't disrespect the audience by being caught underdressed. You can always take a jacket off.
- **Be event-appropriate:** Plan as carefully for the company retreat in July and the holiday dinner in December as you would for the April board meeting.
- **Express a subtle personality:** A distinctive jacket cut or a flattering piece of jewelry makes a better statement than tiger prints and sequins.
- **Have great hair:** If it has been a while since you visited a good

salon, get a contemporary, flattering style that doesn't hide your eyes or fall in your face.

- **Support "the girls"**: You don't need to shrink wrap yourself in Spandex, but when was the last time you were measured for a bra?

Step 3: Event-Ready Wear

Without fail, the room temperature will either be too hot or too cold. Layering gives you options. You can leave the jacket off until it is your turn to speak. Be sure the top underneath is professional. Short sleeves are okay, but avoid tank tops and other sleeveless options. If you perspire heavily, wear thin layers to cover up wet spots. Also, avoid shirts that have to be tucked into your pants or skirt. They bunch, wrinkle, and dampen with perspiration. Try a shorter tunic style or shell that doesn't require tucking—it will be cooler and won't wrinkle. A man's-style dress shirt with buttons can be unflattering if the fit is too tight across the bustline, resulting in gaps.

A fitted dress with sleeves is not the best option if you will use a lavalier microphone because there is nothing to attach the clip to. A suit with pants or skirt is better because the battery pack can be attached to the waistband. If wearing a suit, one in a solid color will be more slimming. If you are wearing separates of mismatched colors, the jacket should be the lighter or brighter color, and the bottom should be in a darker color. If you normally wear high heels, assess how comfortable they will be after you stand in them for an extended period. It might be wise to wear a lower heel and make arrangements to have a podium to stand on.

Wrinkle Busting

Road warriors logging thousands of airline miles will get their money's worth out of better-quality suits. If you travel frequently, don't hesitate to invest in outfits that can withstand the rigors of airport delays and a crammed suitcase. The wrinkles will fall out overnight in a suit made of a high-quality fabric, a bargain in the long run. Also, blends of synthetic fibers with wools, cottons, and silks help clothes go the distance. Another great investment for travelers is a three-season raincoat with a hood.

Expect spills, drips, and stains of every sort. Dark colors are better at hiding accidents. It is always a good idea to bring a backup blouse and pantyhose. Checked luggage disappears all too frequently, so carry on a small bag with makeup and grooming essentials.

Special-Occasion Dressing

The association where you work is honoring Angelina Jolie at its annual awards luncheon, and you have been asked to introduce the movie star. An Aspen resort is the site for a meeting to pitch your services to wealthy high-tech entrepreneurs. The temperature is expected to be a sweltering 95 degrees, and you must walk in an Independence Day parade. You will give an acceptance speech at a gala sponsored by a large charitable organization. *Good Morning America* would like you to appear in the studio with George Stephanopoulos to discuss your research. The company's annual retreat will be held at a conference center in a national park, and you will give a motivational talk to senior staff.

Don't let these special-occasion events cause last-minute panic because you don't have anything suitable to wear. These are not the events where you want to show up wearing that old navy suit. The higher you rise up the ladder, the more opportunities you will have to appear in the media and to network at high-profile gatherings. It takes time to build a professional wardrobe. If you haven't a clue about what to wear, then seek help so you can avoid the fashion disasters below. Enlist the help of a personal shopper to figure out what is best suited to your body type and the occasion. Most major department stores provide the service free of charge.

What Never to Wear

- Schoolgirl flourishes—ruffles, bows, hair ribbons, fabrics with cutesy prints
- See-through blouses, plunging necklines, and short skirts with slits
- Flip-flops and extreme high heels
- False eyelashes, bright eye shadow, and heavy eyeliner
- Dangling earrings and clinking bracelets
- Super-long, brightly colored fingernails
- Tight buns, "helmet" hair, or big hair

STANDING OVATION POINT: IMPRESSION MANAGEMENT IS IN YOUR HANDS

First Lady Michelle Obama arrived in Copenhagen two days before her speech to the International Olympic Committee. From the moment she stepped off the plane, she was caught in a whirlwind of activities—lobbying, visits to the royal family, formal dinners, and Olympic committee meetings. Despite the hectic pace, the First Lady scheduled four practice sessions in fewer than forty-eight hours. Amid the hubbub, those focused sessions provided the quiet time she needed to prepare herself for her speech.

The last rehearsal was at 6:00 a.m. on the day of the event. The hour was early, but the setting was elaborate. A limo picked me up at my hotel for the ride to the ambassador's residence where the First Lady was staying. We worked in a glass-enclosed porch near the swimming pool and manicured gardens. When the First Lady came downstairs, she was in full hair and makeup but dressed for comfort in capri pants and ballet slippers. She would put on the designer gown selected for the occasion just before leaving for the event. By managing her schedule and making time for multiple practice sessions, she made sure the final run-through was not a panicked rush filled with last-minute changes. Rather, it was a chance to calmly review the text and read it aloud so it would be fresh in her mind when she delivered it later that morning. And she did a superb job, as CNN so glowingly reported.

If you are going to give a big presentation, it is imperative that you schedule extra practice time. Otherwise, the days leading up to the occasion slip away, and the night before, you find yourself unprepared. Block off several hour-long slots for writing, editing, and rehearsing. After the speech, the learning shouldn't stop. Schedule another hour to review a tape of the presentation. Taking the time to watch how the performance unfolded will help you pinpoint any habits that need to be ironed out.

Coach Summitt devotes considerable time to practice and to watching game tapes. Viewing videos is not limited to the players, as Summitt practices what she preaches by watching her own courtside performance. Seeing herself in action caused Summit to realize that her demonstrative manner was sometimes over the top. It was clear she needed more balance between doling out criticism of player technique and paying compliments to motivate. Start getting yourself in shape with the champion stance and the well-spoken woman's playbook exercises. With taped practice and review, the new techniques will soon become second nature, and you will be taking victory laps.

Applause Principles: Body Language Fundamentals

- Actions do speak louder than words, and proactive body language will increase your ability to express what you mean.
- The eyes say it all, so use the four-box play to really look at the audience.
- The champion stance projects confidence and conviction.
- Preplan the opening to create the strongest possible first impression.
- Suit up for the occasion with a good-looking uniform.

5

MINDING THE MESSAGE

A woman with a voice is by definition a strong woman. But the search to find that voice can be remarkably difficult.

—Melinda Gates, "Melinda Gates Goes Public," October 2007

"What if it was me? What if I was a woman who grew up in Malawi? What would I do? How would I begin to think about raising a child?" Melinda Gates says these are the questions that run through her mind as she travels the world working to end maternal and childhood death. The woman she was referring to was forced to deliver her baby on the side of a road after failing to reach a health clinic in time. She didn't make it because walking was her only means of transportation. Three hours later, when the woman and newborn finally reached the clinic, the baby was gasping for air and died shortly thereafter.

The story of the newborn riveted the audience that had gathered to honor Gates for her leadership as cochair of the Bill and Melinda Gates Foundation. The evening was a special opportunity to hear directly from the woman who is a guiding hand of a foundation committed to "the belief that every human being has equal worth." I was struck by the assured way she addressed the crowd of over one thousand gathered for the awards ceremony. Speaking without notes, Gates shared the purpose of what she says is the second act of her life. She is pouring herself into identifying what is doable in the fight to save lives so babies like the one in Malawi are not lost. In the process, she has emerged from the shadow of her husband and is being recognized as an articulate, compassionate voice of the world's largest private foundation. Gates says the decision to become a public role model came about as her daughters have grown up: "As I thought about the strong women of history, I realized that they had stepped out in some way."[1]

Gates is speaking out in speeches and television interviews to reframe the conversation on global health. In 2009, the foundation launched a public awareness campaign called the Living Proof Project. The project's goal is to share the good news about the results being achieved through the foundation's investments in health. An integral part of the message strategy is to tell stories about programs that are working, like one called Kangaroo Care. Kangaroo Care saves low-birth-weight babies by simply wrapping them to the mother's chest. The skin-on-skin contact provides the newborn with access to heat, breast-feeding, and love.

The foundation's message strategy for the awareness campaign was designed to combat the generally negative tone of news media coverage about foreign aid. The media's focus on "problems, pessimism, and guilt" in foreign assistance has left the public misinformed about the impact of tax dollars overseas. Gates believes highlighting progress with optimistic stories about curing disease and eradicating poverty is a means to counteract the misperceptions. By highlighting the success of US-funded efforts, the foundation expects to be able to leverage more support from governments and other large philanthropic organizations worldwide.

Melinda Gates in Africa

STORYTELLING: WITH A POINT OF VIEW

An effective advocacy message is a story with a purpose. Think of strategic message development as storytelling on steroids. It is a way to package what you want to say into an accessible narrative that defines a problem and articulates solutions. It is more than informing or educating about a topic. It is about presenting a point of view that provides a context for an audience response, whether individual or collective. With storytelling, we address the third of the three Vs of communication—the verbal. Along with vocal quality and visual style, the verbal or message content ensures you build a solid connection with the audience.

The fundamental principles that comprise an effective message are the well-spoken woman's five Cs of message development. These underlying principles ensure a message reaches a target audience and accomplishes its intended effect. The five Cs provide a foundation on which you can build a "message map." The message map is a tool to create and articulate the right idea to the right audience at the right time. With a strategic message, it is possible to handle difficult situations such as delivering bad news and responding to tough questions. A message map clarifies thinking in advance so you know what to say, as well as what not to say. Sometimes what you don't say is all-important. A map prevents this scenario: you listen to the words coming out of your mouth and wonder: "What the heck am I saying? And how the heck am I going to get back on track?" With a message map, you will be much less likely to utter something you later regret.

It is nearly impossible to be a consistently strong messenger without a strategic message. In the summer of 2010, BP oil executive Tony Hayward struggled to communicate an informed, coherent response to the devastating oil spill in the Gulf of Mexico. His initial misstatements about the size of the spill made him appear ill informed and out of touch. The handwriting was on the wall for his ouster when, attempting to say something sympathetic, he stated: "There is no one who wants this over more than I do. I would like my life back."[2] Hayward's insensitive remark poured salt in the wounds of those who had suffered tragic losses and was evidence that he lacked a message that was focused and purposeful.

The Message Equation

Wouldn't it be nice if exactly the right thing to say would pop into your head when you most need it? The real magic of messaging is that you don't have to rely on divine inspiration or a message fairy godmother. You can use an equation with three elements that summarizes the core components of a strategic message. First, there is a clear statement of a position on an issue or policy. Second, the position needs to be supported by values that are shared with the audience. Finally, the message must include an action step that specifies what the audience should do once they've heard the message. A message is a combination of ideas, beliefs, and deeds. It is the articulation of what you care about,

Message =

Ideals + Ideas + Goals

Message Equation

why the audience should care, and what you are trying to accomplish.

The message equation should be structured to resonate with what the intended audience cares about by speaking to the values they hold. Values are the intrinsic beliefs we learn as youngsters and hold onto throughout life. Social science researchers have identified core values that make up commonly held belief systems. Phrases that resonate with many Americans are based on the primary values of fairness and equality. The Communications Consortium Media Center (CCMC) helps nonprofit organizations influence public policy debates by developing value-based messages. When we worked together on a campaign to advocate for raising the minimum wage, we used concepts such as "leveling the playing field" and "fair wages for hard work" to speak to deeply held beliefs.

A message grounded in shared values increases the likelihood that an appeal will be acted upon. Every ten years, the US Census Bureau undertakes the largest nonmilitary operation of the federal government: counting the population. The census count is used to redraw congressional district lines and to determine how federal funds will be allocated among communities. Locales with larger populations get a bigger slice of the pie. In 2000, I helped the bureau develop the message it used to motivate the public to take the time to fill out and return census forms. The collection of data was linked to the distribution of monies that could be used to fund programs such as disaster readiness, construction of new schools and roads, and resources for job training centers. Educating the public about how their community would benefit from federal resources helped increase the overall rate of return.

Values-based messages elicit strong audience responses:

- Wow! Did you hear that?
- Hmmm. I never thought of it that way before.
- That's not right! We've got to do something.
- Yeah! Sign me up.

Storytelling: What an Advocacy Message Is Not

An advocacy message is different from other types of messages. This chapter is not about developing a brand, creating advertising slogans, or writing an academic paper. Advocacy messages do share characteristics with other forms of communication, but they are not the same. Branding is a marketing concept that individuals and companies use to help us feel good about whatever they are selling. It is about setting a mood and creating an emotional attachment to the coffee we drink, the jeans we wear, and the politicians we support. We know Coke® "Is the Real Thing," and President Ronald Reagan promised us "Morning in America, again."

Effective branding captures the spirit or ethos of a product, but cleverly worded campaigns aren't enough when you need to communicate to broad audiences about complicated policies or to respond in a crisis. Toyota was celebrated for engineering reliable and environmentally friendly cars. That reliability was called directly into question with allegations of sticky gas pedals that caused the cars to accelerate mysteriously. It takes more than a feel-good campaign to address real-life calamities. The car maker needed specific answers to direct questions about what was wrong and what they were doing to fix the problem. "Does she...or doesn't she?" sold buckets of Clairol shampoo. But it wouldn't be much of an answer if a shampoo caused a woman's hair to fall out.

Conversely, a message is not a dissertation. Readers of academic writing expect that substantial research will have been conducted to compile the evidence used to argue in defense of a thesis. Conclusions are drawn based upon facts. There is a strong emphasis on following the stringent rules of formal grammar. Colloquialisms, humor, and slang are shunned. The spice and flavor of everyday conversation is edited out. All advocacy messages should be fact based, but facts alone are not enough. Audiences tend to tune out scientists reciting data from competing studies, especially if the listeners do not understand the science. Messages are more convincing when connected to personal beliefs and convictions.

Similarly, a three-ring binder does not a message make. Too much information is not a good thing. When I signed on to help Lieutenant Governor Bev Perdue run for governor of North Carolina, I was handed a four-inch, three-ring binder. The binder contained background on every position and vote Perdue had taken over the course of her two decades in public service. It was an impressive display of comprehensive research, but it was not a tool that would prepare the candidate to answer questions during live televised debates.

The best-laid messages incorporate some of the elements from advertising campaigns and analytical writing. A savvy message will address primary values by using succinct, memorable language. It will be supported with research but be concise enough to fit on a five-by-eight-inch card. It is brief so that the audience is able to retain the essential points. When combined in the right mix, these ingredients prepare you to tell a story with a purpose.

Storytelling: Efficient Packaging

The storytelling approach avoids the glitz of a slogan and the glut of data overload. A story has a beginning, middle, and end. It takes the listeners somewhere. A good story makes them laugh, entices them to listen, and helps them learn something. A good storyteller draws the audience in through context, characters, and plot. Audiences are familiar and comfortable with stories, as they are a part of everyday conversation. Stories can relax tensions and

A Good Story Is . . .

- relevant to the audience
- purposeful
- simple but not simplistic
- based on policy and research
- arresting, unexpected, different, or new

open minds to new ideas. They are often unforgettable. Think about the stories you heard as a child and the timeless lessons they imparted.

Storytelling: Complexity Is Confusing

High-level managers and policy experts may resist storytelling, preferring to present facts and data. They may be overly concerned about peer judgment and fret that if they convey simple messages, their intellectual aptitude will be questioned. When speaking to insiders about a technical subject, jargon can help move the discussion along. When speaking to external audiences, the challenge is How do you reach them? Don't confuse savvy messaging with reaching out to the least common denominator. The real challenge is to figure out how to reach the *most* common denominator. This isn't about lowering standards; it is about setting high standards for effectiveness. Never assume what the audience knows and understands about the topic. The message will be lost in translation with the following mistakes.

- **Knee-jerk reaction:** With the denial "I am not a witch," failed US Senate candidate Christine O'Donnell attempted to reassure voters that she was one of them. Instead, she came across as bizarrely defensive, especially to anyone who did not know she had formerly dabbled in witchcraft.
- **Laundry list:** Don't be the Al Gore of information overload with a litany of issues. If you talk about everything, your audience is likely to remember nothing.
- **Complexity:** Avoid diving into the weeds by belaboring the minutia and fine points of an argument. Senator John Kerry is infamous for explaining in detail why he voted for something after he voted against it.
- **Gobbledygook:** If you are a rocket scientist talking to another rocket scientist, then technical language is necessary and appropriate. But don't assume knowledge or awareness on the part of a lay audience.
- **Explainer:** Avoid a five-minute stream-of-consciousness answer starting with the history of the problem from decades ago when a sixty-second summary will suffice.

- **Johnny One-Note:** Don't be that person who talks about the same thing over and over again as if she has no idea that she is the person who is notorious for talking about the same thing over and over.

FIVE Cs OF MESSAGE DEVELOPMENT

The well-spoken woman's five Cs of message development provide a framework that ensures a message is not a big, muddled mess. The five Cs are fundamental principles that help you think strategically about what you must say to have an impact on a policy discussion or public debate. The principles will prepare you for a wide range of scenarios, including a live radio interview, a speech to five hundred, a contentious board meeting, a one-on-one with a VIP, questions from a newspaper reporter, the Q&A session at a conference, and a panel discussion talk. The principles of *clarity, connection, compelling, concise*, and *continual* ensure that preparation is geared to a specific audience with a specific purpose.

Principle 1. Clarity

We are a message-saturated culture with much of the information bombarding us from screens—handheld ones; small ones in taxis and elevators; larger ones in lobbies, airports, and living rooms; and Jumbotrons® in auditoriums and sports complexes. Much of the information on those screens is advertising. It is estimated that the average person in the United States is hit with thousands of ads daily. It is nearly impossible to escape this distracting and annoying overload. Principle number one is the need for clarity. Clarity is achieved by narrowing the agenda. With a limited number of messages, it is possible to cut through the clutter of overload.

Limit yourself to three or four main points about a topic: "three or four, no more." A twelve-point agenda contributes to message static. Limiting the overall number of messages increases the likelihood the audience hears and retains what you want them to remember. Political candidates with narrowly defined agendas position themselves with the voters they need to win. When Senator Barack Obama sought the White House, he used a three-point message that articulated who he was and what he stood for. Obama presented the rationale for his candidacy by exclaiming that Americans have the opportunity to choose hope over fear, unite rather than divide, and send a powerful message that change is coming.

Obama Campaign Message

The Obama message with the three values-based themes of change, hope, and unity succinctly positioned him as an outsider who would shake up Washington. The "Yes we can!" slogan was used to inspire voters to mobilize behind the vision. Successful candidates of all parties use a similar type of message construction.

Principle 2. Connection

A limited-message agenda requires a strong editing pen. You can't say everything, so you must decide what fits and what doesn't. Begin the process of prioritizing by asking a fundamental question: "Who is my audience? Whom do I need to talk to?" You are not talking to everyone. If you try to talk to everyone, you risk not talking to anyone. There are always three potential audiences. One group is the people who already agree with you and support you. Second are those people who, no matter what you say, will never agree. The third group is the people in the middle. They are referred to as the *persuadables*, or the ones who haven't yet made up their minds. They are open to hearing your side of the story, and you may be able to convince them to support your position or cause.

The Persuadables

To reach the people in the middle, you need to identify them demographically and geographically. Who are they, what do they do, and where do they come from? Establish the "who" first. Then you can move on to what will "move" them. What will get them to respond? What are their beliefs and values? What do they care about? What do they need? Draft your message so that it will resonate with the target audience. Use language that will catch their attention and draw them in.

The Women's Collective is a nonprofit organization that provides care and support to women living with HIV/AIDS. The collective has a number of AIDS prevention programs aimed at helping women protect themselves, including one affectionately referred to as OPRAH. OPRAH is an easy-to-remember acronym for how to properly use condoms. *O* stands for open the condom carefully. *P* is for pinch the tip as it is put on. *R* means roll it all the way up. *A*: enjoy the action. And *H*: hold the condom snug until it is removed.

If the message isn't tailored to the audience, you run the risk of being misunderstood, maligned, and misquoted. For years, climate scientists have attempted to educate the public about the dangers of greenhouse gases and the impact of climate change. The effort has been stymied by the use of dense, incomprehensible language. Here is a typical example of a scientific explanation. Does the following definition of greenhouse gases illuminate or obfuscate?

> These are gases which allow direct sunlight (relatively shortwave energy) to reach the Earth's surface unimpeded. As the shortwave energy (that in the visible and ultraviolet portion of the spectra) heats the surface, longer-wave (infrared) energy (heat) is reradiated to the atmosphere. Greenhouse gases absorb this energy, thereby allowing less heat to escape back to space, and "trapping" it in the lower atmosphere.[3]

Unfortunately, many scientists struggle to translate their work because they are overly dependent on jargon. As a result, nonscientists have been confused about the dangers associated with greenhouse gases. Aren't greenhouses nice, warm places where plants grow? Thus, couldn't greenhouse gases be beneficial to the environment? Brenda Ekwurzel is a leading climate scientist who has been trying to clear up the confusion. When appearing on cable TV, Ekwurzel doesn't use the detailed charts and graphs she brings to professional conferences. Rather, she utilizes simple analogies, referring to climate scientists as essentially doctors who have been monitoring the earth's temperature and have diagnosed a fever.

The warming effect is caused by heat-trapping emissions from activities such as driving cars and burning coal in power plants. The more complex the point, the more essential it is to choose language that clarifies rather than obscures.

Principle 3. Compelling

Facts are not as effective as emotional appeals in motivating an audience. A climate-related scenario that is helping the public understand the impact of global warming is the melting of the polar ice cap. Photographs of polar bears on shrinking ice floes riveted audiences in a way the science never has. The pictures hit an emotional chord, raising awareness and concern about rising temperatures. According to psychologist and neuroscientist Drew Westen, facts and statistics alone are not persuasive and often raise more questions than they answer. Westen says: "There are a few things if you know about the brain, they change the way you think.... If you understand we evolved the capacity to feel long before we evolved the capacity to think, instead of barraging people with facts you speak to people's core values and concerns."[4]

Leaders of the tea party movement seemingly embraced Westen's advice with a message loaded with rhetoric that nearly derailed the passage of healthcare reform. A well-orchestrated campaign led by talk radio host Rush Limbaugh tapped into the anxiety felt by people who didn't know how reform would affect the quality and cost of care. At town hall meetings, tea party activists deployed a disciplined message to argue against proposals put forth by the White House and congressional leaders. The theme with the greatest resonance was "death panels." The death-panel claim lacked veracity but nonetheless was successful in causing fear, particularly among senior citizens.

In a controversial debate, the side that makes the stronger emotional appeal often gains greater, more broad-based support. Unfortunately, some advocates have been willing to throw facts and reasoning out the window in order to win policy debates. In the long run, win-at-all-costs rhetoric can backfire, and it is a disservice that undermines the efforts of well-intentioned policy makers. The key is to make an emotional appeal while remaining intellectually honest. A message needs to feel like there is a person behind it with a heart and a brain. Facts lend legitimacy to an argument but are open to interpretation. Emotions amplify an issue, making it more comprehensible. Balance hard data with a passionate appeal.

Principle 4. Concise

In E. B. White's classic tale *Charlotte's Web*, a spider named Charlotte spins a simple message to save her friend Wilbur the pig from the butcher's knife. In the ceiling beams above Wilbur's pen, Charlotte spun a web that read: "Some Pig." The succinct message quickly convinced Wilbur's farm family that he was no ordinary barnyard animal and should be spared. Charlotte's web mastery demonstrates that much can be said with just a few well-chosen words.

Communication today demands brevity. Audience attention spans continue to shrink. Twitter® has a 140-character limit. Network TV reporters want sound-bite answers in roughly ten to twenty seconds. This is as much about self-restraint as it is about finding the right words to fit a limited space. Mark Twain quipped that he would have written a shorter letter if he had more time. Less is always more, but less can take more time. Simple and short doesn't mean simplistic.

Principle 5. Continual

Creating an echo chamber with a message that reverberates is another way to break through clutter. It takes many repetitions to hit a nerve with audiences reeling from information overload. Listeners need to hear, see, or read a message between seven and twelve times before they get it. Advertisers strive to create a "wear in" effect so that consumers experience an ad enough times that it prompts a response. That's why we keep hearing about how the Energizer bunny's battery is going and going and going.

In the 2002 State of the Union address, President George W. Bush used the occasion to present his rationale for the war with Iraq. The address was the first time the president had spoken directly to the American public about the need to send US troops into war overseas. The message was intended to resonate with a nation that was still reeling from the unexpected 9/11 attack.

Bush said the war was necessary because of the following:

1. We need to take out Saddam Hussein, a nasty dictator who used "weapons of mass destruction" against his own people.
2. The Cold War is over, but the world is still a dangerous place. There exists an "axis of evil," namely, Iraq, Iran, and North Korea.
3. We need to fight the "war on terror," and it is better to fight it over there than to have to fight it here at home.
4. It is up to America to bring "freedom and democracy to the Iraqi people," and our troops will be welcomed on the streets of Baghdad as liberators.

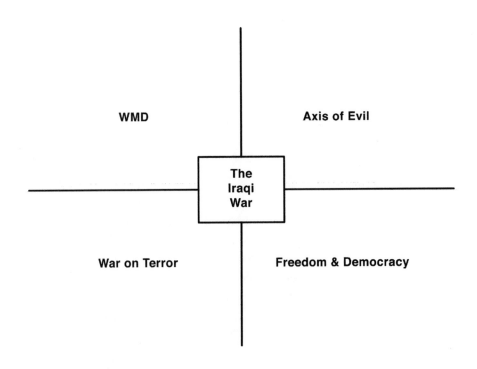

Bush Iraqi War Message

The Bush administration demonstrated a steely discipline in the repetitive articulation of the war message. The president along with top spokespeople repeated the themes time and again. Colin Powell gave a PowerPoint® presentation that contained "evidence" of the weapons of mass destruction. Vice President Dick Cheney, Secretary of Defense Donald Rumsfeld, and National Security Adviser Condoleezza Rice remained "on message" for years. The message was repeated enough times that later surveys show some Americans believe weapons of mass destruction were found in Iraq.

Repetition of message is an effective way to break through information noise and is mandatory if you want to motivate or persuade. It is never enough to say something once, assume the audience heard it, and then move on to something new. Consider how this plays out in daily living. How many times do you have to ask your partner or your kids to do something before they respond? You need to feel worn out from communicating the message before it reaches the point of wear in.

The five Cs are a fundamental guide to strategic message building. By identifying the primary audience, it is possible to streamline the message agenda into three or four main points. With a tight agenda, the message can be delivered repeatedly. Abiding by the principles of clarity, connection, compelling, concise, and continual ensures a storyteller achieves results.

MESSAGE STEADINESS

If you are successful, remember it is because somewhere, sometime, someone gave you a life or an idea that started you in the right direction. Remember also that you are indebted to life until you help some less fortunate person, just as you were helped.
> —Melinda Gates, valedictorian, Ursuline Academy, 1982

A consistency of message has followed Gates throughout her life. The motto of Ursuline Academy, the all-girl preparatory high school she attended, is "*Serviam*" (I will serve). The school was founded by Roman Catholic nuns with the sole purpose of educating young girls in a community invested in volunteerism. The nuns established the school in 1874 in what was then the frontier town of Dallas, Texas. Gates says the school and her teachers had a tremendous impact on her life path and worldview. It was Sister Judith Marie who recognized and nurtured Gates's math talents in the seventh grade.

Gates first encountered a computer when her father, Raymond French, an engineer who worked on the space program, purchased one. It was, as is well-known, an Apple®. Melinda grew familiar with the technology entering financial records for a family business and playing games. A standout student, Gates choose to attend Duke University after learning the school was expanding its Computer Science Department. In five years, she earned undergraduate and MBA degrees in economics and computers. In 1987, Gates headed west to a young company based in Seattle called Microsoft®. At Microsoft, she helped develop the products Encarta® and Expedia® and then fell in the love with the boss. Her mother disapproved because she didn't think her daughter should be involved with someone at work, and at times it was lonely for Melinda. She found herself eating lunch by herself in the company cafeteria, as some co-workers seemed intimidated by her boyfriend.

Saving the World

When the couple married, Bill's mom wrote them a letter encouraging the newlyweds to seize the rare opportunity presented by their wealth: "From those to whom much is given, much is expected."[5] The couple needed a giving plan because they were besieged by countless letters from people in need. Installing Bill's father at the helm, they initially started the Bill and Melinda Gates Foundation to provide schools with computers. The effort was criticized for being too self-serving, and Gates says she soon realized it wasn't nearly enough in the face of the daunting challenges faced by public schools.

Gates retired from Microsoft in 1996 when the couple's first child was born, and the family has since expanded to two daughters and a son. As the children have grown, Gates has devoted more time to figuring out how the foundation can serve as a catalyst to tackle the enormous needs in education and global health. Some estimates say that the Gates have the potential to give away $100 billion, but that sum isn't enough given the scale of the problems. To put $100 billion in perspective, the National Institutes of Health, the federal government's research center, has an annual budget of $29 billion. The reality of the numbers is a driving force behind the Living Proof Project and the need to seek funding partners.

Saving the world is hard work. If Gates is frustrated with the slow grind of leveraging resources or exasperated with the process of convincing skeptical governments, it doesn't show in her demeanor. She doesn't come across as someone who is overwhelmed by the desperate circumstances of the villagers she meets in remote places. She maintains a consistent, steady focus on what can and should be done next. The message is not pie in the sky, nor is it seeped in angry insinuations attempting to guilt-trip people into action. Pointing fingers and assigning blame are not effective motivating strategies. Advocates who attempt to goad people with defensive or accusatory messages find no one wants to hear what they have to say.

At a Women Deliver conference, Gates was on message about the need for the world to come together on maternal healthcare. She shared a story about a mom named Rukmini and how the birth of a child is celebrated in India. According to custom, Rukmini and her newborn remained together for six days in the birth room. Then she donned a crimson sari and dressed the baby, and they emerged to the singing of family and neighbors who thanked the sun god for the birth. Gates expressed her own joy at the birth of her children and urged the policy makers to try harder, saying more can be done for the millions of women who never experience the beauty of holding a healthy baby.

The personalized narrative about her childbirth experience made the story even more powerful. The message map is a tool that provides a structure for storytelling to ensure that stories are focused and purposeful.

CREATING A MESSAGE MAP

The message map allows you to communicate more than a slogan but less than a three-ring binder. It organizes and prioritizes information into a manageable package that can be delivered more effectively. With the map, you will develop the skill of message discipline—staying focused on the important stuff and not getting sidetracked by trivia. The structure of the message map is based on the motivated sequence developed by Professor Alan H. Monroe in the 1930s.[6] The motivated sequence is particularly suitable to persuading or inspiring audiences. The sequence allows the presenter to frame an existing problem or challenge in such a way that it touches a nerve with the target audience. Once the problem is framed, then solutions are presented. The audience is motivated to address the problem because it is clear that doing so will bring positive change to an issue that is of concern to them.

Step 1: Create a One-Page Map

The message map approach modifies Monroe's motivated sequence into a streamlined storytelling structure with four themes. The themes make up the outline of a narrative that tells a story about a particular issue or policy. The narrative allows you to frame a problem, offer solutions, and put forth a call to action that is tailored to the audience's interests. The benefit is the incentive to the audience to help you reach the goal.

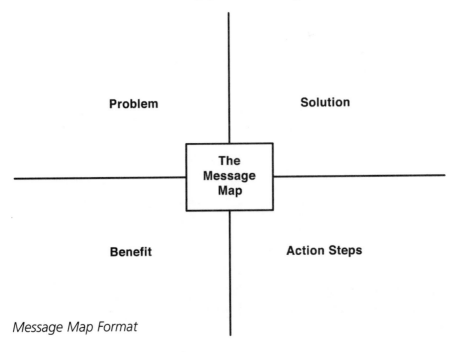

Message Map Format

The message map is laid out on a grid so that the entire message is visible on one sheet of paper. The design promotes brevity and makes the map a handy tool for preparation and practice. No more thumbing through talking points or three-ring binders. No more trying to read messy notes. The easy-to-read visual layout will help you see and remember what you want to say. The grids can be drawn on PowerPoint slides so they are portable. Some clients laminate their messages onto wallet-sized cards so they don't leave home without them.

An added bonus of the message map design is its functionality in responding to questions. As you listen to a question, you can decide how you want to answer by selecting one theme from the grid. The map facilitates fielding questions and bridging your responses back to your message. This skill provides message discipline, especially when taking tough questions from skeptical audiences or aggressive news reporters. It is the ultimate preparation guide for all types of media interviews, including print, radio, television, and online distribution.

Step 2: Name It and Frame It

The template message map can be used to develop a strategic message on any topic. Put the template to work in a message-storming or brainstorming session. The most productive message-storming sessions involve individuals with a range of backgrounds who bring unique perspectives and relevant experience to the topic at hand. Ideally, the group should include a mix of communications professionals, policy types, and senior staff. Below are questions to jump-start the message-storming process.

Message-Storming Questions

- What is the problem or challenge we face?
- What's at stake?
- What doesn't the audience know?
- From whom do we need buy-in to fix the problem?
- How is our solution different, better?
- What is the impact on the target audience?
- How will the audience benefit?

Once you have completed the message storming, review the notes on all the ideas that were discussed. The goal is to winnow the points down to three or four main themes. It will be apparent that many of the brainstormed ideas can be lumped together, as the same thought is often restated several times. It will also be clear that some ideas and words should be edited out. Eliminate any information that dilutes the main purpose of the messaging. Weed out ideas that are negative, defensive, inaccurate, or tangential. Working with the pared-down list, now draft the four headline points. Start by framing the problem and then work through the solution, action step, and benefit to audience.

Frame the Problem

What is the issue at hand, and what is the best way to frame it so it will resonate with the target audience? Framing puts the problem into a context that is relevant to your listeners. An example is the message antismoking advocates used to win big victories against tobacco companies. The advocates successfully exposed how cigarette advertising targeted children. Most people would agree that smoking is an undesirable habit. The advocates generated outrage at R. J. Reynolds when it was revealed that the company's Joe Camel character was as recognizable to kids as Mickey Mouse®. The new frame was that the tobacco companies were inducing children and adolescents to start smoking by appealing to them with a "smooth character."

Provide a Solution

Lay out a concrete, practical solution. Be wary of solutions that are too big and cumbersome. Banning all tobacco products would be an effective way to prevent kids from smoking, but it is not a solution that is feasible in the short term. The antismoking advocates went to court to argue for resources that could be used to counter the impact of the Joe Camel ads. In the settlement of a lawsuit filed in California, R. J. Reynolds agreed to a $10 million payment, $9 million of which would be used by cities and communities to fund educational campaigns to prevent children from smoking.

Detail a Specific Action Plan

What specifically do you want the audience to do? It is not uncommon for advocates to forget to make the "ask." The action step may seem obvious to you, but it is not so obvious to others. If you want them to write a blog or call a member of Congress, ask them to do so. To keep up the pressure on R. J. Reynolds, a coalition of antismoking groups initiated a consumer boycott. It targeted the food products of companies like Nabisco, which was owned by the tobacco company, and asked shoppers to avoid buying specific food products unrelated to tobacco.

What Is the Benefit to the Audience?

Make it clear to the audience why they should respond to the call for action. You must give them a compelling rationale for taking time out of their busy lives to join the effort. According to the Federal Trade Commission, after the Joe Camel campaign was launched, the percentage of children who smoked Camels was higher than the percentage of adults. The health benefits and cost savings of preventing children from lighting up resonated with parents and anyone concerned with the serious risks and high healthcare costs known to be associated with the habit.

Step 3: Plot the Message Map

Fill in the message map by drafting the four headline themes: problem, solution, action step, and benefit to audience. Use full sentences to articulate each of the points and avoid incomplete sentences or phrases. For example, the nonprofit National Immigration Forum needed a pro-immigration message after the 9/11 attacks to deal with concerns about other terrorists entering the country. The forum's response was designed to remind Americans about the long tradition of immigration to counter arguments for closing the borders. Forum spokespeople drew a distinction between terrorists and immigrants. The problem was framed by stating: "Terrorism is the problem, not immigration." The spokespeople then called on policy leaders to fix the broken system and institute comprehensive reforms that would address both security and economic concerns.

As you draft the headline points, make strategic decisions about word choice. The words that work best are simple, conversational, attention getting, and visual. Pro-life groups brilliantly labeled an obscure procedure "partial-birth abortion" to argue against a woman's right to comprehensive reproductive healthcare. Never mind that the phrase is not found in medical dictionaries or used by doctors. It was a concise, graphic description that generated antiabortion sentiment.

Terms of Expression

Researchers have grown ever more sophisticated in their ability to identify words that influence how we feel about an issue. Was President Bush's decision to send additional troops to Iraq "an escalation," or was it a "surge"? People who supported the war tended to view the president's decision to raise the level of troops as a surge. *Surge* implied a short-term show of force that would overwhelm the enemy and hasten the war's end. Those opposed to the war saw a rise in troop numbers as an escalation of the war effort that would prolong the conflict, resulting in more casualties and further depletion of limited sources.

Large organizations and corporations hire polling firms to conduct focus groups that test language. They want to pinpoint the words that will elicit a desired response. With the right phrasing, public sentiment about issues and products can be dramatically changed. Pollster Frank Lutz tapped into antitax sentiment by calling the estate tax, a fairly obscure provision in the tax code, the "death tax." Nobody wants to pay taxes, especially after they have died. Supporters of offshore drilling for oil are encouraged to call it "exploring for energy." As Luntz says, "Drilling for oil sounds dirty," while "exploring for energy" creates a positive visual and "has a more patriotic feel to it."[7]

Step 4: Make It Memorable

Not every organization has the resources to invest in research and focus groups. And sometimes you need to respond quickly. It is possible to write your own great lines. With the quotable quote techniques, you can create Twitter-sized messages that pack a big bang for the buck. Quotable quotes are the types of lines that appear on the front page and that generate sustained applause. "Let there be light" and "I have a dream" are messages that stick in our consciousness. Paint pictures with illustrative words, and what you say will break through the din and be remembered for some time to come.

Organizers of the Susan G. Komen Global Race for the Cure® creatively draw attention to the 5 km event that raises funds for prevention of breast cancer. During the race, thousands of runners wear brightly colored pink and white T-shirts adorned with inspiring and heartbreaking messages, such as "Yes, they are fake. My real ones tried to kill me." "Operation Support 2nd Base" is another example. For some race participants, humor tells the story: "Walkers for Knockers," "Taking Care of the Girls," and "Tata Sisterhood."[8] Use the sound-bite ("ink-bite") techniques below to craft bold statements that will draw attention to your cause.

- **One-liners:** These are not jokes but well-thought-out, well-crafted phrases.

"More children will live through their parents' bankruptcy than will live through their parents' divorce."

—Elizabeth Warren

"This is a pivotal moment for women's and children's health; this is our moment."

—Melinda Gates

"Failure is impossible."

—Susan B. Anthony

"The truth will set you free. But, first it will piss you off."

—Gloria Steinem

- **Clichés:** The utility of clichés is that everyone understands them.

"Caught between a rock and a hard place."

"Don't throw the baby out with the bathwater."

"There's no silver bullet, but there may be a silver lining."

Analogies: Sports analogies are popular with media reporters.

"Three strikes and you're out."
—state statutes requiring mandatory prison time
for a series of three offenses

"Our struggle today is not to have a female Einstein appointed as an assistant professor. It is for a female schlemiel to get as quickly promoted as a male schlemiel."
—Bella Abzug

"Gumbo was meant to keep us together. You stir in the good times. You stir in the bad times."
—Donna Brazile

- **Startling number:** Numbers are more powerful when put into context.

"The 3 billion dollars Americans spent on potato chips in 2007 would fund the National Institutes of Health obesity research for more than three years."
—Centers for Disease Control

"Domestic violence is an epidemic. One in three women worldwide has been a victim of violence."
—Vital Voices Global Partnership

"Each day a cruise ship generates 30,000 gallons of raw sewage which they can dump into pristine ocean waters three miles off shore."
—Oceana

- **Contemporary reference:** Use catchy lines from popular culture.

"Show me the money."

"Go ahead, make my day."

"Where's the beef?"

- **Quote an unlikely source:** It gives your message more credibility.

"Even President George W. Bush agrees that climate change is caused by manmade activity."

"I may sometimes be willing to teach for nothing, but if paid at all, I shall never do a man's work for less than a man's pay."
>   —Clara Barton, American Red Cross founder
>   and early proponent of equal pay

"Pope Benedict agrees that the use of condoms can reduce the risk of HIV/AIDS infection."

- **Colorful language:** The more vivid, the more impact it has.

"The women's libbers are radicals who are waging a total assault on the family, on marriage, and on children."
>   —Phyllis Schlafly, Eagle Forum

"And Hubble has become the people's telescope. It has its own Web site and it gets its own email. What I love the most are the messages from children. They talk to the Hubble as if it were a person. They send emails that say, 'Did you see God today? Have you met an angel? Is there another universe? What does it look like?' Hubble gets kids excited about science, inspiring our next generation of scientists and engineers."
>   —Senator Barbara Mikulski

STANDING OVATION POINT: MESSAGE IS QUEEN

An enduring quote used by Melinda Gates is from anthropologist Margaret Mead: "Never doubt that a small group of thoughtful, committed citizens can change the world. Indeed it is the only thing that ever has." Gates is adept with the sound bite when it comes to characterizing the success of the Living Proof Project. Both she and husband Bill are self-described "impatient optimists." The phrase neatly sums up the sentiment that much has been accomplished but much more remains to be done to improve global health. The following is an excerpt from the inaugural presentation of the Living Proof Project.

> We're optimistic because of the people that we meet on the ground, in the developing world, whose lives are absolutely transformed by American investments. Just a couple of years ago, Bill and I visited an AIDS clinic in Durbin, South Africa, and we expected to see in this clinic what we see a lot of places in the developing world, an overworked staff, long waiting lines, not many drugs available.
>
> But, in fact, we saw something completely different than that in this AIDS clinic. We saw a well-trained staff, we saw an ample supply of medical drugs, and we saw patients being counseled about how to live with HIV. And this clinic was completely paid for by the American people....
>
> So, we are optimists: The world is definitely getting better. But it's not getting better fast enough, and it's certainly not getting better for everyone. For every two people who go on the antiretroviral treatments that we saw in this clinic in Durbin, South Africa, five more people become infected.
>
> Now, we know how to prevent these infections, but they do happen anyway, and that's the kind of thing that makes us impatient optimists.[9]

Audiences would pay attention without regard to the savviness of Gates's message. The billions distributed in charitable contributions guarantee people will listen. In just a few years, the foundation has donated more than all of the money given away by the Rockefeller Foundation since it was founded in 1913. The business of the foundation is carefully managed; so, too, is the work of communicating its progress. The carefully constructed message about global health keeps the public's attention focused on results. Melinda is a messenger who holds the hand of a woman dying of AIDS in a rural village in Kenya as readily as she shakes hands with presidents, prime ministers, and rock stars. Strategic messaging ensures the spotlight is not on celebrity or wealth but on the work that remains to be done.

Applause Principles:
Be Clear, Concise, and Compelling

- Effective advocacy messages tell a story with a point of view.
- The five Cs of message development are timeless principles that ensure your point sticks.
- Relevant messages are value based, compelling, and well documented.
- Use the message map to motivate or persuade with credibility and passion.
- Craft attention-catching language using the sound-bite techniques.

PART 3

THE OUTWARD TRAPPINGS

6

PREPLANNED SPONTANEITY

One of the basic causes for all the trouble in the world today is that people talk too much and think too little. They act impulsively without thinking. I always try to think before I talk.

—US Senator Margaret Chase Smith

Before she was a celebrity with her own reality TV show, an unknown Sarah Palin exceeded all expectations in her first nationally televised address with a humorous and rousing endorsement of her running mate. Since that historic night, Palin has stumbled and then regained her footing with an inconsistency that can be likened to the Dickens classic *A Tale of Two Cities*. It is as if there are two Sarahs, in that she can be the best of speakers, and she can be the worst of speakers. When prepared and rehearsed, she can speak to the age of wisdom; when not, to the age of foolishness. When ready, the epoch of belief; when not, the epoch of incredulity. With her everywoman's sentiments, she is the spring of hope; with her cringe-inducing quips, the winter of despair.

While Dickens provides a literary comparison, it is difficult to compare Palin to any other speaker past, present, or in the imaginable future. While everyone experiences ups and downs on the public stage, Palin's swings tend to be more like a roller coaster ride, with dramatic climbs followed by free falls. The pressure of the nominating speech was handled without a gaffe. She owned that speech, having helped rewrite the original draft, which was written assuming a man would deliver it. The funniest line about lipstick, hockey moms, and pit bulls was a last-minute insertion but not a lucky fluke. Palin could bet on the line delivering a laugh because she had used it before.

As the roller coaster roared on, the spirit of Sarah the Barracuda was missing in an interview with Katie Couric when she was unable to say what magazines and newspapers she reads. Palin later admitted she was unprepared for the encounter, and her defensive answers opened her up to fair criticism about her qualifications for the vice presidency. So few women reach the top echelons of any field, it is difficult to watch one who does stumble and be relentlessly pummeled. While Palin's candor, energy, and ambition are worth emulating, the inevitable mistakes and inflammatory rhetoric that go hand in hand with a "going rogue" style are not. Fortunately, they can be sidestepped by taking a different approach.

Going Rogue Goes Only So Far

A rogue speaking style is a high-wire act that is difficult for anyone to maintain. So too is its polar opposite—being overly organized. An overly organized speaker tends to stick to the script word for word at all times and can become easily rattled should something go wrong. An excessively scripted presentation, like a wildly irregular one, lacks balance. Both of these styles can prevent the speaker from making a real connection with the audience.

Elizabeth Dole has developed a balance as a speaker between her desire to be organized and the need to be able to react in the moment. Renowned for her acute attention to detail and exhaustive practice schedule, Dole is said to have a photographic memory, and her methodical preparation could be described as epitomizing the exacting standards of a perfectionist. Dole has never denied the criticism and gets high marks for telling an audience: "Some pundits say I'm scripted . . . but according to my notes, that is not true."[1]

The self-deprecating humor proved to be a handy tool for a woman of many remarkable firsts. Dole was one of the few women to be admitted to Harvard Law School in the 1950s and went on to be a cabinet secretary, American Red Cross executive, presidential candidate, and US senator. In college, Dole said she worked twice as hard as her male classmates to counter their belief that her presence was wasting a classroom seat that would be better filled by a man. Yet she admits that striving for perfection can become "a kind of social tyranny, and that there is most definitely a point of diminishing returns."[2]

A THIRD WAY: PREPLANNED SPONTANEITY

"Preplanned spontaneity" breaks loose from both manic inflexibility and the unpredictability of anything goes. Preplanned spontaneity (PS) is just what it sounds like: being ready to experience the moment. The approach is a balance between being excessively scripted and being unprepared. It combines the freshness of resourcefulness with the steadiness of skilled competence. It isn't a strict formula or regimented routine, which drains originality and stifles inventiveness. It is the habit of developing and executing best practices, practices that allow you to exercise control so you consistently deliver at a level that earns the audience's approval.

Consistency is more than being predictable or reliable. It is about meeting the audience's expectations and not disappointing. Presenters who repeatedly throw caution to the wind eventually try an audience's patience, especially when it is clear the speaker's interests come first. Seasoned pros draw upon their experience to consistently meet and even exceed an audience's expectations. Dole's attention to detail ensured she didn't disappoint when a big opportunity came her way.

Preplanned Spontaneity at Work

An unprecedented appearance at a political convention positioned Dole as presidential material. Ironically, Elizabeth was speaking on behalf of husband Bob Dole's presidential bid when she broke with a long-held tradition. Rather than remaining a podium hugger, she became a floor walker. In a stunning canary-yellow suit and three-inch heels, she skillfully descended twelve steps and navigated a crowded floor to walk among thousands of "friends." The seemingly risky move wasn't so, if you understood Dole's preparation regimen. The talk-show delivery style wasn't an eleventh-hour decision. Rather, it was a well-rehearsed, choreographed routine that she had been refining during months of practice on the campaign trail. The made-for-TV speech wasn't a "going rogue" move but well-executed stagecraft; it was an excellent example of preplanned spontaneity in action. It had such a "wow" factor that it led to immediate speculation that Elizabeth should be on the ticket rather than her husband.

Elizabeth Dole

In fact, Dole went on to use her star power to make her own run for the presidency three years later.

Born in Salisbury, North Carolina, Dole and her older brother were raised in a comfortable middle-class home. Her father was a florist, and her mother was a stay-at-home mom. Dole strived to satisfy her goal-oriented parents, who taught her that "self-improvement was a measure of personal growth."[3] At the knee of her grandmother, she developed a familiarity with and devotion to Bible scripture. On Sunday afternoons, she would sit with her cousins listening to Bible stories. Those early religious lessons resonate in Dole's speeches, as she often articulates the strength and comfort she has found in her faith.

Dole says that as a young girl, she "caught the rhythm of a different drummer" and for her, "life was more than a spectator sport." The conventional wisdom at Duke University when she enrolled as a political science major was that "there were girls with dates and girls with data." Dole happened to possess both. In 1958, her senior year of college, she was crowned May Queen and elected president of the student government. The poise she acquired as a debutante who attended cotillion balls later proved to be a good defense against the naysayers.

At Harvard Law School, professors and classmates openly expressed hostility toward Dole and her five female classmates. A professor of property law pretended the women didn't exist except on "Professor Leach's Ladies' Day," when they "were summoned to the front of the room to read a poem of their own composition."[4] When finished, the women were pelted with questions from the men. When Dole graduated in 1965, the chauvinism that existed in the classroom was evident at the major law firms. None were recruiting women, so Dole decided to put her legal education to work in what would become a lifelong career in public service.

Dole went on to distinguish herself by serving as a cabinet secretary for two presidents. Ronald Reagan appointed her secretary of transportation, and under President George H. W. Bush she was secretary of labor. In 1991, she left government to spearhead the American Red Cross until she resigned to make her presidential bid. Dole said it was during her tenure at the Red Cross that she became comfortable with moving out from behind the podium to visit with people in the audience. The conversational style stemmed from her days as a student teacher "when you are walking up and down the aisle."[5]

The style was popular with audiences, and she used it repeatedly throughout her presidential and US Senate campaigns. While Dole's agility made the movement appear spontaneous, she wasn't speaking impromptu. Rather, she had rehearsed the speech enough times that it was in her head. The five steps to preplanned spontaneity ensure that you aren't either shooting from the hip or glued to a script. Preplanned spontaneity ensures you will be ready to handle the foreseen as well as the unforeseen situations that occur with live audiences.

PS Step 1: Channeling Nancy Drew

Make preplanned spontaneity work for you by taking the time to get a sense of what you are getting yourself into and how you can maximize the situation. All aspects of a presentation need to be given deliberate advance attention, including audience, event, setting, and room and equipment setup. Pull out your Nancy Drew sleuthing tools to learn as much as you can about the who, what, where, when, and why of the occasion. Like the "girl detective," investigate to compile the clues that will take any mystery out of what is expected of you.

Ask questions before you accept an invitation. That way you can decide whether the event is worth the investment in preparation time before you commit. Some program chairs will overestimate the audience size and clout. Some programs lack focus or are not germane to your interests. Don't be afraid to decline; otherwise, the speaking date will hang over you like a black cloud. Better to say no immediately so you don't waste time regretting the acceptance.

Audience Profile

- Who are they? What is their level of education? What is their profession or occupation? Are they male/female, young/old, urban/rural, black/white?
- How many people are expected to attend?
- What is the audience's level of experience/familiarity with the topic? Do they know less than they think they know?
- What is your relationship to them? How well do they know you? Have you spoken to them before? What is their opinion of you?
- What is the audience's attitude toward the subject matter? Are there any sensitive or controversial pressure points? Are there areas of disagreement?
- What potential impact could the subject matter have on them? How important is it to their decision making?
- How will they benefit from your talk? What do they want to take away from the presentation?
- What are your goals? What do you need them to take away?
- Are they expecting handouts or other takeaway documentation?
- What follow-up should take place after the event is over? How do they contact you? Whom do you want to stay in touch with?

When you are an invited guest speaker, reach out to the event sponsor or host to get the logistical intelligence you need. Some sponsors are experienced and know how to help; some don't. Early reconnaissance starts with getting a read on the audience's composition and what they expect the topic will be. When people make an effort to show up, they come with a certain predisposition about what they will hear. These expectations and the expectations of the host should guide your decision about whether the event is a good fit for you.

Event Profile

- Who is hosting the event and why?
- What do they want you to talk about?
- When and where will the event take place?
- When do you speak and for how long?
- What is the full agenda?
- Are there other speakers on the program?
- Who will introduce you?
- Will there be a question-and-answer period?
- Will the news media be present?
- Who is your contact for logistics and program?
- What is the dress code?

The Event

As you gain a better sense of the audience members, you need to investigate what type of event is being planned. Are you speaking to five decision makers in a boardroom, fifty video conference participants, or five hundred annual meeting attendees? Is the agenda well organized, and does it outline a program in which you are excited to participate? Use the following list of event-profile questions to ensure you have a thorough understanding of the program and your role.

Work with the event organizers to select your time slot on the agenda. The morning hours are better than immediately before or after lunch, when people are either hungry or digesting food. Post lunch is not a good time to dim the lights for a PowerPoint® presentation. The most challenging time slot is at the end of the day or during evening events. Speaking before or after dinner presents a multitude of challenges, as most people are tired and some may have been drinking. The rule of thumb for the evening presentation is to keep it short and keep it moving. Pull out your most entertaining stories or, better yet, hire a professional speechwriter to add humor.

Find out who is going to introduce you and what she plans to say. Offer to provide a draft introduction. Writing it yourself ensures that the relevant pieces of your résumé and experience will be showcased. The event organizers will be grateful for your input and relieved that they have one less task to complete. Keep the introduction short. It shouldn't run longer than a couple of paragraphs. If your last name is unusual or difficult to pronounce, provide a phonetic pronunciation.

PS Step 2: Stage Setting

Set the stage so that you are comfortable with the room and equipment arrangement and they suit your objectives. The setting and your proximity to the audience will have a direct impact on your ability to engage and interact with them. What is the planned setup, and to what extent can you change it to suit your preferences? If you stand behind a lectern, it can be more difficult to interact with individual members of the audience. Can you easily access the audio/video controls, or is the setup awkward? Will you be able to see the screen and the audience? The following setting-profile questions will help you use the available space and equipment to greatest effect.

Setting Profile

- How large is the space?
- How far is the presenter from the audience?
- What is the room setup, and can tables and chairs be rearranged?
- Is a speaker's lectern available?
- What type of microphone is available?
- What audio/video equipment is available? When can it be tested?
- Will anyone speak before you? Is there a break before you go on?
- Where are the restrooms?
- Will food or drinks be served? Where will they be located?
- If the event is outdoors, what is the contingency plan for foul weather?

Find out when the room is available for a walk-through prior to the event. The evening before is an ideal time to check out the arrangements so any necessary changes don't have to be made in a last-minute rush. At a minimum, be sure to make time the morning of your speech to acclimate yourself. Many speakers skip this step, setting themselves up for problems when they stand before the live audience.

A well-laid-out room will be conducive to engaging the audience. But keep in mind that you may still need to warm them up. As a young trainer, I was most uncomfortable speaking to groups of older men who would stare back at me with blank expressions that were intimidating. What I interpreted as disinterest or hostility was nearly always not the case. Most often they were an audience being an audience and not secretly plotting schemes to derail me. Audiences tend to be initially cool because they are dealing with their own issues and distractions. They may not want to be called on or be singled out. They may feign indifference because they don't want to volunteer to talk about an issue they don't feel comfortable addressing.

Step off on the right foot by modeling the behavior you seek from your audience. The professional dancers on TV's *Dancing with the Stars* lead with sure footwork that helps their celebrity partners complete audience-pleasing routines. Start with a question if you want the session to be more interactive. Move out from behind the lectern to set a conversational tone. A technique Dole uses to involve the audience is to ask them to give themselves a round of applause or to stand up and be acknowledged. In the kickoff speech of her US Senate campaign, she said: "I know some of our veterans are with us today, and I promise you that one of my top priorities is to stand up for you and our men and women in uniform. Now, would all of you please stand up, so we can show our appreciation for your service and your sacrifice?"[6] The applause creates a social atmosphere, and the audience members are more likely to relax and enjoy themselves.

PS Step 3: Break Murphy's Law

Dole was in top form the night of the convention address with the assistance of a professional team of stage managers and technical crew. Walking and talking isn't as easy as it looks, and she demonstrated true grace under fire when three minutes into the presentation, her lavalier microphone hissed, sputtered, and cut out. Although the speech was being broadcast live, no look of panic crossed her face. She paused and waited for an aide, who appeared from off camera and handed her a backup microphone. Without missing a beat, Dole smiled to the audience, and they responded with warm applause. Anticipating the equipment breakdown prevented a nationally televised embarrassment. The speaker and the advance team had done their jobs.

Murphy's law holds that "anything that can go wrong will go wrong," and it is particularly applicable when technology is involved. In fact, a corollary law holds that "to err is human, but to really foul things up requires a computer." Sometimes the stiffest competition you face in getting the audience's attention is the room environment. Waiters drop trays. Technicians fuss with a balky audiovisual system. People arrive late, and the program starts behind schedule.

Most speakers perform at a peak level when challenged constructively. Encountering the unexpected and unpleasant can leave you flustered. Have you walked into a room minutes before you are scheduled to speak to find a mess? People are crammed into a too-tight, too-hot space littered with debris. The LCD projector is on the fritz, so the PowerPoint slides don't appear, and nobody knows how to fix it. What should have been a no-brainer becomes a disaster that leaves you frazzled. The following are some of the most common logistical problems and solutions for solving them in advance.

Annoying Ambient Distractions

- **Extraneous noise:** Ringing cell phones, clattering dinnerware, and buzzing air-circulation units can drown you out. The only noise more distracting is the jackhammer of a nearby work crew or the cheering Amway® crowd on the other side of the folding partition. (Amway salespeople are notorious for spirited team chants.) Woe to the presenter who finds herself in competition with a raucous neighbor. Check the sound system in advance, especially if you are speaking to a large group in a large room. If your voice is soft or hushed, you need quality amplification to be heard. If the sound system is weak, ask if it can be replaced. If not, position yourself at a spot in the room so you are close to the audience and they can easily hear you. It may be helpful to stand on a riser, as this will help you project to the back corners. A strong voice may project over a noisy disturbance, but don't shout, as shouting strains the vocal cords and is hard on the ears.

- **Extreme temperature:** Expect the air to be either arctic cold or stifling hot, and expect the temperature to be the first thing audience members complain about. If you are on early in the morning, the room temperature may have been lowered overnight. Adjust it before-hand so that it reaches a comfortable setting. Monitor it throughout the day, too, as any mass of bodies will raise the temperature. A lack of ventilation or vents that blast cold or hot air will also affect the room temperature. If the ventilation is inadequate, open windows or doors to circulate the air. If you open doors, be sure the areas around them are kept clear and quiet. Try not to stand directly in the line of fire from a vent. The blowing air may irritate your vocal chords.

- **Bad lighting:** Is there an appropriate level of lighting so that you and any visuals can be seen? Astonishingly, many hotel conference rooms have dim lights or lights that are not adjustable. Check to see if the room has a separate control that can lower the lights when you are ready to show slides or video. Rooms with large windows can create an inviting aesthetic, particularly for daylong conferences. But win-dows can be a disaster if you plan to use large-screen projection. Glass creates glare from the sun, and the room may heat up in the afternoon. Are you able to adjust the drapes or blinds? If not, try to position screens so the glare does not hit them directly. If you are taking the stage in a large auditorium or at an evening event, check beforehand to see if the speaker's lectern will be lit by a spotlight. The intense glare may blind you or impede your ability to read from your notes. Ask the technical crew to make the necessary adjustments.

- **Uncomfortable seating:** Work with the event planner to select a seating arrangement that is conducive to the goal of the presenta-tion. Most hotels and conference centers can provide a variety of chair and table combinations. If your presentation lends itself to note taking, request round tables or rows of chairs and short tables. If you want to create a dialogue among the audience members, consider a U shape. If the rows are placed in a slight curve rather than straight across, the presenter and audience members see more of each other; the listeners aren't stuck looking at the backs of heads.

- **Sufficient seating:** Try to estimate the crowd size so the appropriate number of chairs is available. Don't put out too many, because people tend to fill in the back first, forcing late arrivals to create distractions as they reluctantly walk to the front. Have extra chairs available in the back of the room. Many people prefer to sit on the aisle, so avoid having long rows that prohibit movement and create a cramped atmosphere. Check the sight lines by standing in the back of the room. Will people have a clear view of you and the visual aids? Can any distracting decorations or wall hangings be removed? Do you need to move any equipment so that it is not blocking someone's view?

- **Dysfunctional microphone:** It's comical to watch what happens when a speaker is handed a microphone. Inevitably, they do three things in this order: (1) stare at it as if they have never seen one before; (2) blow into it; and (3) ask two questions: "Is it on?" and "Can you hear me?" Always test the microphone setup beforehand. When using a mike that is attached to a lectern, position it just below the mouth, about six inches away. If the previous speaker was taller or shorter, adjust it before you begin speaking. When you speak over the top of the mike instead of down into it, the quality of the sound will be better. Never blow into the microphone or tap on it. Use a normal speaking level and let the system do the broadcasting. The lavalier is easy to use because it attaches to a jacket lapel or shirt collar, thus freeing the hands. Position it about three inches below the collarbone and attach the battery pack to the waistband in the back of your pants or skirt to ensure the wire trails behind you.

- **Malfunctioning hardware:** An embarrassing computer malfunction occurred during a presentation by Bill Gates when he was CEO of Microsoft Corporation. While he was rolling out Windows 98 at the Comdex Computer Show, gremlins caused the operating system to crash. Gates had the wherewithal to quip that the snafu might explain why the company wasn't ready to ship the new product. For less experienced presenters, this type of glitch can induce a panic attack. There are two solutions. First, don't become overly reliant on any piece of equipment. Expect bugs and be prepared to sail ahead if they can't be fixed. It is always a good idea to prepare a set of note cards with your speech outline as backup. If you are nervous about the setup, bring a copy of the entire speech and have photocopies of the PowerPoint slides available for distribution. Second, it is imperative to arrive early so you have plenty of time to test the equipment. This is particularly necessary if you will be using an unfamiliar setup. Even simple things like a mouse can cause aggravation. I've seen PowerPoint clickers that are shaped like doughnuts. Not only is an unusual shape difficult to hold, it can be tricky to operate.

PS Step 4: Notes That Work

The presenter who speaks from a written text that was designed to be read aloud will give a better presentation than someone struggling to decipher handwritten notes. Mistakes are more likely to occur if the script is not legible. It is not enough to lay out a speech in a standard document format. When you are standing at a lectern with the lights dimmed, twelve-point font will not suffice. Neither will crossed-out lines and last-minute notes scribbled in the margins. Sloppy notes lead to a sloppy presentation.

Several options can work for the speech script: word-for-word text, a detailed outline, or bullet points. Some clients come in with the notion that they don't need a script because they will memorize the speech. The executive director of an international nonprofit was convinced it would be okay to memorize the opening remarks she would deliver to over three hundred people after logging a fifteen-hour flight to New Delhi. The stress of the travel could be enough to block her ability to recall main points, much less every single word. Who wants to suffer through the discomfort of going blank? A well-laid-out text is an important tool, whether you are an experienced speaker or a novice. It can ensure a strong performance, especially when the stakes are high—you've earned the promotion, you're testifying for the record, you're running for high office, you're chairing the big meeting. If you are starting out in your career, learning how to use a script early on will help you improve more quickly.

Full-Text Script

The advantage of having the full text is that you can focus on delivery because the burden of figuring out what to say is lifted. The words are in front of you, and you can deliver the presentation the way it was written without major deviation or digressions. This approach is a must if you are concerned about leaving something out or in a formal situation when every word counts. However, a full text is not meant to be read word for word. Once the speech is written, you will want to reformat it so that it is easy to see and doesn't prevent you from making eye contact with the audience. It should resemble the teleprompter copy shown in the example below. Notice the margin width. The margins are wide so the eye doesn't have to scan across the page. Rather, with practice you can quickly glance down and scoop up chunks of information. This will prevent you from looking like you are overly dependent on your script.

The font should be as large as you need it to be. Double-space the lines and indent all paragraphs. Avoid using all CAPITAL LETTERS. Upper-case and lowercase are more familiar and thus easier to read. The words should start at the top of the page and only run about two-thirds of the way down. The closer the words are to the bottom, the farther your head must dip so you can read them, and you lose eye contact with the audience. There will likely be many more pages, so number them.

Notice that the sample page has delivery cues embedded in the text. These cues are reminders for specific techniques; for example, pause, smile, or pick up the pace. All commands should be placed in parentheses so you don't inadvertently read them aloud. Words in bold or underlined are places to use inflection or add emphasis with a pace or volume change. Once you have the full-text script formatted, then you will want to practice with it aloud several times before the day of the event.

Use standard 8½-by-11-inch sheets of white paper. Water-resistant paper is available for outdoor events when weather may be an issue. Never staple the pages together because it makes them more difficult to turn. Experiment with the pages in a three-ring binder. This is when a three-ring binder can come in handy. The weight of a binder allows you to place it at the top of the lectern so you don't have to look down as far to see the pages. Insert the pages into clear plastic sleeves so they turn more smoothly. The sleeves are also helpful if you are concerned about wind or rain.

Four score and seven years ago, our fathers brought forth on this continent a **new nation**, conceived in liberty, and dedicated to the proposition that **all** men **are created equal**.

(PAUSE)

Now we are engaged in a great civil war, testing whether that nation or **any** nation so conceived and so dedicated, can long endure.

The Outline

The outline is a good option if you are familiar with what you are going to say and just need prompts to help you remember order, flow, and key points. The outline ensures that you are prepared, and it provides the flexibility to add or subtract material. Most speakers use an outline after they've given a presentation several times. They start with a full text and then reduce it to an outline when they feel confident with the material.

The outline used during the presentation will likely be very similar to the original outline used to develop the speech. Example speech outlines are provided in chapter 7. In addition to the main points and supporting material, you may want to indicate where you'll add a story or a statistic. The format should incorporate a large font with plenty of white space, similar to the teleprompter layout.

Note Cards

Five-by-eight-inch note cards are useful for a few bullet points, an outline, or a full text. Full sheets of paper can be cut and pasted to fit or reformatted on the computer. The cards are stiffer than regular paper and are thus easier to hold and less distracting. Note cards are especially handy when you want the session to be interactive and you want to be able to stand closer to the audience. Only use full-size typing paper when speaking at a lectern, however. Be careful not to wave the cards around while gesturing; hold them in the hand you are not using to gesture. Glance at them now and then to refresh your memory. Be sure to number them so you won't panic should you drop the stack.

Teleprompter

As Diane Sawyer delivers the evening news from the anchor desk, watch her eyes. Sometimes you can see them moving back and forth ever so slightly. News anchors rely on the teleprompter, and the nearly invisible eye movement is not distracting. Some speakers resist the teleprompter, believing that the use of what was once facetiously called the "sincerity machine" makes them appear less genuine. There isn't much difference between reading words from a piece of paper and reading from a screen. The trick to using the teleprompter is not to look as if you are reading every word. The setup involves two textbook-sized clear screens on either side of the presenter positioned about six feet away. The speech text is projected onto the screens from monitors on the floor beneath the screens. Rehearsal will allow you to get the hang of it and avoid looking like a mechanical doll.

PS Step 5: Visual Aids

Which do you remember best, names or faces? Most people who are hard-pressed to recall a name can readily remember a face. A study conducted at Harvard University found that audience retention can be increased by as much as 40 percent with the use of visual aids such as slides, flip charts, props, and video.[7] Visuals also help polish the image of the presenter. Audiences view speakers with well-constructed visuals as more professional, persuasive, interesting, and prepared. Presenters get themselves in trouble, however, when they overuse or misuse what are intended to be aids, not crutches. Poorly planned, dull visuals can drag down a presentation.

PowerPoint

For some presenters, PowerPoint (PPT) is the crutch of choice, and in some organizations the use of the software is mandatory. An advantage to PPT slides is the ease with which you can add pictures and illustrations. The dark underbelly is that all text must fit into template slides consisting primarily of headers and bullet points. Thus, the template controls what information will fit or how it must be skewed to fit. The limitations of the technology led one Marine Corps general to declare that "PowerPoint makes us stupid."[8] Essays have expounded upon how it oversimplifies complex ideas, reduces dialogue, and stifles creativity.

The poster child for how bad PPT can be is a slide that was intended to depict the US military's strategy in Afghanistan. The one-frame diagram looked more like a huge bowl of spaghetti and meatballs than a coherent outline of troop movements. The drawing was so outrageous, it caused some commanders to forbid the use of PowerPoint for any presentation on military strategy. One general was quoted as saying: "Some problems in the world are not bullet-izable."[9]

Unlike the military, other organizations have mandated the slides for board meetings, sales talks, and training exercises. If PowerPoint is de rigueur in your workplace, avoid the common mistake of beginning the speech-preparation process with the creation of slides. This can waste time as you struggle to make what you want to say fit into a limited format. Outline what you want to say and only then decide if the use of visuals is appropriate to clarify your points. Visuals are meant to support explanations, not give them.

If you elect to use PowerPoint, design the slides to look like highway billboards, which can be read by drivers going fifty-five miles per hour. The use of multiple colors is risky. Yellow fades out, and some audience members may be color-blind and thus unable to distinguish between red and green. ALL CAPITALS IS DIFFICULT TO READ, as are fancy, unfamiliar fonts and *italics*. Don't forget to use spell check and to proofread carefully.

PowerPoint Design Flaws

- Busy illustrations
- Too much text
- Illegible fonts
- Poor color choices
- Flying bullet points and ricocheting words

> ## PowerPoint Design Perfection
>
> - Simple charts and graphs
> - Six lines, five words per line max
> - Photographs
> - Simple animation, if any
> - Brief video clips

Flip Charts and Erasable Boards

Don't presume that high-tech visuals will be more effective than a flip chart or erasable board. Low-tech can be the way to go for training scenarios because the tools are more interactive than slides. Some rooms are not set up for electronic displays, and charts and boards don't require extension cords or connector cables. Hardly anything can go wrong with a low-tech approach, especially if you bring your own supply of fresh markers. A great trick with the flip chart is to write down the entire presentation in advance. Do it with a light pencil, and no one in the audience will be able to see it. Charts and boards are not effective, however, in more formal settings or with large groups. They are difficult to see in rooms with more than forty people or in an auditorium with theater-style seating.

Props

Did you see Oprah's "fat wagon"? It was a prop the TV hostess used to show how much weight she had lost. A red wagon filled with a sixty-seven-pound mound of lard was wheeled onto the studio set to dramatically illustrate a successful diet. Three-dimensional props are creative and memorable. A well-selected prop can tell a story more effectively than words. The introduction of something novel while you are talking also focuses the audience's attention on what you are saying.

Props have been used in the theater and movies to illustrate story lines and enhance the characters' personalities. The word *prop* comes from the theatrical term "company property." Some are as well-known as the character that used them, like Dorothy's ruby-red slippers in *The Wizard of Oz* and Laura's figurines in *The Glass Menagerie*. Simple props can be arresting. During her maiden congressional speech, newly elected Senator Dole held up an oddly shaped sweet potato. The potato couldn't be sold because of its shape, even though it was edible. It was an effective example of how food is wasted that could feed the hungry.

Multimedia

Multimedia presentations incorporating video and other visuals are more common and easier to use now that they can be run off of a computer. All visuals should tell a story that is germane to a main theme. Check to make sure the format of your material is compatible with the technology available at the event site. Always test for picture and audio quality. Most computers have weak speakers, so you will likely need additional amplification. Be careful about the running time. Video has to be well produced if it runs longer than a couple of minutes. Think twice about showing a low-production piece with grainy pictures.

Handouts

A supplementary handout should not be the outline or text of the speech. Handouts are takeaways that embellish what was discussed during the presentation and provide additional information. They can include detailed graphs, charts, and spreadsheets that are not readable when projected onto a screen. Audiences can forget as much as 90 percent of what is said, so handouts help people recall and apply details. Handouts are more likely to be read if they are well designed.

Let the audience know at the beginning that you have prepared materials so they can decide whether or not to take notes. Distribute the handouts at the end of your presentation unless you want the audience to read while you're talking. Inevitably they won't follow along but will skip ahead. Handouts can be shared at the beginning if there are exercise sheets to fill in; this is an effective approach for training seminars. When speaking to a

> ## All-Time Great Line
>
> Women have had to be overachievers to succeed. We worked twice as hard as men to be considered as good.
> —Elizabeth Dole

group larger than two hundred people, the logistics of producing and distributing handouts may be prohibitive. It might save time and resources to send supplementary information electronically.

UNPLUGGED BUT NOT UNSCRIPTED

There are situations when going with the flow can create a magical moment. Jazz musicians instinctively know when to break into a riff that will thrill listeners. The ability to improvise can save the day when the unexpected happens. Letting go of inhibitions and exploring an unforeseen opportunity can reap tremendous rewards. In these situations, audiences sense vulnerability and cut the speaker some slack. When you pull it off, they doubly appreciate your ability to react, and if it doesn't go perfectly, at least you get credit for trying. Near the end of Elizabeth Dole's convention address, she let pass an opportunity to seize a spontaneous reaction. From the back of the hall, a faint chant broke out, but Dole quickly hushed the crowd. The unplanned, unscripted response might have been a high point if Dole had allowed the enthusiasm to build to a crescendo. Instead, bound to the script in her head and mindful of the tight time schedule, she pressed on with her memorized remarks.

Improv is the skill of knowing how to respond to what is happening in the moment. Actors and comedians rehearse techniques to think on their feet by learning how to anticipate, react, and adjust. Improv is not about crossing your fingers and winging it. The rules of the road employed by improvisation troupes will boost your confidence about being spontaneous and your ability to carry it off. These techniques help you make informed decisions about when to change direction for greater effect.

- **Stay in the moment:** Don't allow your mind to race ahead. Focus on what has just happened and allow yourself to respond spontaneously to the unexpected.
- **Acknowledge aloud the unexpected:** There is no sense pretending the lights have not gone out or someone has not just fainted. Take a moment to allow yourself and the audience to adjust. If someone has taken ill, that takes precedence. Keep in mind that no one is blaming you if something goes wrong, so don't get stuck on what could have or should have been.
- **Unscripted isn't necessarily unprepared:** You did your homework. You know the topic and the audience. Allow yourself the luxury of digressing when an interesting, relevant point pops into your head. Feel free to expand on an area of expertise with a good story.
- **Move on:** Once a distracting moment has passed, the audience will turn back to you. It is up to you as the presenter to get the program moving again. A technique that improv actors use to prevent getting stuck in awkward dialogue is to say: "And, yes..." They use the phrase to keep the dialogue flowing. No matter what is thrown at them, they verbally agree with it and go forward.
- **Accept help:** When an airline passenger falls ill, it always seems as if there is a doctor onboard. Same is true for public speaking. Often someone in the room knows how to fix the computer glitch. Audience members will jump in with an insightful comment or even a touch of humor. Be sure to thank them!
- **Go with your gut:** Eventually, you will begin to trust your instincts.

TODAY'S THE DAY

If God isn't in the details, then the devil sure is. Paying attention to the small stuff means you are not sweating the details in front of the audience. It can also mean the difference between giving a professional presentation versus coming off as an amateur who is out of her league. Here is a final checklist to handle any last-minute changes and ensure all systems are go.

PS Final Checklist

- Do you have your speech text or notes? Are they in order?
- Look at today's paper and check your e-mail. Did anything happen overnight that affects your talk? Be prepared to make changes and update material.
- Arrive early to verify room setup.
- Is audiovisual equipment working properly?
- Test the microphone.
- Meet host and greet audience members beforehand.
- Ask if there have been any last-minute changes to the program or agenda.
- Request room-temperature water or bring your own.
- Do relaxation and deep-breathing exercises offstage.
- Use the power of positive thinking.
- Do a final bathroom mirror check. How is your hair? Are all buttons buttoned and zippers zipped?
- Record the performance for later review.

STANDING OVATION POINT: PREPARATION BRINGS PEACE OF MIND

For most women, going rogue is a risky business, as we are still judged more critically than men. Elizabeth Dole could certainly attest to the peace of mind that comes with the knowledge you have done everything you can to maximize what is within your control. A lifelong glass-ceiling buster, Dole's 2000 presidential candidacy was the first serious effort by a credible woman in decades. The campaign fell short not because of a subpar candidate but for a lack of campaign funds. Her poise and strength on the stump paved the way for her victory as the first woman to serve as US senator from North Carolina.

Finding the time to prepare is a challenge, whether you are running for office, positioning for a promotion, or holding a staff meeting. There will always be competing demands on your time as you juggle the responsibilities of work with home and personal life. The solution is to be realistic about the time commitment it will take for you to improve and plan accordingly so your communications skill building doesn't fall by the wayside.

Preplanned spontaneity will help you achieve the balance between being ready for anything versus anything goes. As you gain more experience, it is possible to gauge improvement with the following measures. Preplanned spontaneity is working for you when you experience the following:

- You are given high marks in speaker evaluations.
- People flock around you to introduce themselves afterward.
- You are invited back next year.
- You receive invitations to more prestigious events.
- You receive a promotion, public acknowledgment, gratitude for inspiring others.

Applause Principles: Planning for Success

- Preplanned spontaneity ensures you don't have to rely on your wits alone when something goes wrong, as it inevitably will.
- The cost of winging it is too high.
- Make it a habit to get the lowdown on the audience, the event, and the setting to reduce the chance of a last-minute surprise.
- Audiences appreciate the presenter who can handle equipment malfunctions and environmental disturbances without becoming flustered.
- View challenges or missteps as feedback, not failure. With that attitude, you can adjust and do better the next time out.

7

WELL-WRITTEN
IS WELL-SPOKEN

The idea is to write so people hear it and it slides through the brain and goes straight to the heart.
—Maya Angelou, interview, Academy of Achievement website

The audience of Washington power brokers was all abuzz with anticipation for the evening's guest speaker, the latest in what was billed as the nation's most distinguished speaker series. Previous gatherings had featured such luminaries as Mikhail Gorbachev, Desmond Tutu, Margaret Thatcher, and Walter Cronkite holding forth on achievement and leadership. When Maya Angelou strode across the stage, she was a resplendent figure in a white satin gown that glowed in the soft lights of the darkened performing arts center. As Angelou gazed out on the plush seats filled with VIPs from the White House, foreign embassies, and halls of Congress, she tilted her head slightly, paused, and began to sing.

It was an unconventional opening for a most conventional crowd. For Angelou, the performance was characteristic of what she had been doing since first taking the stage as a twenty-something calypso singer in a San Francisco cabaret in the 1950s. As she has done countless times before in a myriad of settings, Angelou mesmerized the audience with rich, melodious words that flowed like warm chocolate. She lives the power of words, and they are her central focus whether she is performing on Broadway or delivering a presidential inaugural poem. Angelou says she is driven to take words, the most common things, and bring them to new life: "[I] rearrange them so they come out fresh. Arrange them in one way and make people weep. Arrange them in another way and make them laugh. Ball them up like that 'snap' and throw them up against the wall and make them bounce."[1]

Angelou's relationship with words began early, and like any liaison, it has been tumultuous as well as joyful. As a child, she feared words, believing them to be the cause of terrible harm, and didn't speak for years. While her tongue was silent, the words on the pages of beloved books served as a refuge from pain. Self-educated, she read everything she could get her hands on. During the years she raised her son on her own, words provided a paycheck that put food on the table. Angelou's words now provide sustenance to the millions who have read her six volumes of autobiography, multiple children's books, plays, poetry collections, and Hallmark greeting cards.

Maya Angelou exemplifies the "phenomenal woman" she describes in one of her most acclaimed poems. Indeed, when she enters a room, it is "just as cool as you please." There is a bit of a swagger to the elocution and vocabulary, but the words are not bandied about in an impulsive manner, as she knows firsthand how they can hurt as well as heal. When she is writing, she devotes her whole self to the effort, allowing everything else to shut down. Angelou is well-spoken because she is well-written. It is nearly impossible to say something well if you cannot write it well first. Angelou has committed her life to saying things well: "Use the language, men. Use the language, women. That is the only thing that really separates us from the rats and the rhinoceros. It is the ability to say how we feel. 'I believe this.' 'I need this.'"[2]

WHY PUTTING IT IN WRITING MATTERS

The ability to write a speech may seem like a superfluous skill when Twitter® messages and television sound bites create immediate impact. Why spend time laboring over paragraphs and transitions when Power-Point® bullets will get you through the meeting? Technology has the advantages of being easy, fast, and direct. Then, there are the occasions when what you say really matters. An awards ceremony is an opportunity to publicly thank the people who believed in you more than you believed in yourself. Expressing gratitude requires and deserves more than 140 characters or 20 seconds. In a wired world, giving a talk remains the most fundamental means to express yourself in a meaningful and thoughtful way.

The process of speech writing can be intimidating because what works is different from other forms of writing. The best speeches are written not to be read but to be heard. A speech that reads beautifully may not speak well. Most writing is done for the eye. With a written text, the reader sees the chapters, paragraphs, and sentences. Punctuation helps the reader understand the author's intent. Periods and exclamation points clarify meaning, while question marks and commas add nuance.

A speech, on the other hand, must make sense to the listener even though the listener has no visual cues. Once the words are spoken, they are gone. It is up to the speaker to fill in the blanks with a structure that is explicit and easy to follow. Verbal and vocal signposts are needed to signal transitions. Some of the grammar rules from English 101 work against the speechwriter. This is not an excuse for sloppy writing or incomplete thoughts. It means that speech writing is different from our usual writing.

Distant, Jumbled, Tired Speech Writing

- Compound sentences
- Stream of consciousness
- Abstract rhetoric
- Weak, uncertain wording
- Undecipherable jargon
- Passive or reactive tone
- Rambling, scattered ideas

PUTTING PEN TO PAPER

It can be intimidating to stare at a blank computer screen and wonder: "What am I going to say? Where do I begin?" The initial step in the writing process causes many to procrastinate or to never quite get around to it. Angelou always begins with an old-fashioned legal pad—no iPad® or PC for her. She says a clean sheet of paper scares and thrills her: "I see a yellow pad and my knees get weak and I salivate."[3]

If that clean slate brings you more agony than ecstasy, rest assured that some simple steps can make the writing process less daunting. A manageable approach is to divide the writing into small steps over a few days. The

Direct, Clear, Appealing Speech Writing

- Shorter sentences
- Sentences of varying length
- Concrete ideas
- Fewer words
- Many more short words
- Active tense
- Repetition of main points

Maya Angelou

general rule of thumb is that for every minute you plan to speak, you should schedule an hour of preparation time. The preparation includes writing and rewriting and rehearsal. Of course, it is not possible to devote so much time to every speaking event, but for the more important occasions, you must make sure to put prep time on your calendar.

Steps to Speech-Writing Success

1. Begin by establishing the speech's purpose. What type of speech is it, and why are you giving it?
2. Identify the main theme you want to convey. The theme is more than a topic statement. It is the central point of the speech.
3. Draft an outline with main points and supporting material. The outline is the skeleton to which you will add the muscle and flesh that bring it to life. It may take several drafts and rewrites to express your thoughts.
4. Write the introduction and conclusion. Then elaborate on the main points.
5. Read through the script aloud to make final decisions about flow and organization.

Speech Writing Step 1: What Am I Doing Up Here?

A speech without a purpose is either an ego trip or a murky mess. Decide what you want to accomplish and what you can accomplish given the setting, audience, and occasion. Is this a presentation at an annual board meeting or an evening address at a charity event? There is a tremendous difference in atmosphere depending on the type of event and audience expectations. Writing the remarks for the installation of a new board member is a far cry from penning a call to action at a protest rally.

There are four general types of speeches: inspirational, informative, persuasive, and entertaining. To determine which is appropriate, consider the reason the audience has gathered and the response you seek from them. Once you are clear about the purpose, the speech will begin to have direction and form.

Purpose	Desired Audience Response
To inspire	Heighten appreciation, pay tribute
To inform	Create fuller understanding, educate
To persuade	Change behavior and/or beliefs
To entertain	Relax the audience, enjoyment

Speaking to Inspire

Inspirational speeches heighten the audience's appreciation for someone or something for which they already feel devotion or respect. This speech is most frequently heard when people gather to pay tribute, such as at a retirement dinner, sports banquet, or award ceremony. Musician Alicia Keys articulated the appeal of the artist Prince on the occasion of his induction into the Rock and Roll Hall of Fame: "There is only one man who is so loud, he makes you soft, so strong, he makes you weak...so honest, you feel kinda bashful."[4]

Eulogies and remembrances are another example of inspirational addresses. The mourners at Coretta Scott King's funeral celebrated the legacy of a woman who embodied the heart and soul of the civil rights movement. In her remarks, Maya Angelou spoke of her personal friend who was a national treasure.

> In the midst of national tumult, in the medium of international violent uproar, Coretta Scott King's face remained a study in serenity. In times of interior violent storms she sat, her hands resting in her lap calmly, like good children sleeping.
>
> Her passion was never spent in public display. She offered her industry and her energies to action, toward righting ancient and current wrongs in this world.
>
> She believed religiously in non-violent protest.
>
> She believed it could heal a nation mired in a history of slavery and all its excesses.
>
> She believed non-violent protest religiously could lift up a nation rife with racial prejudices and racial bias.
>
> She was a quintessential African American woman, born in the small town repressive South, born of flesh and destined to become iron, born—born a cornflower and destined to become a steel magnolia.[5]

Speaking to Inform

Informative speeches seek to teach, educate, or enlighten. Nearly all talks to some extent include aspects of the informative speech. The challenge is to present practical material the audience will understand and remember. The speaker is not necessarily trying to persuade or convince the listeners to take one course of action over another. The point may be to provide options or alternatives. Training workshops and educational classes are informational, whether they take place in a classroom, at a work site, in a conference room, or on an athletic field. Highly skilled informative speakers use a variety of methods to increase the audience's ability to comprehend and retain information. Visual aids, demonstrations, role-playing, storytelling, and handout materials are all tools that reinforce learning points.

Musician Caroline Phillips is bringing an old-world instrument to new-age audiences. When the folk artist performs, she treats her audiences to a beginner's lesson on the hurdy-gurdy. The one-thousand-year-old string instrument looks like a cross between a violin and a large vacuum cleaner. Accompanied by a slide presentation with photos of the instrument, Phillips presents the hurdy-gurdy for dummies.

> The hurdy gurdy or wheel fiddle. [As you can see on the slides] these are the different types and shapes of the hurdy-gurdy. It is the only musical instrument that uses a crank to turn a wheel that rubs against strings. It has three different types of strings. The second string is a melody string. It is played on a wooden keyboard tuned like a piano. The third string, it activates what is called the buzzing bridge or the dog. When I turn the crank or apply pressure it makes it sound like a barking dog.
>
> This is all pretty innovative if you consider the instrument first appeared about one thousand years ago. It originally took two people to play it. This all changed a couple of centuries ago. One to turn the crank and another person to play the melody. It has been used historically through the ages mostly for dance music because of the uniqueness of the melody combined with the acoustic boom box.
>
> It is used in all kinds of music today. Dance, contemporary and world music. In the U.K., France and Spain. It takes between three and five years to make one. It is made by specialized artisans in Europe. It is very difficult to tune. So, without further ado, would you like to hear it?[6]

Speaking to Persuade

If the informative speaker is a teacher, then a persuasive speaker is a leader. The persuasive speaker is asking for a commitment from the audience. The speaker's goal is to change the listener's views and urge a course of action in accordance with those beliefs. The persuasive speaker identifies the exact steps the audience should take, such as voting yes on a referendum, buying a new product, donating to a charity, or contacting their member of Congress.

Persuasive speeches often attempt to appeal to the listener's emotions and/or deeply held values. A consumer is urged to buy a home alarm system to ensure her family's safety and security. A political candidate bases an appeal on the value of hard work by sharing a "pulled myself up by my bootstraps" story. Another common persuasive technique is the bandwagon effect. The speaker urges the audience to do or believe in something because "everyone else does." Persuasive speeches are heard in nearly all forums where the audience has a hand in determining an outcome, such as political conventions, organizational business meetings, and sales presentations.

Robin Chase is a remarkable innovator and a bit of a transportation geek. In 2000 she used her MIT business training to found Zipcar Inc., now the world's largest car-sharing business. At a gathering of technology bigwigs, she explained why her customers—particularly women—are super satisfied with the company's product.

> How does it feel to be a person using a Zipcar®? It means that I pay only for what I need. All these hours for a car sitting idle, I'm not paying for it. It means that I can choose a car exactly for that particular trip. So here's a woman that reserved a Mini-Mia and she had her day. I could take a BMW when I'm seeing clients. I can drive my Toyota Element when I want to go on that surfing trip. You know? And, the other remarkable thing is that it's the highest status of car ownership. Not only do I have a fleet of cars available to me in seven cities around the world that I can have at my beck and call. But heaven forbid that I would ever maintain or deal with the repair or have anything to do with it. It's like the car that you always wanted that your mom said you couldn't have. I get all the good stuff and none of the bad.[7]

Speaking to Entertain

Speaking to entertain can have more impact than you might expect because most such speeches take place at social events when the audience is relaxed and receptive. People remember the speaker who helped them kick back and have a good time. While humor is almost always an element, there should still be a topic or point of view. This speech lends itself to the incorporation of unusual props, dramatic video, and/or music. First Lady Laura Bush stole the show when she showed her funny bone at a White

House Correspondents Dinner. The gala event comingles the Washington press corps, political heavyweights, and Hollywood celebrities in an evening of toasts and roasts. In 2005, the First Lady said she'd had enough of sitting quietly by and had a few things to share about her husband, President George W. Bush:

> George always says he's delighted to come to these press dinners. Baloney. He's usually in bed by now. I'm not kidding. I said to him the other day: "George, if you really want to end tyranny in the world, you're going to have to stay up later."
>
> I am married to the president of the United States, and here's our typical evening: Nine o'clock, Mr. Excitement here is sound asleep, and I'm watching *Desperate Housewives*—with Lynne Cheney. Ladies and gentlemen, I am a desperate housewife. I mean, if those women on that show think they're desperate, they oughta be with George.
>
> One night, after George went to bed, Lynne Cheney, Condi Rice, Karen Hughes, and I went to Chippendale's. I wouldn't even mention it except Justices Ruth Ginsberg and Sandra Day O'Connor saw us there. I won't tell you what happened, but Lynne's Secret Service codename is now "Dollar Bill."
>
> George and I are complete opposites—I'm quiet, he's talkative, I'm introverted, he's extroverted. I can pronounce *nuclear*.
>
> The amazing thing, however, is that George and I were just meant to be. I was the librarian who spent 12 hours a day in the library, yet somehow I met George.[8]

Speech Writing Step 2: Select a Theme

Once you have decided on the type of speech, whether inspirational, informative, persuasive, or entertaining, then establish the theme. The theme is the single most important idea or message you want to convey. It is the core point you return to throughout the speech. The renewal of hope is the theme of Angelou's poem "On the Pulse of the Morning." She develops it with the line: "For this bright morning dawning for you...." She returns to it with: "Give birth again, To the dream" and "Each new hour holds new chances." The theme is not the same as the statement of topic.

The topic statement should be narrowly defined, while the theme is usually broad and encompasses a value or belief. For example, Angelou talks about the topic of rap music lyrics by relating it to the theme of respect.

Identify the theme by responding to the following five questions. The responses will help you organize and prioritize your thoughts so you can pinpoint the main idea you want to elevate and embellish. Responding to the questions will also put the entire speech into context. Be as specific as you can when responding to the questions; otherwise, the theme will lack focus, and the speech will lack overall direction.

Identify the Speech Theme

Topic statement—what is it about?
Audience—who's out there?
Goal—what do you want to accomplish?
Benefit—why should the audience members care?
Common bond—where do your interests intersect
  with those of the audience?

Got Topic?

Effective topic statements are a concise wording of exactly what you plan to talk about. With any subject, there are endless possible approaches and different aspects that could be covered. It is impossible to organize and develop the remainder of the speech if you lack a clear statement of topic. A common mistake is to select a topic that is too broad to cover in the allotted time. Try to define the subject narrowly. For example, this topic statement is too broad: "The importance of public education." A crisper topic statement would be "A high level of parental involvement spells success for our public schools." This is too vague: "Support the referendum on civil unions." This is more direct: "The civil union referendum should be supported because all citizens deserve to be treated equally and fairly."

Can You Hear Me Now?

Don't be satisfied with a vague sense of who will attend or make assumptions about how much they know about the topic. Chapter 6 details how to work with the event host to get a good read on the audience's vital statistics. Examples of clearly defined audiences include NASCAR dads, suburban soccer moms, male high-tech entrepreneurs age twenty to forty, or senior citizens living on fixed incomes in Arizona.

What's the Point?

Once you have a clear understanding of the audience, then pinpoint what you want to accomplish. Zero in on specifics so the goal statement is not empty rhetoric or meaningless platitudes. "Raising public awareness" is too squishy. What is it exactly that you want the listeners to do? Former First Lady Nancy Reagan publicly endorsed stem cell research and made an impassioned plea to take the politics out of this scientific issue to ensure funding for researchers. Reagan spoke out in favor of human embryo research, which could help cure diseases like Alzheimer's that afflicted her husband, former president Ronald Reagan.

WHAM Them

All audience members ask themselves the WHAM question. WHAM is an acronym that stands for "What Here Applies to Me?" Your listeners want to know what's in it for them, so you must address this question up front. Don't save it for the conclusion. The WHAM factor is the hook that will engage them and keep them listening. The audience will care more about your topic when it aligns with what they value. For example, Americans love dogs and cats, but not everyone is ready to adopt an abandoned animal from a shelter. The Humane Society of the United States makes it possible for animal lovers to assist by writing a check to fund the organization's efforts.

E Pluribus Unum—*Out of Many, One*

What common bond do you share with the audience? Sometimes it is obvious, such as when you are speaking at a professional conference that draws like-minded individuals. Wendy Kopp, the founder of Teach for America, has likely given more college commencement addresses than anyone else her age. The requests roll in because her story embodies a belief in the unlimited potential of America's youth. While a college senior, Kopp came up with the idea for Teach for America as a way to deal with inequities in the classroom. In her first year, she recruited 500 college graduates to teach in distressed schools, and 20 years later, nearly 30,000 teachers have served low-income communities.

Identifying the bond is more difficult when the audience is unfamiliar, skeptical, or hostile. It wouldn't seem that members of the American Bird Conservancy—people who like to watch birds—would have much in common with members of Ducks Unlimited—people who hunt birds. The point where their interests do align is on the issue of preserving wetlands and open space for wildlife habitats. Both groups agree that too much land is threatened by the encroachment of strip malls and tract housing.

Poet, Performer, Plus More

Angelou says she is a dancer at heart, but when her knees started to give out, she turned her creative energies to singing and acting. The description barely covers the richness of her life experience. The singer became a stage performer when invited to join the European cast of *Porgy and Bess*, and she spent a year touring in Paris, Rome, and Cairo. Following the show's success and relocation to New York, she joined the Harlem Writers Guild, home to some of America's most creative writers, historians, and novelists. The return to the states reunited Angelou with her much-loved son, Clyde. Her only child was born just after Angelou graduated from high school. The boy's father was absent, and her family stepped in as Angelou struggled to care for her son. While taking dance and singing lessons, she had held a variety of jobs, including stints as the first black female streetcar operator in San Francisco and as a brothel manager. Angelou married, but the unions didn't last. She built a community of love and support with her family and a large, extended network of friends.

In the late 1960s, Angelou was working as a playwright and poet when she was asked to develop a television series on African American culture for public television. She had never written for TV but poured herself into creating *Black, Blues, Black!* The achievement readied her for the next challenge, which would establish her as one of America's most gifted voices. In 1970, her autobiography, *I Know Why the Caged Bird Sings*, was published and became a bestseller. She said the book was more than a coming-of-age story about a black child in the segregated South. It was intended as an affirmation of the African American experience and a celebration of the human spirit.

In the book, Angelou bares the details of the childhood tragedy that caused her to remain speechless for six years. She chose to silence her voice because she blamed herself for the death of the man who raped her at the age of seven. The abuser was her mother's boyfriend, and after his trial, it is believed that Angelou's uncles murdered him. Angelou thought her voice had killed him because she gave the man's name to relatives. Angelou and her younger brother, Bailey, were sent to live with their grandmother, Annie Henderson, in Stamps, Arkansas. Henderson was a formidable presence in the lives of her grandchildren and in the segregated community, where she ran a general store on the black side of town. Henderson accepted her granddaughter's muteness, convinced she would speak when she was ready. While Maya's voice was silent, she devoured books from the public library. It was a friend of her grandmother's, Bertha Flowers, who helped her reclaim her desire to speak. Mrs. Flowers said it was not possible to really love poetry until she had read it aloud: "Not until you speak it, till you feel it across your tongue, till it comes out your lips, you will never really love poetry."[9]

Angelou says she hears poetry when she's writing it and thus always writes for the voice, not the eye. "I listened, I

All-Time Great Line

Life is not measured by the number of breaths we take, but by the moments that take our breath away.
—Maya Angelou

listened to the radio. I listened to the church music. I listened to poetry as it was spoken and I thought of my whole body as an ear and I could go into any room and absorb sound particularly and somatically through my pores."[10] Poetry frees a writer to draw upon all five of the senses—what you heard, saw, tasted, smelled, and felt. The poem "Still I Rise" gives voice to the determination people find within themselves to do more than just persevere. To read the poem aloud is to experience Angelou's ability to express emotion with sparse, clear writing. It is possible to feel what it is like to rise even when downtrodden, to rise with a sassiness and haughtiness that may upset and offend. The discipline of poetry writing teaches you how to say nothing more than what needs to be said.

Speech Writing Step 3: Organize the Flow

A stream of consciousness running out of your mouth is not a speech—that is called rambling. Poets use patterns to express what they want to communicate, often in thirty lines or less. Literary devices like rhyming, imagery, and meter enhance the meaning of words. Ideas and emotion flow in a particular rhythm, whether in the form of rap, haiku, or sonnet. It's been said that a novel is "words in the best order" and poetry is "the best words in the best order." Then a speech can be "the best words spoken in the best order."

A speech should have a flow that the audience can discern and follow. It shouldn't be a deluge of information, nor should it be a linear stream of data. A speech should not start at point *A* and end up at point *Z*. When you are writing for the eye, the information can be laid out in a straight line. The reader can go back and reread something she missed the first time. A more holistic or full-circle approach will ensure that the listeners hear your main points and that they stick. Good speech writing is literally well rounded, meaning you end where you began. The speech's opening should lay out the topic and purpose and foreshadow the theme. The body of the speech covers the main points that

---

Speech Flow

Open—tell them what you are going to talk about.

Body—tell the main points.

Close—tell them what you told them.

support the goal and objectives. The conclusion isn't something new. The conclusion summarizes the main points and revisits the main theme.

Outline the Body of the Speech

The body of the speech is the speech. Organize the main points by developing an outline that divides the content into limited, manageable parts. With an outline, you will be able to maintain order and balance throughout and literally see how ideas might flow together. You can also see which ideas have been overemphasized to the exclusion of others. Limit the overall length to no more than three or four main points. There are five primary methods of arranging content.

- **Chronological:** A chronological order arranges ideas in a time sequence. Events can be ordered as they occurred, or a process can be described. Past, present, and future is a common arrangement. A step-by-step pattern is effective when laying out detailed plans or procedures, conducting a training seminar, or presenting historical material. The following example traces the history of the women's movement over the past 150 years:

  I.   The first wave of the women's movement begins in 1848 in Seneca Falls, New York.
       A.   Women in Wyoming are granted the right to vote in 1890.
       B.   In 1920, the suffrage amendment is signed into law.
  II. In the mid-twentieth century, the second wave focuses on gender equality in laws and culture.
       A.   The 1963 Equal Pay Act makes it illegal to discriminate in pay.
       B.   The National Organization for Women is founded in 1966.
  III. The present-day movement is a continuation of the second wave and a response to perceived failures.
       A.   The Hill-Thomas confirmation hearings rivet the nation on workplace sexual discrimination and fuel the 1992 "Year of the Woman" in politics.
       B.   Younger women create the third wave, which heightens awareness of racial issues and generational differences.

- **Topical:** Topical patterns simply divide a speech into categories of a subject. Using this pattern, you list aspects of a person, place, or thing. Resist the temptation to list all the aspects by limiting yourself to those that will be of greatest interest to the audience. The following topic outline is designed for prospective pet owners who are considering adding a Great Pyrenees to the family.

  I.   Great Pyrenees: A Large-Breed Dog
        A.   History of breed
        B.   Breed information
  II.   Temperament and Personality
        A.   Good with children & other animals
        B.   Requires obedience training
  III. Care and Feeding
        A.   Diet
        B.   Exercise

- **Spatial:** A spatial or geographical pattern organizes the major points by position, location, or direction relative to each other. This order can create a visual appreciation for the subject as well as provide an orderly and logical flow. An interior designer might employ a spatial division to describe how a renovation will progress; the designer might start with the kitchen and describe how changes in that room would affect the decor of adjoining rooms. Topics that lend themselves to a spatial arrangement include a description of a hospital campus; a presentation on geological formations of the Grand Canyon; or the explanation of the layout of a museum, library, or airport.

- **Cause and effect:** The cause-and-effect arrangement is a useful format when the speaker's goal is to explain why something is the way it is or to provide a perspective on an issue. This pattern is frequently used for persuasive speeches. It prepares the audience to consider, and then accept, a specific proposal for improvement. For example, a speech about the dangers of offshore oil drilling might argue from the following causal outline:

I.   Three principal causes of offshore oil disasters:
  A.   Poor federal oversight
  B.   Lack of proper equipment maintenance
  C.   Company failure to take preventive steps
II.   The effects of oil spills create additional problems:
  A.   Worker death and injury
  B.   Economic hardship for fishing and tourism industries
  C.   Environmental havoc
III.   What can be done to limit drilling accidents:
  A.   Federal and local legislation
  B.   Corporate responsibility and accountability
  C.   Citizen input

- **Problem and solution:** The problem-and-solution arrangement can be used to advocate for a change in action or thought. This is one of the most frequently used methods, as it is a logical approach and audiences are familiar with the flow. It is similar to the Monroe sequence explained in chapter 5. The first step is to define the problem; then you provide a solution and suggest a course of action that benefits the audience.

Speech Writing Step 4: Open and Close Well

Now that you have established a theme and drafted the outline, write the introduction and the conclusion, starting with the intro. Contrary to popular belief, audiences remember what they hear first better than any other point of the speech. They remember second best what they hear last. The opening is the prologue that sets the stage for the rest of the play. It can be as brief as thirty seconds or as long as two or three minutes, depending on the overall length of the speech. Use the opening to accomplish the four points listed here, and the cell phones will remain in sleep mode.

For many people, the beginning is the most difficult portion to get through. The ability to start well can be hindered by different factors, including a bad introduction, bad acoustics, equipment glitches, and stage fright. Environmental distractions or a case of the nerves can cause speakers to say and do peculiar things. If you don't preplan the opening, you risk permitting something else to become the central focus. Here are the worst ways to start.

> ## Maximize the Opening
>
> - Gain goodwill and respect.
> - Introduce the topic and main theme.
> - Disclose what's in it for the audience.
> - Set the tone and direction.

Busted Openings

- **Tell a joke:** Leave it to pros like Whoopi Goldberg. Comedians diligently perfect their timing and are prepared to recover if nobody laughs.
- **Give logistical information:** Latrine directions are for drill instructors.
- **Admit unpreparedness:** Immediately, everyone does a watch check and looks for the nearest exit.
- **Disclose self-doubt:** Don't give them an excuse to question your expertise or capacity to lead.
- **Apologize:** This draws more attention to nervousness, a misspoken word, or a technical problem. The exception is a late arrival. Then you owe your audience a sincere and humble explanation.
- **Say: "You would rather be somewhere else."** This may be true, but vocalizing it can be a downer.
- **Misstate the host's name:** Save yourself the humiliation by writing it down.
- **Let slip: "Someone else wrote this speech."** This may be true, but you come across as less genuine and committed.

Bang-Up Openings

A good introduction is free of the obvious, ordinary, and offhand. It is a creative articulation of the speech topic and theme. The well-spoken women who delivered the following well-written dynamic openers earned rave reviews.

- **Pose a question:** Legendary marine biologist Sylvia Earle is an eloquent speaker who uses sophisticated multimedia presentations to
  pull listeners deep into her underwater world. Earle has led more
  than fifty deepwater research expeditions, including one that gained
  international headlines when five women aquanauts lived for two
  months in a special laboratory on the ocean floor. Dubbed "her
  deepness" by the *New York Times*, Earle shares her passion for the sea
  by asking the audience members to imagine the fate of the oceans.

Fifty years ago when I began exploring the ocean, no one—not Jacques
Perrin, nor Jacques Cousteau or Rachel Carson—imagined that we could
do anything to harm the ocean by what we put into it. Or by what we took
out of it. It seemed, at the time, to be a sea of Eden, but now we know
and now we are facing Paradise Lost.

I want to share with you my personal view of changes in the sea that
affect all of us. And to consider why it matters that in fifty years we've
lost—actually, we've taken, we've eaten—more than 90 percent of the
big fish in the sea. Why you should care that nearly half of the coral reefs
have disappeared? Why a mysterious depletion of oxygen in large areas
of the Pacific should concern not only the creatures that are dying but it
really should concern you as well?[11]

- **Quote an admired figure:** Civil rights leader Mary McLeod
  Bethune was a teacher who founded schools to educate black students and served as an adviser to President Franklin D. Roosevelt.
  McLeod Bethune celebrated the achievements of African American
  women at the Chicago Women's Federation in 1933 by using the
  time-honored technique of quoting a respected person.

To Frederick Douglass is credited the plea that "the Negro be not judged
by the heights to which he is risen, but by the depths from which he has
climbed." Judged on that basis, the Negro woman embodies one of the
modern miracles of the New World.[12]

- **Recount a personal experience:** Handgun-control activist Sarah
  Brady shared her family's trauma with gun violence. At the Demo-

cratic National Convention in August 1996, Brady took the audience back to the day when her husband and President Reagan were attacked by a would-be assassin.

Fifteen years ago, [my husband] Jim was White House press secretary. Our son Scott was just two years old. All our dreams had come true.

But then one rainy afternoon in March our dreams were shattered by an assassination attempt on Ronald Reagan. President Reagan was shot. And so was Jim. We almost lost Jim that day. And we almost lost the president. But thanks to the heroism of the Secret Service and the determination of the physicians and staff at George Washington Hospital, Jim lived and so did the president. Thank God.

But our lives would never be quite the same. All it took was one gun, one bullet and one man who should never have owned a gun.[13]

- **Specific example:** In 1872, it was illegal for women to vote, but that didn't stop Susan B. Anthony on election day. Her effort to cast a ballot nearly landed her in jail, and she was fined $100. Anthony refused to pay as a protest against the absurdity of the laws that discriminated against women. She defended her actions by asserting her equal rights as a citizen.

Friends and fellow citizens, I stand before you tonight under indictment for the alleged crime of having voted at the last presidential election, without having a lawful right to vote. It shall be my work this evening to prove to you that in thus voting, I not only committed no crime but, instead, simply exercised my citizen's rights, guaranteed to me and all United States citizens by the National Constitution, beyond the power of any state to deny.[14]

- **Colorful language:** US senator Barbara Mikulski's floor speech in support of the anti–wage discrimination legislation known as the Lilly Ledbetter law grabbed attention with its vivid wording.

I take the floor today as the dean of the Democratic women in the Senate. I say to my colleagues and to all who are watching: We women are mad as hell, and we don't want to take it anymore. We are mad that in this institution, when all is said and done, more gets said than gets done.

We are here today, united as Democratic women, to be a voice, a voice for change. We have a checklist for change we think we can do before this Congress adjourns. These are issues that focus on the big picture of what our country is facing, but they also focus on the impact these issues have on families. We look at macro issues that affect the world and the macaroni-and-cheese issues that affect families.[15]

- **Humorous common bond:** "My fellow job seekers...." So said former Hewlett-Packard CEO Carly Fiorina as she greeted the graduates of North Carolina Agricultural and Technical State University. Fiorina delivered the commencement address just months after being fired.

When I first received the invitation to speak here, I was the CEO of an $80 billion Fortune 11 company with 145,000 employees in 178 countries around the world. I held that job for nearly six years. It was also a company that hired its fair share of graduates from North Carolina A&T. You could always tell who they were. For some reason, they were the ones that had stickers on their desks that read, "Beat the Eagles."

But as you may have heard, I don't have that job anymore. After the news of my departure broke, I called the school, and asked: do you still want me to come and be your commencement speaker? Chancellor Renick put my fears to rest. He said, "Carly, if anything, you probably have more in common with these students now than you did before." And he's right. After all, I've been working on my resume. I've been lining up my references. I bought a new interview suit. If there are any recruiters here, I'll be free around 11 a.m.[16]

The Close: Revisit Important Stuff

What do you want the buzz in the room to be once you've finished speaking? End with that. The conclusion is not the time to throw in something new. It is the time to summarize the main points and revisit the theme. All good endings convey a sense of wholeness and finality. The speaker who seems to end one speech only to begin another leaves the audience frustrated and distracted. However, the worst conclusion is no conclusion at all. A young writer for *Salon* was speaking passionately on the impact of sexism in the 2008 presidential campaign when she ran out of gas at a book signing. After reading an emotional passage, she looked up at the audience, and her facial expression said it all: "Well, I guess that's about it. [Pause] Thank you very much. [Awkward pause.] Are there any questions?" The lack of closure is unsatisfying because everyone feels the deficiency. Always preplan the conclusion since it is your last chance to drive home the theme.

- **End on time:** Respect other people's time and busy schedules. If you are given five minutes for the panel discussion, then stick to it out of courtesy. A toast should run thirty to ninety seconds. A summary of a work project should be done in two to three minutes. The adult attention span is less than twenty minutes, so it is always better to come in under that limit.
- **Give a heads-up:** Tell your audience you are about to wrap up by using one of those cliché lines like "Let me wrap this up with a story" or "I will conclude my remarks by reminding you of something I said earlier." Give them fair warning, and they will focus on you.
- **Summarize the main points:** Now that you have your audience's attention, maximize the final moment by reviewing what you want them to remember. Avoid surprise endings that don't relate to the theme. Digressions confuse and frustrate listeners who are waiting for closure.
- **Be believable:** Speakers who scrimp on the conclusion are at a greater risk of leaving the audience hanging. Don't allow the conclusion to feel like an afterthought by running out of content. Use the bang-up techniques below to finish in a strong and convincing manner.

Bang-Up Closers

- **Make a pledge:** There was a moment of absolute silence when Mary Fisher finished her "A Whisper of AIDS" speech, and then the stadium exploded. The speech shook the assembled crowd at the

Republican National Convention and shattered America's sense of complacency about the spread of HIV/AIDS. A divorced, white heterosexual mom delivered a passionate appeal that presented another face of the disease and lifted the shroud of silence surrounding those who were afflicted.

To the millions of you who are grieving, who are frightened, who have suffered the ravages of AIDS firsthand: Have courage and you will find comfort.

To the millions who are strong, I issue this plea: Set aside prejudice and politics to make room for compassion and sound policy.

To my children, I make this pledge: I will not give in, Zachary, because I draw my courage from you. Your silly giggle gives me hope. Your gentle prayers give me strength. And you, my child, give me reason to say to America, "You are at risk." And I will not rest, Max, until I have done all I can to make your world safe. I will seek a place where intimacy is not the prelude to suffering.

I will not hurry to leave you, my children. But when I go, I pray that you will not suffer shame on my account. To all within the sound of my voice, I appeal: Learn with me the lessons of history and of grace, so my children will not be afraid to say the word AIDS when I am gone. Then their children, and yours, may not need to whisper it at all.[17]

- **Pose a rhetorical question:** Suffragist Carrie Chapman Catt was a newspaper reporter from Iowa who reportedly signed a prenuptial agreement with her second husband securing that she would have the time necessary to advocate for the right to vote. Her husband wholeheartedly supported her efforts, saying he would earn a living so she could work for reform. In the winter of 1917, Catt called upon Congress to extend voting rights to women on the national level.

Gentlemen, we hereby petition you, our only designated representatives, to redress our grievances by the immediate passage of the Federal Suffrage Amendment and to use your influence to secure its ratification in your own state, in order that the women of our nation may be endowed with political freedom before the next presidential election, and that our nation may resume its world leadership in democracy.

Woman suffrage is coming—you know it. Will you, Honorable Senators and Members of the House of Representatives, help or hinder it?[18]

- **Get personal:** Author J. K. Rowling, creator of the wildly popular Harry Potter series, shared a personal story and a quote to conclude her commencement address at Harvard University in June 2008.

I am nearly finished. I have one last hope for you, which is something that I already had at 21. The friends with whom I sat on graduation day have been my friends for life. They are my children's godparents, the people to whom I've been able to turn in times of trouble, people who have been kind enough not to sue me when I took their names for Death Eaters. At our graduation we were bound by enormous affection, by our shared experience of a time that could never come again, and, of course, by the knowledge that we held certain photographic evidence that would be exceptionally valuable if any of us ran for Prime Minister.

So today, I wish you nothing better than similar friendships. And tomorrow, I hope that even if you remember not a single word of mine, you remember those of Seneca, another of those old Romans I met when I fled down the classics corridor, in retreat from career ladders, in search of ancient wisdom: "As is a tale, so is life; not how long it is, but how good it is, is what matters."

I wish you all very good lives.[19]

- **Issue a call to action:** In September 2010, actress Meryl Streep addressed "an idea that has yet to become real: a National Women's History Museum that we can all see and touch and feel." At a gala fund-raiser, she spoke about the importance of symbols and why it is necessary to create a building that will house the richness of women's history in America. Streep rallied the crowd with the surprise announcement that she would kick off the fund-raising drive with a pledge of $1 million. She concluded her remarks with a succinct summary of what everyone in the room needed to do.

We need two things tonight: permission from Congress and cash from you.

We will get permission because I cannot imagine that those two Senators who have put "a hold" on our museum have a stomach for war with American women.

And we will get the money to build this tribute. I have no doubt of that. I even have a plan! If each of the 500 of us here tonight can get 50 people (that's less than your Christmas card list), 50 women to put away one $20 bill a week—that's less than $3 a day—that's coffee money. If we make that pledge, in ten years we'll have over $250 million. More than a quarter of a billion dollars![20]

STANDING OVATION POINT: YOUR WORDS MAKE THE MUSIC

Every four years for the past twenty, I've helped the Democratic Party present its message to the American people by prepping the prime-time speakers who appear at the Democratic National Conventions. It's a big operation headed up by Michael Sheehan, who is known as the speech coach to Democratic presidents. With two teams working simultaneously out of rehearsal rooms set up offstage, we ensure that every speaker does a run-through before facing millions of TV viewers. We are assisted by a large production crew and dozens of speechwriters who churn out reams of teleprompter copy, all in the effort to help dignitaries, celebrities, top party officials, and real people present a unified party message.

This practice routine might sound glamorous, but the hours are long, the work is grueling, and the conditions resemble those of a sweatshop. Typically, the famous and not-so-famous flow in and out of the converted locker rooms of whatever sports stadium we are in. There is nothing pleasant about the lingering odor of sweaty socks.

In 2004, Maya Angelou brought a touch of class to the Fleet Center in Boston with her tribute to civil rights activist Fannie Lou Hamer. The night Angelou was scheduled to speak, she arrived for rehearsal in a dazzling black lace evening gown. I was awed by her regal presence, commanding voice, and eloquent prose. As she neared the end of the tribute, Angelou had the entire crowd swaying on their feet as they joined in a song for Fannie Lou. Angelou led the way with an anthem of the civil rights movement, "This Little Light of Mine."

> Preacher, singer, blues singer, jazz singer, rap person, it is so catching, so hypnotic, so wonderful that, as a poet, I continue to try to catch it, to catch the music. If I can catch the music and have the content as well, then I have the ear of the public.[21]

Angelou has broken down barriers with the power of her words. She courageously allows herself to be influenced by her wide-ranging interests and life experiences. Take a risk by moving beyond bullet points and slide presentations. Seek inspiration in the words and lyrics of your favorite writers, singers, and performers. Relishing great words by great writers will enhance your style.

Applause Principles: The Speechwriter's Recipe

- Well-spoken is well-written. Good speech writing catches the listener's ear, not the eye.
- Write so the listener feels like you are talking to her and so she can follow your train of thought.
- Set the stage with a clear statement of topic and purpose.
- Use the opening to ignite imaginations; then close with conviction.
- Dare to be expressive with words that are personal, clear, and relevant.

8

CONQUERING THE CAMERA

I view the camera as a living entity. I flirt with it and have a great time.
—Suze Orman, personal finance expert, interview with the author

Suze Orman's rapport with the camera was nearly as hard-earned as her wealth. It was a trial-by-fire experience that taught Orman how to do television. Her training ground was the cable TV home-shopping behemoth QVC. As she related the story to me, well before Orman was a household name and when TV appearances were still a little scary for her, she was nonetheless the person QVC wanted on its first program to broadcast before a live studio audience. There was a big publicity buildup to create interest in the program. Orman would appear with a lottery winner who said she won after reading Orman's book *You've Earned It, Don't Lose It*.

Arriving at the studio the day of the broadcast, Orman came upon a chaotic scene. The lottery winner had spent the night in Atlantic City and was seriously hungover. The program host, the only professional, was beside herself with anxiety about the live audience. With lights blazing, cameras rolling, and expectation rising from the audience, the program began. Orman found herself seated between the host, who barely talked because she was a nervous wreck, and the lottery winner, who couldn't talk because she was wasted. Through the earpiece, Orman could hear the director screaming at the host to say something. The host was speechless and there was dead silence, so Orman took over carrying the program for the next hour. That wild experience was her introduction to live TV, and it taught her how to conquer the camera. Your first or next appearance doesn't need to be so dramatic.

Are you aware of the twenty-second rule? Do you know when to look directly at the camera? Do you have HDTV makeup? Is a navy-blue suit the best choice? This chapter demystifies the camera so you can exercise more control in broadcast, cable, and online appearances and still be yourself. But being yourself takes a little extra work and some specialized know-how. TV land is different, so you must prepare differently. What works for in-person audiences doesn't necessarily translate well to a television monitor or computer screen. Adjustments are required in delivery technique, messaging, and wardrobe. Knowing how to sit, where to look, and what to wear will help you project a camera-ready well-spoken persona.

THE CAMERA: AN ACQUIRED TASTE

When Orman hears "You're on," her made-for-television personality lights up the small screen. The words that cause others to sweat and stammer are the prompts that energize her rapport with the camera, which comes across as a combination of big-sisterly concern and televangelist intensity. This bond draws millions of viewers to her weekly cable TV talk show, QVC, PBS specials, and countless talk-show appearances. The fans tune in to get a regular dose of commonsense financial advice from a woman they trust with their money decisions. Orman shares a deep affinity with her fan base because she has dug her own way out of what many of them are trying to escape —a money pit.

Suze Orman

A former waitress, Orman doesn't possess the well-modulated voice of a radio announcer or the detached cool of a professional broadcaster. On her cable program, Orman often displays her annoyance with callers who plead for approval of risky schemes that violate her "laws of money." While she doesn't hesitate to express exasperation, her empathy is apparent as she counsels people to change their errant ways. Orman does one of the hardest things in life, and she does it on camera: she appears as who she is. As she explained to me, she hasn't allowed anyone to mold her into being someone she isn't.[1] She has molded herself into what she wants to be. Her persona is abundantly likable, and that's what counts on camera.

The Likability Quotient

On screen, the likability quotient reigns supreme. Television news directors watch anchor audition tapes with the sound turned down because they want to hire newsreaders who project a warm and friendly demeanor. Uptight and arrogant personalities don't attract viewers to the morning shows and evening newscasts. Viewers will stop channel surfing to watch people who make them feel comfortable. It is a popularity contest, and the winners are upbeat, proactive talkers with relevant, colorful messages.

The likability factor can present a double standard for women. The Barbara Lee Family Foundation—a foundation dedicated to women's advancement—has found that women seeking positions of power must prove both their likability and their credibility. It is not enough for a woman gubernatorial candidate to demonstrate that she is capable of doing the job. The woman candidate needs to come across as someone it would be fun to join for happy hour. Men get a pass on likability. If a man is perceived to be doing a good job, he is generally well liked. Women must demonstrate high job performance while projecting a girl-next-door image. Women who are too perfect, too intelligent, and too tough are viewed with suspicion.

Martha Coakley is the whip-smart, hard-edged Massachusetts attorney general who lost to Scott Brown in the US Senate race to fill Ted Kennedy's seat. Brown was a relatively junior state legislator who campaigned in a pickup truck, crisscrossing the state with his daughters in tow. When Coakley was asked to explain why she wasn't campaigning like her opponent, she shot back: "As opposed to standing outside Fenway Park? In the cold? Shaking hands?" Coakley's biting reference to her opponent's glad-handing style cost her more than the votes of Red Sox fans. When the candidates faced off in a televised debate, Coakley's frown and sharp elbows turned plenty of people off.

SHAPE UP TO GO ON CAMERA

The camera changes your demeanor and your appearance in ways that you might not expect. Lieutenant Governor Bev Perdue got an earful about her on-camera appearance from a complete stranger while campaigning in small-town North Carolina. After speaking at a rally, Perdue was approached by an elderly woman who asked to touch her. The request was odd but not the oddest, so the candidate held out her hand. The woman grabbed it, pulled Perdue in close, looked her straight in the eye, and said: "You are not nearly as old or as fat as you look on television."

When I shared this story with a group of women business and political leaders, my intention was to add a touch of levity to a long day of coaching. Instead of a laugh, the reaction was a collective gasp. Each of the women was imagining herself in Perdue's place, smiling through clenched teeth while enduring an unsolicited comment about her appearance. For women in the public eye, the critique of every aspect of their look and wardrobe has long come with the territory. The scrutiny is now intensified with the proliferation of technology that can capture your image anyplace, anytime. A professional once could go her entire career without appearing on camera. Those days are gone. Don't be surprised when your next appearance at an industry conference or association is uploaded to the Internet. Be ready and willing when you are asked to appear on a cable television talk show. And then, brace yourself for the feedback from viewers who will instantly praise your performance or pan your lack of polish. In a digitally connected world, it is vital to add on-camera delivery techniques to your skill set.

Everyone looks larger and taller on TV. Orman says that when she meets people in person, they often comment on how small she is. TV creates something akin to a Renée Zellweger effect, except that the weight gain is an illusion. Zellweger actually bulked up on Snickers® bars to play the character Bridget Jones. When you sit before a camera, the wide-screen lens appears to add as much as fifteen pounds. Cinematographers call the effect "mumping." The other reason people look different on camera is that the technology flattens images. In person, you are a living, breathing, three-dimensional image. The camera reduces the three dimensions to two, even in a high-definition format.

The flattening and fattening effects of the camera technology can be minimized with special techniques. SHAPE UP is an acronym for seven delivery techniques that will help you shape up for the camera without undergoing a Zellweger diet or boot-camp regimen. The SHAPE UP techniques help you project likeability, and they ensure that you look like you. These tips will prepare you for broadcast news interviews, cable talk-show appearances, video blogs, YouTube® videos, and webcasts.

> **SHAPE UP**
>
> **S**mile
> **H**ands
> **A**nimated voice
> **P**osture
> **E**ye contact
>
> **U**pper-body movement
> **P**urposeful practice

Shape Up: Smile

Nearly everyone should smile more than they think they should on camera. Watch the expressions on the faces of the anchors on *Good Morning America*. The pros are very "smile-ly." As inappropriate as this may seem, more facial expression is necessary to compensate for the two-dimensional effect of the camera, which drains away expression. An in-person neutral expression can appear bored or glum on a television or computer screen. An in-person serious expression looks more like a frown or scowl on TV. It may seem counterintuitive to smile broadly, especially when you are talking about a serious subject. But on TV, the smile will not look as big as it does in person, and it can help you project confidence, enthusiasm, and empathy. Be aware that the first time you try this technique, it may feel awkward and forced.

How broadly you should smile depends on the shape of your head and the bone structure of your face. Some people need to grin like the Cheshire Cat. The only way to determine what is appropriate is to practice on camera and review the tape. The most genuine smiles start in the brain and are evident by a sparkle in the eyes. A smile will look contrived if the eyes are dull. Recapture natural enthusiasm by thinking "happy" thoughts. Recall a moment when you heard good news and allow your

On-Camera Smile

brain to power the expression. No one should use a closed-mouth smile, which looks like a smirk.

Shape Up: Hands

As Martha Stewart might say, hand gestures are "a good thing." Hand gestures can be used to underscore key points, and the movement can externalize excess energy to help you relax.

Hand Gesture Box

On-camera hand gestures should be kept in an imaginary "hand box" that is centered at the top of the chest, as shown by figure B. The parameters of the hand box are below the chin, between the shoulders, and above the top of the bra. During a training session for a group of physicians, they reacted to the hand box by saying: "Oh, you mean the scrub zone." The docs were referring to the area in front of the chest where they hold their hands once they've scrubbed up prior to surgery.

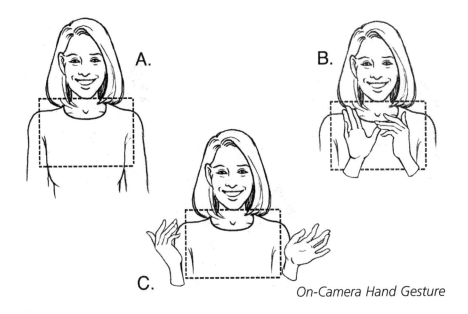

On-Camera Hand Gesture

Use one hand or two, but keep the hand or hands inside the box. Hands bobbing in and out of the box are moving in and out of camera range. The typical camera shot shows the area from the top of your head to the top of your chest. Hands moving beyond the tight frame look like little birds flitting about and are distracting. Pointing with one finger makes you look like a scold. Resist the temptation to reach the hand out to the camera like football players waving to mom on *Monday Night Football.* The hand will be distorted and appear overly large. Hold the hand or hands about six inches or so from the chest. Initially, this positioning may feel tight since the placement is different from how we gesture during regular conversation. Practice several times, and you will get a feel for the movement.

Quiet Hands

There are two good options for the hands when you are not gesturing: place one hand on each leg about midway down the leg with the fingers closed or place one hand on top of the other on one leg. Both are "quiet-hand" positions, meaning they are not distracting to the viewer. Avoid gripping the armrests because you will look as if you are strapped to an electric chair. Don't rest your elbows on the armrests, either, because doing so will cause your posture to slump.

Shape Up: Animated Voice

Use your normal speaking voice. There is no need to dramatically raise the volume level because the microphone will pick it up. But if your voice sounds flat as a sidewalk, your message is easier to disregard. Get a sense of what sounds good by listening to the well-modulated voices of favorite radio announcers or news anchors, perhaps someone like CNN's Candy Crowley. Hear the cadence and the intonation. Notice the inflection and pacing. The five best ways to add interest to the voice are discussed in detail in chapter 3. Good vocal technique is as important on camera as it is in person. Use pace, pitch, pause, pronunciation, and projection to create a sense of interest, urgency, even drama, if the subject matter calls for it.

Shape Up: Posture

How you sit will go a long way toward determining whether or not you gain those extra TV pounds. The correct posture is essential to appearing slimmer and coming across as engaged with the viewer. When you are seated, it is crucial that you sit up straight and tilt forward slightly. Don't relax back in the chair or crouch, hunch, or slouch in the shoulders, as shown in the bad seated posture figure. If you sit back in the chair, you will appear frumpy and wider.

Sit up and tilt forward from the waist about two or three inches to position your head closer to the camera. This helps you look more engaged and will put you in a more conversational mode of talking, as shown in the good seated posture figure. As you lean forward, drop your shoulders back slightly.

You can position your legs and feet three different ways to enable you to lean in comfortably. The position you choose depends on how tall you are, what you are wearing, and the type of chair. If you are tall and wearing pants, use the runner's position, which is just like it sounds. Place one foot slightly in front of the other on the ground as if you were about to take off in a 100-yard dash. This position allows you to balance your body weight forward on your feet as shown in the good seated posture. If you are wearing a dress or a skirt, it is more "ladylike" to cross your legs at the knee. Don't forget to sit up and lean forward, though, as there is a tendency to slouch with the legs crossed.

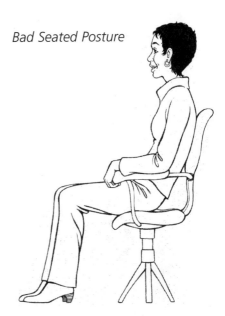

Bad Seated Posture

If you are shorter and/or wearing a shorter dress or skirt, cross your ankles and pull both feet straight back under the chair as shown in the front-view posture. This position will reduce the leg shot: less thigh, more skirt. It is also a more comfortable position if the chair or sofa lacks support. Sit forward, closer to the edge of the furniture, so your body weight is supported by the frame. This will prevent you from sinking into the cushions.

Standing Posture

For standing interviews or press conferences, avoid positioning the feet shoulder-width apart because this

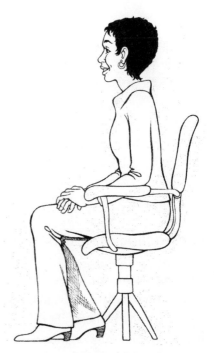

Good Seated Posture

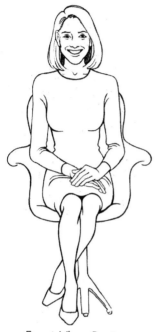

Front-View Posture

stance facilitates swaying back and forth. Try a slight adjustment, using the champion stance detailed in chapter 4; place one foot slightly in front of the other. This stance will look and feel better. With one foot ahead, you will naturally move forward toward the camera and appear more interactive.

Shape Up: Eye Contact

As it is for public speaking, eye contact is the most important nonverbal technique for the camera. Where you focus your eyes depends on the type of appearance. For media interviews with a news reporter or program host, look directly at the reporter and maintain steady eye contact. Focus on one spot on the reporter and don't glance away while speaking. The instant you break eye contact, the movement seems exaggerated and you appear less credible. If the camera catches you looking up, you appear as if you are searching the heavens for the answer. Looking side to side will appear shifty. If you repeatedly look down, you come across as uncertain. Good, steady eye contact on one spot enables you to establish and maintain your credibility with the people watching at home. Look the reporter in the eye or at an earring or a necktie knot. It doesn't matter where you direct your gaze as long as it is in the general direction of the reporter's face.

Satellite and Webcasts

The spot where you direct your eye contact changes if you are doing a satellite interview or a virtual presentation. In those formats, you are often alone with the camera; there is no live audience. In a satellite newscast there is no one to look at because you hear the questions through an earpiece called an IFB. The earpiece allows you to hear what is happening on

On-Camera Eye Contact

air or in the director's control booth. Look directly into the center of the camera lens. The principle of steady eye contact remains unchanged; the only thing that is different is that you are looking into the camera lens— not up, not down, not all around.

When clients review their practice tapes, they are sometimes concerned when they see themselves blink. Blinking can be a problem if it is excessive. Neuropsychologists contend that stress can be measured by how often a person blinks. The normal blink rate for someone speaking on TV is 31 to 50 blinks per minute. People who are nervous can blink as rapidly as over 125 times per minute. If this is a worry, bear in mind that not blinking appears odd. You may come across as a wide-eyed zombie or space alien.

Shape Up: Upper-Body Movement

Upper-body movement helps you appear relaxed and confident, even if you don't feel that way. Many people hold themselves still because they don't know what to do and are worried about making a mistake. Nervous anxiety can also cause people to freeze up. But holding yourself still will look stiff and ill at ease. In daily conversation, most people interact with each other by using nods, shoulder shrugs, and gestures. Experiment with some upper-body movement while you are talking. Avoid swaying from side to side or bobbing your head from shoulder to shoulder. It is more conversational to nod the head forward from time to time. Keep the shoulders relaxed and down so you can shrug for emphasis. Moving forward and back from the waist will help you look engaged in the dialogue.

Shape Up: Purposeful Practice

"I'll just wing it." Nothing causes communications staff more heart palpitations than the spokesperson who doesn't appreciate the value of practice. On the airwaves, a bad performance can result in a major setback. Some clients go to great lengths to avoid on-camera practice—canceling or showing up late—but there is absolutely no substitute for practice. It is the most effective way to zero in on what works and what doesn't. The camera provides the feedback you need to improve. Be objective when viewing practice tapes, especially if you tend to fall victim to negative self-talk. Don't fall into the trap of obsessing about weight gain, and let Nora Ephron worry about the skin under her neck. No one is expecting a camera-ready performance the first time out.

The process isn't rocket science or brain surgery. In fact, I once had a neurologist ask me: "Do they really pay you to do this?" But it does take a commitment to a practice schedule. Practice can be done by hiring a media trainer or working with knowledgeable staff. Prepare for news interviews and talk-show appearances by having someone test your message and delivery techniques through mock interview exercises. Practice fielding a range of questions on a topic using the message map discussed in chapter 5 and the SHAPE UP techniques discussed here. Initially, staying on message and projecting well will take some concentration. With practice, however, you will be able to internalize the techniques, and eventually more of your personality will come through. The techniques are the means to the end. As Orman says, the end is "to be who you are and forget about the camera."

Try, Review, Refine

Some people, when watching their initial round of practice, feel that the SHAPE UP techniques make then appear robotic. Consider that what may feel unfamiliar and awkward to you does not appear that way to the viewing audience. You may be experiencing cognitive dissonance because what you think you are doing is not what you are actually doing. Upper-body animation, facial expression, and vocal inflection help you come across as engaged. In time you will develop muscle memory for the new postures and movements.

Retain new skills by scheduling brief refresher sessions every several months so that you're camera ready when a last-minute call comes in from CNN. Be sure to schedule additional time prior to major interviews and appearances so you can take full advantage of those opportunities. Reinforce the techniques by watching and analyzing the pros. Experienced broadcasters use the SHAPE UP techniques to deliver the news with confidence and poise. Note the vocal inflection and engaging body language of *Today Show* hosts Kathie Lee Gifford and Hoda Kotb. They are eminently watchable personalities with high likeability quotients. Tune into Orman and the women of *The View* to see how they maintain camera rapport while engaged in conversation.

A TV STAR IS MADE

Orman is an unlikely on-camera success story, which is part of what makes her so eminently watchable. As a child, she was an underperformer who suffered from low self-esteem. A speech impediment caused her to slur consonant sounds, and she still worries that if you listen closely, you can hear traces of slurred *s*'s, *t*'s, and *r*'s. In grade school on the South Side of Chicago, Orman's speech impediment made reading aloud an excruciating experience. In college, she majored in social work after being told that with her grades, she wasn't going to amount to much. In 1973, she decided to move to California and spent the next six years waiting tables at a café in Berkeley.

An opportunity to turn the waitress gig into a more financially stable career path came about when several regular customers pooled $50,000 to open a restaurant. Orman jumped at the chance to become an entrepreneur and took the money to a Merrill Lynch broker, requesting that the funds be invested conservatively. The broker didn't follow her instructions, and every penny was lost. Outraged, she applied for a job at Merrill Lynch, figuring she couldn't possibly do worse. Soon she discovered her financial acumen, and after seven years of learning the ropes, she started her own financial-planning firm. Disaster struck again shortly thereafter when an employee stole all the company documents. She spent the next three years struggling to recover the lost money.

Despite setbacks, Orman's dogged enthusiasm for helping people make sound retirement investments began to pay off. When she found herself a wealthy woman in the early 1980s, she was somewhat surprised to realize she was not completely content. There was something missing, so she embarked on another journey, this time a spiritual quest to the Far East. Her travels led to an epiphany about life's meaning and the role money plays in people's lives. She began to develop a financial philosophy based on the principle of "valuing who you are over what you have." The insights about the psychological and spiritual aspects of money were the basis of the first of several popular books. The publishing success led to her first on-camera performance, which ultimately launched "the people's financial planner." QVC gave her a late-night selling slot, and the rest is "her-story." Soon she was making guest appearances on the *Oprah Winfrey Show* and *Larry King Live*, and before you could say, "Lights, camera, action," she had her own show.

Orman believes that if you try to be someone you are not, you will fail miserably, especially on television. The camera magnifies who you are. She says she can see the truth in the eyes of whomever she is talking to. It is apparent whether they are struggling or being sincere. A regular feature on *The Suze Orman Show* is the "Can I Afford It?" segment in which viewers call in to ask permission to buy an object of desire. A middle-aged man who claims he wants to purchase a $60,000 Ferrari "as an investment" immediately gets an Orman eye roll

---

All-Time Great Line

The camera magnifies the truth and it magnifies the lie.
—Suze Orman

and exclamation: "Are you kidding me?" She denies the man on the spot. His car obsession threatens his financial security because he lacks a coherent plan to make the payments. The same reasoning is used to loudly deny a forty-nine-year-old mother's desire for a $7,000 tummy tuck.

Orman's jovial, cajoling manner about the cosmetic surgery is the sugar that helps the blunt retirement savings advice go down. Orman's littered financial past gives her the license and street cred to level with people who are tempted to load up credit card debt and launch get-rich-quick fantasies. The "Suze smackdowns" would be too much tough love if Orman hadn't had to reinvent herself. Underlying the direct, no-nonsense style is genuine compassion that makes for good television.

Camera Savvy Step 1: The Goldilocks Rule

The small screen loves emotion, but a little bit can go a long way. Orman has been known to disregard some of the SHAPE UP techniques when she exaggerates the role of outraged financial therapist. You can avoid the biggest on-camera mistakes with the "Goldilocks rule." Goldilocks didn't want porridge that was too hot or too cold; she preferred porridge that was just right. Overwrought expression will make you appear too hot, and a flat demeanor will make you appear too cold. The middle way is just right.

Presidential candidate Howard Dean learned the Goldilocks rule the hard way with what became known as his "I Have a Scream" speech. After Dean lost a crucial caucus, he attempted to rally his troops with a rousing speech. What sounded like a loud yell to the supporters gathered in a hotel ballroom came across as off-kilter on TV. Six months after dropping out of the race, Dean was scheduled to practice his first national speech since the scream episode at the Democratic convention. I was somewhat apprehensive about what kind of mood he would be in when he arrived for practice. Walking into the rehearsal room, he looked around with a twinkle in his eye and said, "Don't worry, I won't scream." I breathed a sigh of relief. A number of body language and vocal techniques do not work on camera. Avoid the following gestures, expressions, postures, and vocal habits.

No Screaming, Crying, or Flailing on Camera

- A frown looks like a scowl.
- Thrashing your hands makes you look scattered and wild.
- Bobbing your head or swaying your body looks silly.
- A flat voice without inflection communicates dullness.
- A rapid, staccato pace makes you sound rattled.
- Weak eye contact comes across as shifty, distracted, or uncertain.
- Stiff posture makes you look like a patient in a dentist's chair.
- Relaxed posture makes you look too casual and sloppy.
- Leaning backward appears standoffish.
- A high-pitched voice makes you sound overly excited.

Camera Savvy Step 2: Emotional Traction

Orman made it her life's work to talk directly to small investors long before the explosion of money programs on the cable channels. No other on-air personality has touched a nerve the way she has. The critics charge that her advice is way too basic. Perhaps that's because Suze isn't afraid to say what she thinks about how the big banks drive her "nuts." Her practical recommendations on how to manage credit card debt, resolve bankruptcy, save for college, and set up a will are intended to ensure the solvency of the masses. Despite all the Wall Street wizards who preach the complexity of the markets, Orman demystifies the numbers, making it possible for individuals to control their financial futures. Orman says she is the world's personal finance expert because she's "earned it." She has lived the life, mastered the material. This authenticity enables her to speak from the gut.

Orman's message is jargon- and lingo-free. Thus it helps reduce the fear factor associated with finance. A trust is differentiated from a will. She explains how to buy the right life insurance product. What the message may lack in originality and whiz bang is made up for by its accessible packaging, literally. Orman decided she wanted to reach people at the breakfast table, but rather than produce a morning show, she formed a partnership with Total cereal to provide financial tips on the back of cereal boxes.

Suze Speak

Orman preaches that simplicity is what leads to wealth, and she embraces the necessity of hitting her core themes in a mantra-like fashion. As she says: "Forever, I've told you." And, "Don't you watch my show?" It is clear that her message is breaking through when the viewers who call into the show launch into "Suze speak." They will repeat Suze's core money rules about establishing "an eight-month emergency cash fund." Other commonsense refrains they know by heart: "Stay out of credit card debt," "Live on one's salary," and her core philosophy, "If you expect your money to take care of you, you must take care of your money."

There is no audience that Orman targets more consistently than women because she understands firsthand the insecurities they possess about managing a budget and planning for retirement. She cites surveys that reveal 90 percent of women worry about money. Some women admit that "the prospect of ending up a bag lady has crossed their minds." Orman is on a mission to get women to view their financial well-being as personally as they view their health and spirituality. Women callers are her "girlfriends," and she will say to them: "Just between you and me." Orman feels the pain of the stay-at-home mom who wants a $100,000 dream kitchen her family cannot afford, but she won't allow that caller to make a costly mistake. There is no need to decipher the Orman message. The repetition of a simple message packaged with real-life money tales rings loud and clear.

Camera Savvy Step 3: How to Be a Good Guest

Jon Stewart wants you to come on *The Daily Show* to discuss your new book, should you be so lucky. After the euphoria ebbs, don't panic. There is a formula for how to do more than not make a fool of yourself. Making a successful in-studio appearance is very similar to being a good dinner party guest. Arrive at the appointed hour dressed appropriately. Don't be a conversation hog, droning on about nothing. Engage others in lively repartee and tell a humorous story. Leave when there is a break. TV producers, like dinner-party hosts, consider the event a success if the guests were entertained. On *The Today Show*, guests who give long, technical answers will be interrupted in twenty seconds or less to keep the pace of the program moving.

When sitting across from a celebrity host, above all else you need to understand your host is the star of the show. It is not your job to upstage or out-funny her. Your job is to be a supporting player in her drama. Be ready for a fast pace—it will be over before it feels like it started. Don't expect much of a warm-up. Stewart may pop into the green room or warm up the audience for only a minute or two. Sometimes you are led to the studio just moments before the camera goes live. When seated on the set, avoid being distracted by the studio audience and by the image of your face popping up on monitors scattered around the stage: don't look at the monitors, the audience, or the cameras. Keep your eye contact focused on the host or whoever is asking the questions. Once you are seated on set, you may have a few seconds before the show begins to get a sense of what is coming. In a friendly, polite way, ask the host how he or she plans to start. At that moment, the host very likely will give you a heads-up about how the opening will go. This gives you a few seconds to massage the message you've prepped in advance.

Meet the Press

For twenty-five years, Larry King and his suspenders were a top draw on CNN. Celebrity guests flocked to the show in anticipation of such probing questions as "What's it like to be you?" Not every program host will lob softballs at you. On the talk-show circuit, know exactly what you are getting yourself into. Are you dealing with an amiable host, or will you face a grilling by multiple inquisitors? Is there time for thoughtful conversation, or will you be interrupted? What is the host's agenda, and will you be given a fair chance to air your opinion?

On MSNBC's *Morning Joe,* Joe Scarborough and Mika Brzezinski often team up with one or two guest commentators to pummel interviewees. The president of the American Federation of Teachers, Randi Weingarten, found herself outnumbered when she was asked to justify why the union protects bad teachers. Weingarten was ready for the onslaught and resisted the temptation to lash back. When finally given a chance to make the union's case about its commitment to the success of every teacher and every student, she did so in a positive, proactive way. Her calm under fire was acknowledged by the hosts, who invited her back to follow up on the union's progress.

If you are unfamiliar with a program, the best way to prepare yourself is to watch a couple of episodes in advance. Most are available online. Getting a feel for the lay of the land will reduce anxiety. Expect a telephone call with the associate producer the day before you are scheduled to go on. This is essentially an audition, so be ready to shine with your best quotes. Don't hold back but treat the call as if it were the real deal. If the pre-interview doesn't go well, don't be surprised if you get a message later saying that you have been bumped by breaking news, though the show will try to get you on in the future. During the pre-interview process, you can also get debriefed on the interview logistics. Be ready to ask the following questions so you know what to expect.

Interview the Interviewer First

- Will the appearance be live or taped? If it is live, then whatever you say goes straight from your mouth into your mother's ear. There is no pulling it back. Taped appearances will be edited into bite-sized answers, so keep yours succinct.
- What is the topic? Ask for clarification about the angle. If answers are not forthcoming, you may want to reconsider the invite.
- What type of program is it? Is this a food-fight show on cable TV or a roundtable discussion on public television? Is the host more likely to ask lifestyle questions? Or will there be a deeper focus on substance?
- Who is the reporter or program host? What is his or her reporting style? Does the host ask personal questions like Barbara Walters? Well-informed ones like Christiane Amanpour? Or does the host go for laughs like Chelsea Handler?
- Treat pre-interviews on the telephone like the real thing. It is an audition, and not everyone makes the cut.
- Will there be other guests? Don't allow yourself to be sandbagged,

particularly if you are addressing a controversial subject. If there are other guests, will you all be on at the same time? Or will you appear consecutively? Always ask to go first, since doing so allows you to frame the debate and the other guests will need to respond to the overview you lay out.

- Always ask for the questions in advance. You will be surprised at how often they will be handed over. But expect a few new ones to pop up during the interview.

Every television studio is a little different. Arrive early, and if the crew allows, see the set before the interview begins. Meet the floor director who is in charge of the studio set. Check out the furniture arrangement to know where you will sit and what type of chair you will be sitting in. You may be asked to cool your heels in the "green room," a small space offstage where guests wait their turn. If others are milling about, don't allow chatter to distract you. Use the time to get physically and mentally set. Here's a checklist of what to do while you are waiting in the wings.

Live on the Set

1. Greet the crew. The studio staff, camera operators, and audio technicians can do a great deal to help you look and sound your best.
2. Seek out the room for the interview beforehand. Choose the chair closest to the host. This ensures more flattering camera angles.
3. Do a final mirror check of wardrobe, hair, teeth, and makeup.
4. Drink room-temperature water or warm tea to relax the vocal cords.
5. Do some deep breathing and other relaxation exercises.
6. While you are being introduced, make a strong, confident first impression with a friendly smile and a "thank you" to the host.
7. Start with your most important message. Don't expect the reporter to be a mind reader. Don't wait for the right question; it is rarely ever asked.
8. Keep answers short and simple. Use words and phrases that are easy to understand and jargon-free.

The Butt Rule

No, this is not a special diet to help you contend with the additional pounds the camera lens may add. The "butt rule" is a reminder to comport yourself as if the camera is rolling and the microphones are live even if you don't think they are. Former HP executive Carly Fiorina was caught on an open mike making fun of Senator Barbara Boxer's hair during their Senate race. While getting made up in a Sacramento TV studio, Fiorina was seated on the set fiddling with her phone when she blurted out: "God, what is that hair. Soooo yesterday." Her laughter ended abruptly when someone offstage motioned to the live mike.

The butt rule is in effect from the moment your butt hits the interview chair until you leave the studio. Throughout, you need to act as if everything you say and do is broadcast live. Never assume the camera is off when you are not talking. We have all laughed at TV reporters in the field caught primping on camera as they waited for the studio host to throw the interview to them. During talk shows, the director will cut away from whoever is speaking to get a reaction shot of other guests. Resist the temptation to roll your eyes or shake your head in disgust. Split-screen technology is common on the cable shows, and you may be visible the entire time someone else is talking.

When you want to interject or communicate that you disagree with what is being said, shake your head back and forth slowly. Do this calmly for three or four seconds. When the host notices the head shake, she will likely ask you for a comment, so this is a good way to signal you want to jump into the conversation. The butt rule remains in effect until a member of the studio crew removes your microphone and you exit. It is not an unusual mistake for a spokesperson to let out a long sigh of relief when she thinks the experience is over but the camera is still live.

Camera Savvy Step 4: Handling Interruptions

Don't try to interrupt another guest by attempting to talk over her. It is more effective to show you have something to say with the nonverbal signal of shaking your head "no." If that doesn't work, hold your hand up as to signal "stop" when you want someone to stop talking. The hand signal may momentarily distract the other speaker, and when she pauses, that's your opportunity to starting talking. If someone is trying to interrupt you, resist the temptation to speak more quickly and to raise your pitch. Rather, be politely assertive by continuing to speak, but slow your pace and lower your pitch. By speaking low and slow, you will be able to hold the floor, and the person who is trying to cut in will appear rude.

If you are a guest on a political commentary show, you need to have appropriate expectations about what you can accomplish when you know in advance the host disagrees with you. On programs like *The O'Reilly Factor* and *The Colbert Report*, you are not invited on to do real interviews. You are there to serve as fodder for the pundit's commentary on the issue of the day. Expect to be interrupted, and on O'Reilly's show, it is not unheard of for the director to silence you by turning off your microphone. You will not be aware that this has happened until you realize no one is listening to you. These programs are not the place for reasoned arguments or a critical analysis of the facts. It's political theater, and your best bet is to laugh at the host's antics.

The ability not to take yourself too seriously is a must. Colbert is known for his absurd queries and ridiculous line of questioning. If you can't laugh at yourself, be sure that the audience is ready to laugh at you. But do try to work in a good sound bite, and if you can, then consider the outing a huge success. Above all else, keep your cool. The ability to weather antagonistic questions and silly stunts can win the sympathy of the viewers. If the host steps over a line with something really ridiculous, the audience's allegiance can easily shift to you. Once the experience is over, you can always take it to the Internet and post a reaction or commentary on a website or blog.

It's a Wrap

Don't just breathe a sigh of relief that it is over and you survived. Exit like a true pro who recognizes there is something to be learned from every outing.

1. Give a word of thanks to the host, other guests, and the studio crew.
2. Follow up with a thank-you e-mail or call and to offer ideas for future interviews.
3. Review the interview tape. Analyze what worked and what didn't.
4. Inform the producer if any mistakes were made so they can be edited out of future online airings.
5. Monitor the program on an ongoing basis so you can offer yourself as a guest when appropriate.

Camera Savvy Step 5: TV-Ready Attire

Suze Orman's signature look can be spotted across a busy airport. She is a visual punctuation point in loud leather jackets and white-blonde highlights that contrast with her dark tan and royalty-sized jewelry. If she's not wearing yellow, orange, or purple, expect a bold animal print. The wardrobe, like the personality, is purposefully hard to ignore. Orman says publicists are constantly suggesting clothes for photo shoots that she will not wear because the clothes are not her. She dresses like Suze Orman, and she doesn't care if people don't like it. As an established quantity, Orman can wear almost anything and get away with it. When you have your own show, you can, too.

Until then, following some simple rules will improve your on-camera appearance by minimizing the unflattering aspects of the camera. With smart choices, you can camouflage any real or perceived problem areas.

The most slimming look is well-tailored tops and bottoms in dark colors. If you need to add a few pieces, consider those purchases to be an integral part of professional development. The media made much ado about the big bucks spent on clothes for Sarah Palin's vice-presidential wardrobe. Imagine the criticism if she hadn't looked good!

Skin Deep

High-definition television is loved by sports fans, who feel as if they have courtside seats when watching their favorite athletes. The camera picks up every tiny bead of sweat, so the action looks nearly real. The digital technology that produces staggeringly lifelike images is not so kind to human skin in close-ups. Spots are magnified, pores enlarged, wrinkles deepened, and shine looks like a hot spot.

Nearly all TV news programs are broadcast in high-definition, so makeup is imperative. You're not trying to achieve a Hollywood glam facade but to look natural. Every complexion needs concealer, liquid foundation, and powder. Concealer is used to diminish dark circles under the eyes and skin imperfections. Use a liquid foundation, not cake or powder. Liquid smoothes out flaws and doesn't settle so noticeably in wrinkles. The dusting of powder absorbs perspiration and reduces shiny, hot spots on the forehead and nose. Women should always wear lipstick on camera. Select a flattering shade in a matte finish. Avoid high gloss and frosted shades. If you don't normally wear makeup, get some help to learn how to apply the right products properly. Major department and cosmetic stores selling name brands have makeup artists who can provide instruction.

Taming TV Tresses

Stylist Isabelle Goetz has been cutting hair since she was fifteen-and-a-half years old, and she was the magic behind the care and upkeep of Hillary Clinton's gold-highlighted tresses during the grueling grind of the presidential campaign. Goetz jokes that it doesn't have to take a village to have camera-ready hair but cautions that the camera does change how hair looks by making it appear darker and more poufy.[2] The best tip for TV

Ten Absolutely Best Things to Wear on Camera

1. Contemporary business suit with pants or skirt, long-sleeved dress, or a dress with matching jacket.
2. Clothes that fit properly. Every piece must be tailored; otherwise, you will look sloppy and heavier. Find a reliable tailor.
3. Fabrics with rough or bumpy textures. Look for blends of wool, linen, and cotton. Try a tailored sweater in a classic style, like a twinset.
4. Solid, rich colors: turquoise, red, deep fuchsia, royal purple, and emerald green. Darker jewel-toned colors are beautiful on TV, but select a color that flatters your skin tone.
5. What color is the backdrop of the studio set? If it is a light-colored room with beige furniture, wear a dark color so you don't fade into the background. If there are lots of busy graphics and TV monitors, wear a dark color so you will stand out.
6. Choose a light-colored blouse under the jacket. A cream or pastel top will draw the viewer's eye to your face.
7. Long sleeves. Short sleeves are not as professional as long sleeves; remember, the cartoon character Dilbert wears short-sleeve dress shirts with a pocket protector.
8. Dull-finished jewelry like pearls or beads. Bright, shiny metals reflect glare under the lights.
9. Eyeglasses should be rimless or have light-colored frames. Have a nonreflective coating put on your lenses to reduce glare from the lights.
10. HDTV makeup and matte lipstick.

appearances is to keep hair off the face, especially out of the eyes. Goetz says the secret to candidate Clinton's fashionable cut was the addition of layers that flattered her face and were easier to style.

The biggest mistake women make is overprocessed hair color, which can fade skin tone. The right color and/or highlights will soften a look and

Ten Most Outrageous Things to Wear on Camera

1. Black and white fabrics can be unflattering under intense studio lights.
2. Shiny fabrics, such as some silks and synthetics, will glare under the lights.
3. Patterns create what's called the moiré effect, meaning they appear to be moving. Avoid paisley blouses, striped shirts, glen plaid suits, and floral dresses.
4. Pleats will make you look like you covered yourself with a circus tent.
5. If your top and bottom are different colors, you will look heavier than if you wear one, solid color.
6. Necklines appear lower on camera than in person. That's what created all the controversy about Hillary Clinton's cleavage. In person, the neckline was modest; on C-SPAN, it looked like it was plunging.
7. Avoid large, dangling, or flashy jewelry. Remember the adage about quickly looking in the mirror before leaving the house and removing whatever catches your eye. Microphones pick up jangling bracelets and necklaces. Earrings that swing are distracting.
8. Expensive watches and rings can send the wrong signal.
9. Don't let hair fall in your face or over your eyes.
10. Candy-red lipstick makes you look like you're headed to an audition for a daytime soap.

help older women appear younger. Hot rollers can be every woman's best friend. Goetz says runway models use large ones to keep a style fresh a day or two after a visit to the salon. The rollers can be a simple part of a morning routine because they are quicker and easier than a blow dry. Put them in, keep them in until they are cold, and your hands are free to do other stuff.

STANDING OVATION POINT: THE CAMERA IS THE WELL-SPOKEN WOMAN'S FRIEND

Orman has gone where very few women aside from Oprah have gone in the realm of television, and now she will be a regular on Oprah's new network OWN. She has reached the stratosphere of motivational speakers—up there with the likes of Deepak Chopra and Tony Robbins. Her personal magnetism and straight talk are well suited for the medium: "I am exactly who I am in everything I do." The Orman mantra has served her well, and it is good advice for you, too. Orman's confidence stems from her knowledge that she knows her stuff and is prepared. This is what allows her to be who she is.

Learn from Orman's well-spoken techniques so you can prepare to enter the TV and cable landscape. Women remain dramatically underrepresented, with even fewer minority women appearing as guests and commentators on news programs. The cable networks remain a white, male ghetto with nearly 70 percent of all guests on MSNBC, CNN, and Fox being male and nearly 85 percent of those white. The prestigious Sunday morning talk shows are another bastion of white, male dominance. Fewer than 15 percent of all decision makers who appear on shows like *Meet the Press* are women.

In recent years, women have ascended to the evening anchor desks, but don't let that progress lull you into a false sense that women have reached parity. The networks have finally elevated women, but their audience continues to shrink due to competition from cable and the Internet. More women are needed to host broadcast and cable programs, moderate online panels, appear as expert guests, and provide analysis and commentary. With the addition of more women and the female perspective, the dialogue on the issues of the day will be richer and fuller.

Applause Principles:
SHAPE UP to Be Camera Ready

- In a YouTube world, cameras are everywhere. There's no longer any excuse for not acquiring and polishing on-camera skills.
- Looking good on camera can be a bit trickier than it sounds. Give yourself time to learn the SHAPE UP techniques.
- Viewers want to watch and will listen to spokespeople who project likability.
- A guest appearance on a TV talk show is about entertainment first and foremost.
- Simple clothing and accessories keep the focus on the message rather than on a messenger's fashion mistake.

PART 4

THE FINISHING TOUCHES

THE ART OF DIPLOMACY: WELL-SPOKEN UNDER FIRE

Women have to be active listeners and interrupters—but when you interrupt, you have to know what you are talking about.
—Madeleine Albright, interview with Ed Bradley,
60 Minutes, January 2008

The art of diplomacy speaks to dealing with difficult audiences. Most people do not arrive at an event with an ax to grind or with the intention of ruffling feathers. That being said, at some point you could face a disruption. Congresswoman Tammy Baldwin has learned to be ready for anything when she visits with constituents in her home district of Madison, Wisconsin. In 1998, Baldwin smashed double glass ceilings when she became the first woman to serve in the state's congressional delegation and the first openly gay person elected to Congress. Since her victory, she has become a national leader on civil rights and a voice for millions of Americans who face discrimination. Given the controversy surrounding gay rights, Baldwin has dealt with her share of rabble-rousers. Nonetheless, she was caught off guard by a man with a crude handmade sign who showed up at a town hall meeting.

When Representative Baldwin walked into the meeting room in the village of Poynette, her eyes immediately locked onto the sign, which read: "Terminate Unwanted Lesbians." The sign holder was an older man with scraggly long hair and a bushy white beard. He had positioned himself in the front row, and Baldwin realized that no one else could see what she was seeing. Thus, there was no empathy or support from the other people in the room until the man stood and turned to face them to speak. When they read his message, an audible groan was heard. He then launched into a diatribe on the virtue of free speech and asked Baldwin if she considered his sign to be a hate crime.

Baldwin responded that the sign was "odious" but that it did not constitute an arrestable offense. Since the man did not threaten her physically, she decided to turn the disconcerting situation into a teachable moment by calmly outlining the rationale for the hate-crime legislation that was pending on Capitol Hill. As she shared with me when we spoke about the incident later, the practice of "turning the other cheek" is a technique that has served her well.[1] For years, she has been dogged by protesters with ugly chants and placards. Once on a bike tour in the district, she was followed by a man who yelled at her all day through a bullhorn. It bothers Baldwin when protesters show up at places like senior centers because it is her constituents who often feel intimidated. On some occasions, she will have police protection, and she always abides by the practice of not engaging harassers. She maintains her composure by taking a deep breath and staying calm.

Jeers, Not Cheers

The man with the detestable sign was an exceptional case. Most audience members are not openly hostile or there to cause trouble. Most are rooting for the presenter to do a good job. They show up anticipating they will take something positive away from the event. They are impressed with the speaker's credentials and hope to gain a fresh insight, learn something new, or do a little networking on the side. One possible upside to an agitator or unfriendly crowd is that at least you know where you stand. In some situations, it is the seemingly neutral audience members who catch you off guard. A sea of poker faces is impossible to interpret. Are they into you or not? A nonresponsive audience can be frustrating because you may not know what is silencing them.

Members of the news media can also be a challenging audience. A reporter letting loose with gotcha questions can make you appear defensive. Reporters have a bag of tricks they use to try to pull spokespeople off of preplanned messages. Some attempt to ingratiate themselves to get you to relax and lower your guard. Others have a thinly veiled agenda to put words in your mouth. On some talk shows, expect incoming fire from the host and other guests.

What Won't Work

When dealing with a difficult questioner or a trying audience, the first rule of thumb is to avoid reacting emotionally. It is best to maintain your composure rather than try to engage a disruptive person. Otherwise, the encounter can leave you looking petty, angry, or insensitive. It might be tempting to let loose in a moment of frustration, but as Scarlett O'Hara said: "Tomorrow is another day." Losing your cool won't solve anything and likely will make the situation more unpleasant for everyone.

Diplomacy can ease the situation. Defined as the art and practice of conducting negotiations, diplomatic skills can help you handle messy situations without arousing hostility. How you react to an eruption matters because all eyes are fixed on you. It is, in many respects, a test. The audience is watching to see if you can keep your professional wits about you. What a gift it would be to be able to fire back at a heckler with a cutting Joan Rivers–style quip. For those of us who lack the comedian's forty years of stage experience, coming up with a brilliant retort on the spot is unlikely. Most people think of the perfect thing to say a day later. It is better to concentrate on diffusing the situation firmly and fairly with a proactive response.

In some scenarios, it's necessary to set realistic expectations in advance about what can and cannot be accomplished. This may mean you will need to lower expectations. Sometimes the most favorable outcome may be the one in which resistance is neutralized. With others, the only recourse is to cut losses. Deflecting or neutralizing negativism is not about knuckling under. It is about staying calm so you can remain in con-

High-Drama Don'ts

Argue defensively.
Lecture or scold.
Ridicule or criticize.
Use sarcasm or judge.
Tell someone to shut up.
Yell or swear.
Display anger.
Break down in tears.

trol, earn the audience's respect, and salvage what is salvageable. This chapter gives you the diplomatic cache to never let them see you sweat.

CALM, COOL, COLLECTED

The daughter of a Czechoslovakian diplomat who fled the Nazis and then the communists, Madeleine Albright has encountered a variety of tense situations and demanding personalities. Within days of her becoming the first woman secretary of state, a *Washington Post* reporter attempted to damage her reputation for candor. On the campus of Ohio State University, she was nearly drowned out by antiwar protesters. And Saddam Hussein called her a serpent. If Secretary Albright needed extra-strength aspirin to deal with those headaches, it never showed.

Albright's communication style came to the fore in her first diplomatic posting when she served as the US ambassador to the United Nations. There she learned that it was no longer possible to hesitate or be intimidated; she was obligated to speak up. When she walked into a UN Security Council meeting in 1993, she was, not surprisingly, the only woman in the room. The fifteen other nation-states were represented by men sitting with their arms across their chests. "There are lots of women who have walked into rooms like that." Albright said that in the past, she would have followed her instincts by getting a feel for the mood before uttering a word. Then it dawned on her that it was imperative for the US representative to put aside any ambivalent feelings: "If I don't speak now, America's position won't be known.... OK, I'm a woman—I should wait. No, I'm the United States—I must speak."[2] Albright says that inner dialogue helped her find and use her voice.

In her jewel-hued dresses and signature pins, Albright brought a personal savoir faire to international relations. The introduction of line dancing to the Security Council chamber may have been considered "undiplomatic" by detractors. Yet, when Albright showed the minister of Botswana how to do the macarena, she was demonstrating more than dance steps. Her unconventional approach endeared her to the public and eased tensions with colleagues. Albright has said her adult life has been much more fun than her childhood because as a youngster, she was always very serious.

At the age of eleven, the Korbel family immigrated to America, eventually settling in Denver. Her father, Josef, a former diplomat, became a professor of international relations, and her mother, Anna, worked as a secretary. Madeleine attended a private all-girl high school where she participated in debate and founded an international relations club because "I was pretty boring in high school. I was a foreign-

Madeleine Albright

policy wonk even then."[3] Her extracurricular activities and good grades secured a scholarship to Wellesley College, and in the fall of 1955, she headed east to study political science.

Thirty years later, when her alma mater announced the creation of an international studies school called the Madeleine Korbel Albright Institute for Global Affairs, Albright was "over the moon." She credits her Wellesley education with providing the analytical skills that prepared her to serve as a diplomat. After college, however, the international stage would need to wait a few decades for Albright to emerge. Despite a passion for world affairs, three days after her college graduation, Korbel married Joe Albright, a wealthy newspaper heir. The Albrights lived in New York and later Washington, DC. Joe joined the family business as a reporter, and Madeleine raised three daughters, including twins, while earning a PhD in Russian studies. After twenty-three years of marriage, Madeleine says she was stunned the day her husband announced he was leaving for another woman.

Zig-zaggy is the word Albright uses to describe her career. During what she termed "my time of good works," she was a fund-raiser at a prestigious private school and worked on political campaigns. Her first full-time job was as a staff member for the National Security Council during the Carter administration. Her political résumé was polished as a staff assistant on Capitol Hill and at Georgetown University's School of Foreign Service, and she was a foreign-policy adviser for Democratic presidential candidates. Albright wrote in her biography that as she rose through the ranks, no matter her accomplishments, she felt some people "would forever see me as their wife's friend or the cooperative mother who arranged car pools."[4]

KNOW YOUR TROUBLEMAKERS

A hallmark of Secretary Albright's tenure at the State Department was her determined effort to make foreign policy seem less foreign to the American people. She pledged to "tell it like it is," even when the audience didn't agree. At Ohio State University, Albright was a study in diplomacy when a town hall meeting on the possibility of bombing Iraq turned into a rowdy demonstration of unruly democracy. The forum, which was hosted and broadcast live by CNN, nearly turned into a free-for-all, with war protesters attempting to drown out Albright and other administration spokespeople with chants of "One-two-three-four, we don't want your racist war!"

Without assistance from the moderators, Albright steadfastly weathered repeated boos and angry interruptions as she laid out the Clinton administration's concerns about the intentions of Saddam Hussein. While she spoke, the more aggressive hecklers had to be physically removed from the arena. Afterward, there was much finger-pointing about how and why the event had spun out of control. The protesters may have decided to disrupt the event when they learned they would not be given an open microphone. Albright kept her emotions in check throughout the ordeal and commented later that the forum "shows what a vibrant democracy" we have.[5]

Anticipating trouble greatly increases the likelihood that you can manage it before it spirals out of control. When addressing a hot-button issue, it is important to know why people are attending. Are they carrying unresolved issues or other baggage? Do they want to listen, or do they expect to be heard? Have they been told they will have a chance to voice objections? If people are coming loaded for bear, the room temperature can be lowered by providing an opportunity for individuals to speak at the beginning. Set aside time for a public comment period so audience members can blow off steam. Speakers from the audience should have an agreed-upon time limit so everyone has a chance to be heard. Assign a note taker with a flip chart positioned at the front of the room. Jotting down the comments reinforces the sense that each speaker is being listened to.

Troublemakers fall into two general categories: aggressive and passive. The aggressive ones disrupt proceedings with outbursts, banners, and other visual or noise distractions. These tactics are often deployed at open hearings, town hall meetings, and rallies. Passive troublemakers can show up anywhere, and some may work in your office. They are not as demonstrative as the aggressive ones, but their tactics can get under your skin, so they must be handled with care.

Aggressive Troublemakers

Let's discuss the aggressive troublemakers first.

The Challenger

This individual attempts to control the room and pointedly disagrees by saying, "Yes, but...." Challengers love to put on a display of verbal tug-of-war by engaging the presenter in a public debate. If you anticipate challengers in the group, head them off at the pass. Start by explaining that new information will be introduced and ask everyone to listen with an open mind, holding comments until the end. Another tactic to defuse the challenger is to agree with the emotion she expresses but not necessarily with the point she is trying to make.

Mask any frustration or resentment with a neutral facial expression. Hear out the challenger by allowing him to share his wisdom or grievance. Don't engage in a power struggle. As you listen, maintain steady eye contact and, once he has finished, say, "It looks like we have a different opinion on this. Why don't we discuss it in more detail after the meeting? Now let's move on to the other items on the agenda." Usually, the challenger will not take the time to meet. If he does, it is easier to deal with him one-on-one.

Interrupter

A subspecies of the challenger is the interrupter who cuts off the presenter and others. She may not intend to be rude but may lack basic manners or be overly excited about sharing an idea. With the interrupter, immediately call her out on her behavior by saying, "Mary, let's allow John to finish his point." Once you've done this a few times, she usually gets the message. Other polite ways to tell an interrupter to shut up: "Please, just a moment, I haven't finished my thought," "Kindly hold your comments until the end of the presentation, and I'll be happy to take questions then," and "These interruptions are distracting us from the subject at hand."

The Heckler

At a campaign rally, Hillary Clinton encountered two hecklers with signs who taunted, "Iron my shirt." Clinton was quick with a response that received supportive applause: "Ah, the remnants of sexism—alive and well." But the young men persisted until another woman in the audience yelled, "Go iron your own shirt!" At that point, the crowd's reaction reached a crescendo, and the troublemakers were escorted away. A sexist heckler's sole aim may be to embarrass you, so keep your anger in check. If you overreact, you risk alienating the audience. With a lone heckler, try ignoring the outburst and allowing group dynamics to take over. As with the Clinton rally, others were offended and rose to her defense. When the heckler realizes he is outnumbered, he will usually pipe down.

Nearly all women have faced slights and degrading public comments, sometimes lobbed from unseen assailants. How to react can be an agonizing decision when you are on display. Should you get angry, ignore it, or good-naturedly brush it off? Usually your gut instinct is the best barometer of whether or not you should let it slide. Roxanne Rivera runs the Associated Builders and Contractors of New Mexico, and she says trial and error taught her how to be a successful woman in the construction business. Joking is part of what happens with a work crew, but she doesn't indulge crude behavior and nips it in the bud with "That is unacceptable."[6] When she was chief of staff to a US senator, EMILY'S List president

Stephanie Schriock says every week, she would enter staff meetings that felt more like locker rooms. The guys would go on about how they liked women in high heels and their preference for blondes or brunettes. Ever the pragmatist, Schriock made a decision about whether to join in as one of the guys or get offended based on what she needed to get done.[7]

Planned Demonstration

Speaker of the House Nancy Pelosi was invited to appear before what should have been a friendly gathering. But the San Francisco lawmaker was just a couple of minutes into her remarks at a Campaign for America's Future event when disability activists in wheelchairs started to scream: "Our homes, not nursing homes." On cue, others in the crowd unfurled banners, and bodyguards had to circle the podium from which Pelosi was speaking. Organizers of the event tried to shepherd Pelosi offstage until they could quiet the crowd, but she was determined to finish. For the next half hour, while the demonstrators yelled themselves hoarse, Pelosi kept on talking, seemingly unfazed by the ruckus. She even joked: "Listen, I'm used to noise. I speak to the Democratic caucus every single day."[8]

While the experience was excruciating, Pelosi didn't have much of an alternative. If she had stopped, then the protesters would have won a small victory. When outnumbered, you still have the microphone and likely can talk over the hecklers. In a large room with a large crowd, keep going, as many people may not be aware that a disturbance is taking place because they may not see or hear it. At large-scale events, security must be planned in advance and carried out in conjunction with the event organizers.

Passive Troublemakers

Passive troublemakers exhibit many of the symptoms of the passive/aggressive personality type. They appear to be part of the group and seem to be going along, but in reality they are passively resisting. The behavior often comes off as childish but must be managed so they are not allowed to sabotage the presentation. Passive troublemakers talk too much or not at all, speak too loudly and out of turn, blame others, and criticize suggestions.

The Silent Type

Silent troublemakers sit in the back of the room. They may fiddle with papers or electronics. Their body language can be disquieting, as they may appear to be ignoring the presenter or silently disagreeing by shaking their head, rolling their eyes, crossing and uncrossing arms, and so on. It is unclear how they are processing the information being presented. Some may be shy, unassertive, and easily intimidated. They may have difficulty interacting with someone in power and may be trying to avoid being called upon. Others may be preoccupied with something else in their life.

Unfortunately, not much can be done about silent types, and it is usually best to ignore the behavior since it doesn't have much impact on others. Don't waste too much energy on these people, but you can try calling on them by name in a friendly manner. Ask an open-ended question and offer encouragement. You may want to engage them one-on-one during a break or once the talk is completed.

Chatty Cathys

Chatty Cathys don't know when to stop talking. They talk too much, too loudly, and often ask off-point questions. Try to cope by changing the physical dynamic. Move closer to them when they are chatting and maintain eye contact. The speaker's physical presence will often make them aware of their behavior, and they will stop. If they persist, continue to hold eye contact and say, "I appreciate your comments, but we would like to hear from others." Then turn away and continue your presentation. Another strategy is to give them a task so they will be busy and distracted. During a break, ask them to take notes or list questions.

Cathy's cousins are the whisperers who sit off to the side or in the back of the room and share running commentary. Try the technique of moving closer to them. If that doesn't work, stop talking and allow them to be embarrassed when their noise fills the dead silence. Another approach is to call them out on their behavior by asking them a question: "Do you have something you would like to share with the group?"

The Know-It-All

The know-it-all will often start with a phase like "In my twenty-five years of experience..." or "I have a PhD in economics, and...." The unstated assumption is that this individual is right and therefore the speaker is wrong. The key to dealing with the know-it-all is to stick to the facts. Don't theorize or speculate. You can also share personal experience, as it is very difficult for anyone to question someone else's personal experience. Another technique is to use a quotation from an expert whose credentials are greater than those of the know-it-all. The know-it-alls are well practiced at asking a question that isn't really a question but an excuse to deliver a monologue.

Time Abusers

Latecomers, early leavers, and constantly moving troublemakers are a variation of the silent type. These individuals seemingly have no respect for other people's time. The constantly moving individuals are ducking in and out to receive messages and take calls. If this person is the senior person, her behavior can bring the presentation to a standstill as you wait for her to rejoin the group. Try to nip this conduct in the bud by announcing in advance the time and duration of breaks and when the program will end.

For the latecomer, pick a start time such as 9:17. The unusual time should get his attention and is a tip-off that the meeting is really going to start at 9:17. If someone still shows up late, make a casual remark, such as "I'm sorry. I must have started early." Be sure to smile and keep talking about the subject matter at hand. Or try announcing to the latecomer that he has been volunteered to do some follow-up staff work.

It can also be disconcerting to have someone stand up and walk out in the middle of your presentation. Stop the early leavers by getting an agreement in advance about the end time and announcing it to the group. This is nearly impossible when speaking to a large crowd in a conference setting, however. Don't be overly concerned, as people often have planes to catch and kids to pick up.

HANDLING LIVE-AUDIENCE Q&A

The question-and-answer session following a presentation is an opportunity for direct interaction with the audience. It provides a chance to reinforce key message points, raising the audience's retention level. If you unintentionally left something out of the talk, you can work it into an answer. And this is a final chance to clarify any misconceptions or misunderstandings.

Q&A Protocol

- Advise the audience when you prefer to take questions. You may elect to respond to queries during your talk or ask them to hold off until you have finished your prepared remarks.
- Inform the audience how you will field questions. Are there microphones available on the floor, or should questions be written down and handed to the front of the room?
- Request that questioners provide their name and affiliation. It is always helpful to know something about the person who is doing the asking.
- Limit the amount of time available for questions. Fifteen minutes should be plenty. However, if the topic is controversial, plan to stay until everyone has had a chance to speak their piece.
- With a noncontroversial topic, limit the number of questions. After you've fielded about ten, the quality generally takes a nosedive because questions are redundant or off-topic.
- It can be deflating for no one to ask any questions. A tried-and-true method to stimulate questions is to lead off with one of your own: "People often ask me if...." Or plant a question with a colleague in the audience.

Audiences know no bounds when it comes to what they will ask. Whoever said there is no such thing as a bad question hasn't spent much time fielding questions. North Dakota attorney general Heidi Heitkamp was repeatedly asked about the age of her children while running for governor. She considered this a sneaky way to imply she was an unfit mother. Heitkamp's response was to explain that her kids were the same age as the children of her male opponents. Questions based on stereotypes tell you more than you may want to know about the questioner. Manage the Q&A session by setting ground rules at the start. The rules help you handle off-the-wall and hostile questions so the presentation is not pulled astray.

Q&A Strategies

- State the ground rules prior to taking any questions.
- If possible, move from behind the lectern so you are closer to the audience.
- Have a prepared question to break the ice, such as "A question often asked is…."
- Be sure you understand the question before giving a response.
- Address each individual with courtesy and respect.
- Avoid judging questions: "That is an excellent question." Were the other questions not so excellent?
- Use a strategic pause. Silence is an excellent technique to maintain audience attention, and it provides a chance to think about your response.
- Keep your answers short and to the point.
- Bring the Q&A session to a close by saying, "I have time for one or two more questions." End with the next question you answer well.
- Close with a mini summary that includes a key message.

Emotional Outbursts

The perturbed questioner may combine the tactics of the challenger, heckler, and know-it-all. Senator Kay Hagan bungled an exchange with a constituent who appeared to be upset about the cost of healthcare for her chronically ill children. The senator interrupted the woman as she was describing her children's medication regimen. Rather than listening

Perturbed Questioner Prescription

1. Allow the questioner to speak unfettered for as long as she needs. A minute or two will feel longer than it is. While she is speaking, maintain solid, steady eye contact with her to demonstrate to everyone you are being attentive and respectful.
2. Once the questioner has finished, tell her you hear what she said and understand she feels emotional. At this point, the angry questioner may interrupt you. Again, let her speak her mind.
3. When she's finished, begin your response by looking and talking directly to the individual. After about twenty seconds, break eye contact and physically turn to others in the room. At this point, bring the rest of the audience into the dialogue and signal that intention by looking at them.
4. If the same questioner pops up again, let her proceed one more time. It's fair game for her to follow up. When you respond, follow the same technique of looking at her and then breaking eye contact. Then call on someone else in the room.
5. If the angry questioner interrupts again, now her behavior is out of line. Group dynamics often take over, with other audience members jumping in to hush her. If the group doesn't provide assistance, calmly explain to the questioner that it is time to hear from others and you will be available to talk with her in greater detail at some later time. Patience is the key with the perturbed questioner. But, once you've given her every opportunity to be heard, everyone else will be ready to move on.

patiently, Hagan tried to move on with what sounded like a canned response. The brusque dismissal caused the mother to shout: "We want the benefits you have!" referring to the taxpayer-funded healthcare provided to all members of Congress. The audience's sympathies were with the mother, and they responded with a loud "Amen!"[9]

Failing to hear out an emotional questioner appears insensitive or downright cold. In the heat of the moment, be careful not to judge too quickly. It may not be possible to understand the motivation or intention behind the question. The woman could have been a political activist from an opposing campaign trying to discredit the senator. Or she may well have been distraught and making an awkward plea for help. When confronted with a perturbed questioner, follow these steps.

THE NEW MEDIA WORLD

President Bill Clinton said that Secretary Albright's line about the Cuban fighter pilots who shot down two civilian aircraft with

> ### All-Time Great Line
>
> "Frankly, this is not *cojones* [slang for balls]. This is cowardice."
> —Secretary of State Madeleine Albright, 1996

Americans aboard was one of the best in the administration's foreign policy. The remark was delivered at a press conference after the cowardice of the crime was revealed; evidence showed that the fighter planes fired outside of Cuba's territorial limits. The statement, which "would never in a thousand years have been cleared by the State Department if she had submitted it in advance,"[10] was a shocker in the staid world of diplomatic nuance. Albright defended it, given the Cubans' lack of regret about the loss of life and refusal to acknowledge a violation of the law.

Vowing to speak the language of everyday people and not the vernacular of a policy wonk endeared Albright to the public and the media. Wise to the ways of Washington, she courted the press and hired top-notch staff to build goodwill. But those relations didn't preclude becoming the subject of a tough interview just days into her job as secretary of state. Michael Dobbs of the *Washington Post* said he "stumbled across an extraordinary story" when he found evidence that Albright's family was Jewish and that her grandparents and cousins had perished in the Holocaust. In a meeting in her office, Dobbs pressed Albright on her forthrightness about the family's Jewish ancestry.[11]

Albright and her team immediately took proactive steps to prevent Dobbs from attempting to portray her as unwilling to be frank and open. It was necessary to counter Dobbs's insinuations, which created a firestorm of press. If allowed to fester, rumor and innuendo could have impeded Albright's efforts to stay focused on foreign affairs. On *60 Minutes*, Albright said she was raised a Roman Catholic and knew nothing of this story.[12] By responding quickly, Albright was able to exercise more control over the story and maintain her credibility.

DEALING WITH HOSTILE MEDIA

In a new media world, it is more necessary than ever to take extra precautions to protect yourself from inaccurate reporting and unfair tactics. Anyone with a camera can upload video online, and bloggers are bound by no limits. Dealing with social media technology and contentious reporters requires an astute understanding of what you are getting yourself into and additional techniques to exercise control over the process. The next section outlines the well-spoken woman's rules for dealing with aggressive reporters and hostile interview situations. The rules ensure you stay focused on delivering your message and don't allow yourself to be sidetracked. Exercise the following precautions, and you will enjoy more success with the press.

Rule 1: Expect Negativity

"Senator, when did you stop cheating on your spouse?"

Try to answer that question without sounding defensive. It presumes guilt on the part of the interviewee. There is much back-and-forth about the cultural bias of news organizations—the *New York Times* is called a liberal rag, while talk radio is termed a wasteland of conservative extremists.

Whatever a particular outlet's ideological bent, don't allow it to distract attention away from the overwhelmingly pervasive bias in all media: negativism. It starts with the questions "Why not? Whose fault? What went wrong?" If you are not ready for the onslaught of negativism, you can get swept away by a tidal wave and find yourself struggling to keep your head above water. The negativism is evident in how the news is covered. Reporters and editors are drawn to conflict like moths to a flame. The most typical story lines are he-said versus she-said and winners and losers. The formula of covering two sides of an issue fits nicely into a 90-second broadcast story and 700-word newspaper article. The press does less well when an issue is nuanced. And when isn't an issue nuanced? Analysis and thoughtful reportage are in short supply when newspapers, radio stations, television news programs, and cable talk shows have online platforms that require constant feeding. The churn of news creates a cycle of never-ending deadlines. What was once a 24-hour news cycle is now a 1,440-minute news cycle.

Former eBay executive and gubernatorial candidate Meg Whitman learned the hard way about the media's penchant for negativity. Whitman tried to boast that her years spent as a corporate executive ensured she was untainted by politics. The California press corps examined the record and discovered she was so untainted she hadn't voted in nearly thirty years. When Whitman responded by questioning the accuracy of the reporting, she only fanned the media flame. Her troubles were compounded at a press conference organized to apologize to voters, when she responded defensively. As a busy mom she was "focused on raising a family, on my husband's career, and we moved many, many, times."[13] The reaction from women's groups was, predictably, outrage, as Whitman's statement seemed to reinforce the stereotype that politics is the province of men.

Rule 2: Know Thy Reporter

Who are these people posing questions from the other end of a phone line or from behind a camera? Is it possible to be treated fairly? How can you gauge whether a reporter will be objective? Those questions have become more difficult to answer because the definition of who a reporter is has changed. It can be helpful to think of reporters as falling into one of three categories or buckets based on experience, reputation, and skill.

Elite Press

The first bucket contains the elite press. This small group of accomplished journalists have in-depth knowledge of and personal interest in the subject matter. An interview with an elite journalist is distinguished by the fact that the reporter's reputation is on the line as much as yours. She has a real stake in the outcome and cares how her work is viewed, especially by her peers. On any given topic, only a handful of reporters fit the elite description. People like Nina Totenberg, who covers the Supreme Court for NPR; foreign-policy expert Christiane Amanpour, who hosts *This Week* on ABC; and Sue Shellenbarger, who writes about the work-life balancing act at the *Wall Street Journal* qualify. Writers for trade publications focusing on specific industries or topics also fit this category.

Newsroom Journalists

The second bucket contains reporters with journalism training and experience working in newsrooms. Most have degrees in communications, journalism, or broadcast media or have worked their way up the ranks. These individuals are familiar with journalistic principles and professional guidelines. However, they do not necessarily have expertise or interest in the subject matter. They work on assignment under tight deadlines. While not as personally invested in the final product as elite journalists, they can generally be counted on to be objective.

Everyone Else

The last bucket is anyone else—self-described citizen journalists, bloggers, or activists with agendas. These individuals have little or no training and, most notably, no accountability. They write, say, and do what they please. There is little or no fact-checking, and rumor and speculation are sometimes treated as fact. They often create a name for themselves by breaking news before the mainstream press, as was the case with the writer at the *National Enquirer* who broke the story of Tiger Woods's infidelity online. It was an unpaid citizen journalist working for the *Huffington Post* who recorded candidate Barack Obama saying rural Americans are "bitter" and "cling to guns or religion."

In the blogosphere, there is very little verification of information. The online universe is clogged with hearsay or worse. Shirley Sherrod was a government official who lost her job because the White House feared Fox TV would tag her as a racist. Sherrod, formerly an employee at the US Department of Agriculture, was fired when a video appeared on the website of a conservative activist. On the tape, Sherrod, who is black, appeared to be making racist statements at an NAACP conference about a white farm family in Georgia. However, the activist Andrew Breitbart had doctored the tape in an attempt to defame Sherrod and embarrass the White House. What Sherrod was actually doing was expressing gratitude to the farmers for helping her move beyond prejudice.

Rule 3: An Interview Is Not a Conversation

Be extremely wary of the reporter who attempts to sweet-talk you into a false sense of complacency. Skilled journalists are adept at getting their sources to relax and say more than they intended. Some reporters will try to make the interview feel like a conversation at a lively cocktail party. He will posture as a sympathetic friend and give every appearance that he is hanging on your every word. Let's be honest: it's terribly flattering to have someone ask your opinion and seem to care about the answer. Don't be fooled. A reporter's number-one job is to break news.

BBC talk-show host Ruby Wax was a slick operator when it came to getting people to confess outrageous things. Wax charmed her way into Imelda Marcos's closet to reveal the Filipino First Lady's lavish shoe collection. She rummaged through the refrigerator of the Duchess of York and Weight Watchers pitchwoman Sarah Ferguson and coaxed O. J. Simpson into pretending to stab her with a banana. By projecting more like a pussy cat than a pushy broad, Wax was able to soften up her targets to feed the public's insatiable appetite for the foibles of well-known figures.

Neither Friend nor Foe

Reporters should not be viewed as confidants, but neither should you take an adversarial position with them. Reporters are not friends, nor are they enemies. There is nothing to be gained from expressing disdain for them or their profession. This doesn't mean that some interviews shouldn't be off-limits. There are occasions when it makes sense to say no. One can only speculate why Elizabeth Edwards would inflame the media circus with a promotional book tour in the wake of the news about her husband's infidelity. Observers described the book tour as one of the most bizarre publicity jaunts ever, as reporters not surprisingly asked about husband John's cheating while she battled cancer. NPR's Michele Norris's question about the possibility that her children may have a half sister left Elizabeth tongue-tied: "Eh, eh, ugh, am, not that I know of [pause] uhm, ugh, uhm. . . ."[14] Edwards, a veteran of multiple campaigns, needlessly put herself in a vulnerable position. It may have been an effort to control the story, but her nonanswers simply raised more questions.

Rule 4: Dealing with the Gonzo Journalist

It used to be highly entertaining to tune into *60 Minutes* on Sunday nights to watch Mike Wallace show up unannounced on the doorstep of a reticent source with the camera rolling. Who can forget the encounter with the irate guy with the bulldozer who tried to run down the camera operator? It seemed clear that investigative journalists were the good guys going after bad guys to protect the public. Nowadays, the line between what is news and what is entertainment has been sullied. The victims are sometimes innocent, and the tactics are much more nefarious. Ambush interviews, doctored videos, and hidden cameras are now the tactics of activists with political agendas. They are using new media tools to discredit individuals and spread misinformation. If confronted unannounced, you always have the right to decline an interview.

The goal in an unexpected encounter is to disengage as quickly and politely as possible. Assume you are being taped, so be cordial as you take a minute to introduce yourself and shake hands. Resist the temptation to

---

Ambush Interview MO

1. Be friendly and polite.
2. Don't answer any questions on the spot.
3. Calmly disengage and walk away.
4. Decide how to respond later.

---

answer any questions. Firmly, with a smile, say you would be happy to discuss the matter but do not have time right then and there. Exchange business cards and suggest the "journalist" contact you to schedule a time to talk. Then, calmly turn and walk away. The reporter may follow and throw questions. Stay calm and stick to your guns. Don't attempt to respond. You may think you have a good retort, but if the tape is edited out of context, you can end up looking bad. Later, after you have done some checking, decide if you want to do the interview. It is much easier to decline to talk over the telephone.

Rule 5: Avoid Foot-in-Mouth Disease

The irony of the new media age is that more people are providing more news, but the quality hasn't improved. The limitations of the media complicate the process, but not every mistake can be blamed on unskilled or biased reporters hustling to break stories and meet deadlines. Don't aid and abet in your destruction by committing a faux pas. Loose lips can be your undoing, especially now that verbal mistakes move at the speed of sound in the social media world. A well-spoken woman is wise to the ways her own words can be her undoing. Here are strategies to avoid foot-in-mouth disease.

Off-the-Cuff, Digitally Speaking

Off-the-cuff gaffes occur when a spokesperson blurts something out before thinking about how to express what she wants to say. People are now making the same mistake with social media tools. Whether it rolls off your tongue or your Twitter® account, there is no pulling it back. It is going straight into your mother's ears or a digital data bank. Meghan McCain got caught playing hooky from a book tour via her own tweets. The daughter of Senator John McCain canceled a book-signing appearance due to "several unforeseen professional responsibilities."[15] McCain blew her cover when she tweeted that she was "headed to sin city with her favorite crew of sinners."

If you can't resist the impulse to tweet spontaneously, then it is time to close the account. It is possible to delete knee-jerk comments and undisciplined thoughts, but that doesn't prevent them from being cached inside search engines. In the online universe, nothing is ever permanently erased. Your every utterance is findable.

Off the Record

General Stanley McChrystal may have thought he was speaking "off the record" when he criticized his civilian superiors at the White House. But *Rolling Stone* reporter Michael Hastings heard it differently. Hastings was embedded with the general and his staff for several months in Afghanistan and recorded their derogatory statements about Vice President Joe Biden, among others. The resulting headline-grabbing article cost McChrystal his job as the commander of US and NATO forces in Afghanistan.

First off, recognize that the phrase "off the record" is not universally applied and understood. Get clarification before you answer any questions about whether what you say is "off the record" versus "background" or "not for attribution." Set the ground rules beforehand, get the reporter to agree, and then stick to them no matter what. If you throw out juicy comments, you're waving raw meat in front of a hungry reporter. If you offer something tempting and then try to pull it back, you are asking the reporter to forego potentially great publicity for a vague journalistic principle. Some reporters will abide by the ground rules, but others will go with the story. Bear in mind that reporters routinely share information with their colleagues, and e-mail messages are considered fair game.

"No Comment"

Call off the lawyers. This is not a court of law but rather the court of public opinion. If you say, "No comment," you appear guilty as charged or as if you have something to hide. In a crisis situation, there is always a tension that exists between the legal team and communications strategists. The public relations experts want to mollify public anger with expressions of concern, while the lawyers advise against any statement that could be construed as an admission of guilt. Both sides should agree that there is nothing to be gained from saying, "No comment." It doesn't make a bad story go away. Strategize what you want to say so you don't miss the opportunity to communicate your side of the story.

Truthiness

Comedy Central's Steven Colbert has taken the issue of truthfulness to new comic heights with his pillorying of misstatements made by government and business officials. If you fudge the facts, expect it to come back to haunt you sooner rather than later. Guessing, estimating, and speculating can be as bad as making stuff up. Any information that is later found to be inaccurate or misleading damages your credibility.

The Run-on

Knowing when to stop talking can be a lifesaver. Never feel any obligation to fill a pregnant pause. Be wary of the reporter who nods in an encouraging manner when you have finished responding. He is simply trying to egg you on. If no further questions are forthcoming, summarize the key message points and send him packing.

Rule 6: Anticipate the Tough Questions

In the movie *Groundhog Day*, Bill Murray's character is a TV meteorologist caught in a time warp. Day after day he is forced to cover the same story over and over. Will Punxsutawney Phil see his shadow or not? The news media cover the same stories in a near ritual-like fashion, and they ask the same types of questions. The three most commonly asked reporter questions are "Tell me what this means?" "What is your response?" and "How did it feel?" Pay attention, and you begin to recognize the patterns. Listen to the questions on talk radio, the cable shows, and morning television. It quickly becomes apparent that certain questions have inherent traps with the potential to cause harm. Here is the list of the most commonly posed queries and how to avoid stumbling with your answer.

Trickiest Reporter Questions

- **Hypothetical or "What if...?"** Never respond to hypothetical questions. Stick to the facts.
- *USA Today* **or news of the day?** Expect to be asked about breaking news even if it is tangentially related to your topic. Scan the headlines as part of your preparation process.
- **Third party or unknown source?** Always be skeptical when a reporter asks for a response to a comment from an outside source. Who knows if the individual the reporter is quoting actually said what the reporter claims he said. Stick with what you can verify.
- **Wouldn't you agree?** Don't allow the reporter to cajole you into agreeing with something you don't agree with. Respond in a friendly yet firm manner by saying that you disagree and briefly explain why.
- **Ranking or choice?** A reporter may ask you to characterize your answer by deciding if something is better or worse or by choosing *A*, *B*, or *C*. You can say none of the above is accurate.
- **Negative premise?** Don't repeat the negative words that are often embedded in the question.
- **Personal opinion?** Don't ever feel like you must give a personal opinion.
- **Personal attack or cheap shot?** Ignore the pettiness, calmly set the record straight, and quickly bridge to message.
- **False facts?** Inadvertently, you can get a question based on faulty information. Stick to the facts.
- **The softball?** Sometimes the easy question throws you off balance.

If you are asked, "Is there anything else I should know? Or, would you like to add anything?" go straight to your message.

Rule 7: The Bridge Technique

Some questions require a finely calibrated response to prevent getting stuck in a quagmire. The bridging technique helps you maneuver around topics by transitioning back to a preplanned message. When hit with a tricky question, give a concise, direct response and then bridge back to what you want to talk about. The "escape hatches" are phrases that allow you to acknowledge the question and then take control by bridging back to your message. Practice the phrases aloud, and soon you will be adept at keeping the interview on track.

In addition to the escape-hatch phrases, a surefire way to entice a reporter to quote what you want her to quote is to preface your answer with "I shouldn't be telling you this, but...." No reporter can resist that lead-in. The line almost guarantees that whatever you say next survives the editing process.

Escape Hatches

- Here's what I can tell you...
- Let me answer that question this way...
- Your question raises another equally important point that needs to be addressed...
- Your question doesn't directly address what matters most to the people in the audience...
- I wouldn't characterize it that way. What I would say is...
- I'm frequently asked about that, and it reminds me of a story I would like to share now...
- Let me tell you why your question is so important...

Rule 8: The Golden Rule

Finally, there is one golden rule that applies to all your interactions with media reporters. This rule will prevent much heartburn and heartache if you abide by it. It is deceivingly simple: if you don't want to hear it, see it, or read it, then don't say it or don't do it. Reporters can only report what you say and what you do. Spokespeople are most likely to forget the rule when they treat the interview as something other than what it is. It is not a conversation or a chance to settle old scores, take revenge, or vent. First and foremost the interview is an opportunity to tell your side of a story.

STANDING OVATION POINT: WELL-SPOKEN WOMEN KNOW TROUBLE WHEN THEY SEE IT

In her celebrated book *Read My Pins*, Madeleine Albright chronicles how she used jewelry as a "personal diplomatic arsenal." The secretary of state's decision to wear a snake pin came about as she was preparing to meet with representatives of Saddam Hussein. The Iraqi dictator had earlier described Albright as an "unparalleled serpent." She didn't think anyone would notice the gold snake entwined on a stick with a tiny diamond hanging from its mouth, but the press immediately wanted to know its meaning.

Albright has amassed a fascinating collection of bejeweled symbols to "add warmth or a needed edge to a relationship."[16] Albright writes that "the idea of using pins as a diplomatic tool is not found in any State Department manual." This enterprising woman fashioned a unique approach to dealing with prickly personalities while signaling her intentions. It is the rare audience that won't give you a fair hearing, but if you should encounter trouble, avoid returning the fire. Follow a diplomatic protocol, and, like Albright, you will be able to hold your ground firmly and gracefully.

Applause Principles: Diplomatically Speaking

- Troublemakers and interrogators can be placated with tactful maneuvers and composed responses.
- Establishing protocol for the Q&A session wards off unruly behavior and helps maintain control.
- Know what you are getting yourself into when consenting to a media interview.
- Deflect gotcha questions with smooth transitions rehearsed in advance.
- Protect yourself from the traps of social media and gonzo journalists by practicing the golden rule: if you don't do it or say it, they can't report it.

THE WELL-SPOKEN SISTERHOOD IN FLATTERING PANTS

> To my supporters, my champions—my sisterhood of the traveling
> pantsuits—from the bottom of my heart: Thank you. You never gave in.
> You never gave up. And, together we made history.
> —Hillary Clinton, Democratic National Convention, August 2008

Hillary Clinton has taken a lot of unnecessary flack about her closet full of monochromatic pantsuits. *Glamour* magazine got it right when they saluted her for finding a good-looking signature style and sticking with it, no matter what the critics had to say. And, kudos to Clinton for turning an unending stream of commentary about appearance into an affirming statement of gratitude.

The genesis of her pantsuit comment is the coming-of-age story *The Sisterhood of the Traveling Pants*.[1] Four lifelong friends stay linked through a pair of magical blue jeans. Each looks great in the jeans, even though no two are the same shape or size. During their first summer apart, the young women correspond about their adventures in love and loss as they pass the jeans along. The traveling pants represent a bond of support the young women provide to one another as they handle new challenges and overcome feelings of inadequacy. Each woman is preparing to face the world with the knowledge that her friends have, so to speak, got her back.

It's okay that the flattering magical pants don't exist. What really matters is the idea of creating a network of support. A central aim of this book has been to provide inspiring stories of how to become well-spoken, and this final chapter is no exception. A sisterhood of support ensures you are not going it alone as you work to improve your communications skills. Everyone needs a support network to find a mentor; acquire optimal skills, become a role model, and promulgate a woman's perspective. The ultimate benefit of a network can be boiled down into a twofer deal: "American women, ask what your sisters can do for you; also ask what you can do for them." The sisterhood starts with each of us. We need to get our collective selves moving because lots of work remains to be done if our voices are going to ring loud and clear from every corner of the public square.

According to the World Economic Forum, a nonprofit group that studies the gender gap in education, healthcare, economics, and political power, women at the current pace will reach parity with men in school, the office, and life by the year 4000. While women's voices are being heard, when we have a larger chorus, the impact will be greater. US senator Debbie Stabenow dug in her heels to ensure maternity coverage was not eliminated during a legislative debate on healthcare reform. When Senator Jon Kyl stated that his insurer shouldn't have to provide the coverage since he didn't need it, Stabenow shot right back that his mom probably did.[2] Imagine that debate if Stabenow hadn't been in the room. Who would have spoken up on behalf of women? Do you want to speak for yourself or depend on someone else speaking for you?

Many women are joiners who enjoy participating in social clubs to talk about everything from nonfiction to fly-fishing. We need to leverage this inclination to be joiners into a more powerful force. As Madeleine Albright says, women are very good at being friends but we aren't as successful at networking. Albright's philosophy was immortalized on a Starbucks coffee cup: "There is a special place in hell for women who don't help women." We can take greater advantage of the desire to come together by pooling our collective talents to fuel strategic endeavors.

THE NEW GIRLS' NETWORK

She came, she saw, she put the world community on notice. Hillary Clinton championed the rights of women the world over when she traveled to Beijing, China, to speak out against degradation and abuse and

All-Time Great Line

Let it be that human rights are women's rights and women's rights are human rights, once and for all.
—Hillary Clinton, Fourth World Conference on Women, 1995

to stand up for respect and dignity. It was an act of courage for the First Lady to condemn a tyrant on his own turf. No country was singled out in the speech, but it was clear what was meant when Clinton said: "It is a violation of human rights when women are not allowed to plan their own families, and that includes being forced to have abortions or sterilized against their will."[3] The talk was tough, but the goal was illumination, not intimidation. Clinton was raising the legitimate topic of the aspirations of women "in fields and factories, in village markets and supermarkets, and in living rooms and board rooms"[4] who strive for a better life for themselves and their families.

Although she had delivered thousands of speeches, Clinton wrote in her autobiography that she felt nervous before Beijing because the stakes were high. If nothing came out of the conference, an opportunity to advance women's rights would have been squandered, and she didn't want to embarrass herself or her country or let anyone down. Clinton was also aware that the passion she personally felt for issues didn't always translate into a good delivery of the message. Given the emotional nature of the speech, with its focus on injustice, she didn't want the delivery to distract from the blunt language: "Now I had to make sure that the tone or pitch of my voice would not confuse the message."[5]

While Clinton spoke, the audience listened intently, and when she gave the concluding call to action, the crowd's reaction was an instantaneous standing ovation: "the serious and stony-faced delegates suddenly leaped from their seats.... Outside the hall women hung over banisters and rushed down escalators to grab my hand."[6] The Chinese government had forbidden any broadcast on television and radio of the speech, and newspapers were not allowed to print a single word. But nothing could silence the response to what was one of the First Lady's finest moments in public speaking. Clinton says: "To this day, whenever I travel overseas, women come up to me quoting words from the Beijing speech or clutching copies they want me to autograph."[7]

First Ladies Need Role Models, Too

Over a forty-year career in public service, Clinton has drawn upon the intelligence and dedication of an all-female nucleus. "Hillaryland" is the name for the staff and advisers who have provided guidance to her at the White House, in the US Senate, on the presidential campaign, and in the secretary of state's office. Certainly, an honorary member would be Clinton's role model, former First Lady Eleanor Roosevelt. The press infamously reported that one of the activities taking place in Hillaryland during the White House years were "séances" held to communicate with Roosevelt. Speaking at a function sponsored by the Roosevelt Institute, Clinton addressed those who mocked the idea of drawing sustenance from a woman of substance.

> As some of you might remember, I used to have imaginary conversations with Eleanor. And, she gave me a lot of really good advice. I often remarked about how there was nothing I did as First Lady that Eleanor had not already done. I would go to a place in New York or a place in India, and be greeted by some excited person saying, "Oh, we haven't had a First Lady here since Eleanor Roosevelt."
> I discovered that she had blazed trails that were not only unique for her time, but really stood the test of time. But when she visited, it was not just a simple drop-in. She would listen, she would learn, she would bring that information back to her husband, and she would continue to push for the kinds of changes that were absolutely necessary.[8]

Throughout the highs and lows of living a public life, Roosevelt has served as a source of inspiration and solace for Clinton. Roosevelt's unconventional approach to the role of First Lady made her a target for harsh criticism just as Clinton was for her stands on healthcare reform and equal rights. Clinton says whenever she finds herself having to listen to people say unkind things about her, she pinches the skin on her arm to test for its thickness. The pinch is a reminder of Roosevelt's firm belief that every public woman must have skin as thick as a rhinoceros hide.

During the campaign for the Democratic presidential nomination, Clinton endured slings and arrows from all quarters. As a women's adviser to her campaign, I was dumbstruck and angry about the crushing expectations and judgments other women placed on her candidacy. In message workshops and strategy sessions I conducted, the questions women raised frequently had little to do with the candidate's readiness to be commander in chief. Many women were

*Secretary of State
Hillary Clinton*

preoccupied with her marital status, pressing for information about her marriage. It seemed they expected the woman who could be elected president to be perfect in every possible way. While this background noise was confounding, it didn't distract Clinton from delivering expertly in the forum political candidates most dread.

Any woman looking for a master class in performance skills would be well served to review the televised presidential debate tapes. In a seemingly endless number of forums, Clinton consistently demonstrated how a woman can present herself like a leader while facing intense questioning. As the early front-runner, Clinton withstood a barrage of comments from her seven primary opponents, including the inane from John Edwards, who said a jacket she wore looked like asbestos, and Barack Obama, who told her with a smirk, "You are likable enough, Hillary."[9] The debate questions ran the gauntlet, with the silliest coming at a CNN forum: "Do you prefer diamonds or pearls?"[10]

The ability to weather the politicking was only one aspect of Clinton's impressive display of communications acumen. The debates showcased a Clinton who was, as always, in command of the facts and well versed on international affairs and domestic policy. She was clear in her statement that as president she would not sit down with leaders of rogue nations. Her position about standing firm against raising Social Security taxes never wavered. While disagreements remained on policy positions, the debate appearances put to rest lingering questions in this country about whether a woman could be president. Clinton looked ready to lead the nation with substantive responses; a clear-eyed, confident smile; and a good-natured sense of humor.

TALK LIKE A GIRL

An essential question posed by all well-spoken women is "How can my next presentation be better than what I delivered today?" Well-spoken women recognize that outstanding performances are the result of an ongoing process—preparing in advance, delivering the goods, analyzing feedback, and refining technique. Every speaking situation is a chance to learn something new. Don't make the mistake of cooling your heels in the land of the almost famous, stuck in a rut, with skills that have flatlined.

The well-spoken women featured in this book achieved extraordinary success because they expected much of themselves and were supported by a committed team. The well-spoken may appear alone onstage, but they don't fly solo. Colleagues and family members are seated in the audience, staff members watch backstage, and consultants wait expectantly to hear how it went. While preparing for her big convention speech, Ann Richards received drafts from total strangers. People called to volunteer to write it, and people called wanting to get paid to write it. Richards tapped pros like Lily Tomlin as well as John F. Kennedy's speechwriter, Ted Sorensen. She watched videotape of Mario Cuomo and Barbara Jordan. In the end, it does take a village. Becoming well-spoken requires a combination of setting individual goals and asking for and accepting assistance.

Do It for Your Sisters

Here are proactive steps you can take to assist the women you know—and steps to take for yourself.

Give an "Atta Girl!"

Accolades go a long way. If a colleague has done a good job, tell her so on the spot. She may be thinking only about how nervous she was and worry that as a result the performance was subpar. Since she thought she looked and sounded terrible, she likely will not be aware that her ideas were well received. Tell her that people were impressed, and she'll walk away thinking, "Wow, maybe I wasn't so bad." Deserved praise works wonders when it comes to building confidence. On the other hand, if a colleague makes a mistake, help her keep the faux pas in perspective and not blow it out of proportion. Nearly everyone can recall a searing embarrassment in vivid detail, primarily because it was never put into a broader context.

Avon vice president of public relations Debbie Coffee provides balanced feedback to her all-gal staff in the spirit of honesty and kindness. If someone has misspoken, Coffee pulls her aside immediately to provide a clear appraisal and constructive criticism. This process has enabled Coffee to build a team of climbers and pullers. The climbers and pullers are women who climb the ladder of success and pull other women along with them. That's the type of atmosphere in which confidence can flourish. Avoid dragging out a negative situation with a chain of twenty-five e-mails. Acknowledge what went wrong quickly and provide feedback that can be put to constructive use.

Chick-to-Chick Coaching

Soon after Ann Richards won her first race for Travis County commissioner, she and two girlfriends created a "road show" of how-to seminars for the "PTA, garden clubs, [and] country-club ladies."[11] Most women they spoke to were not interested in running for office, but they did want to learn how to raise money and approach someone about a cause. Richards said it was tremendously gratifying to teach women skills and to help them feel better about themselves. She says she "did it for the joy of it. Because it was fun, and because it moved women along."[12]

At work or at home, you could gather a small group to practice with a camera to record one another. It could be a mini version of Toastmasters

International, the nonprofit that for nearly one hundred years has been helping people improve their speaking skills. Toastmasters meetings usually last about an hour, with everybody playing a role in them. Some members practice a prepared speech, while others give impromptu remarks. There is no formal instruction, but rather all participants provide positive feedback. Debbi Fields of Mrs. Fields® cookies and Nancy Brinker, the founder of the Susan G. Komen Breast Cancer Foundation, are famous alumni. Get a tripod for the camera, and you're ready to go.

When not at her day job, running the National Telephone Cooperative Association, which boasts a membership of six hundred companies, CEO Shirley Bloomfield is building a network called GlobalWIN for women in the telecommunications field. Bloomfield says she is still shocked when she walks into meetings and finds there are only one or two senior women in the room. Having spent her share of time on the golf course, Bloomfield makes a point of seeking out young women who will benefit from networking in a safe environment and provides them a space where they can get a little extra push, some training, and exposure.

Say "No" to Mean-Girl Comments

Women can be especially cruel to one another with personal put-downs and petty comments. The godmother of polling, Celinda Lake, says women voters judge women candidates much more harshly than male voters do, particularly when discussing appearance. A focus group can sound like a meeting of the Plastics, the superficial, backstabbing high school clique in the movie *Mean Girls*. An echo of the Plastics reverberated in a comment a state legislator made about a "sister" legislator during a gubernatorial campaign in Minnesota. The Speaker of the House, Margaret Anderson Kelliher, was poised to receive the Democratic Party's endorsement when legislator Sue Halligan told the state's largest newspaper, "I think her stump speech skills just suck."[13] Ouch!

Women don't need to march in lockstep or support each other only because they are women, but when there is a difference of opinion, let's keep it professional. For women in America, being elected governor is as difficult as becoming the CEO of a Fortune 500 company. In 2008, Hillary and Sarah provided an example of how to avoid a public catfight. Neither uttered a word of personal criticism about the other. While the two have fundamental differences, there was no trash talk, and both agreed it would be interesting to sit down over coffee. If women as a whole are to move ahead, then we need to respect differences and each other's choices.

For twelve of the twenty-five years she spent on the US Supreme Court, Sandra Day O'Connor was the lone woman justice. Despite having graduated third in her class at Stanford Law School, O'Connor's only job offer came from a firm that needed a legal secretary: "We don't hire women, but how do you type?"[14] O'Connor says one of her happiest days on the Court was when she was joined by Ruth Bader Ginsburg. She welcomed the newcomer with "enormous pleasure" despite their ideological differences. O'Connor was appointed by President Reagan and was considered a moderate, whereas Ginsberg is a liberal nominated by President Clinton. The pair was dubbed "the New Supremes," and O'Connor said it was liberating not to shoulder the burden of representing the women of America alone.[15]

Call out Sexism

Women of every age have been the targets of demeaning, demoralizing verbal abuse that leaves them feeling violated or physically threatened. Now there are options when it comes to deciding if and how one should respond. During a training workshop for a group of one hundred law enforcement officers, I was conducting a mock news interview with a county sheriff. As part of the exercise, I was firing off some tough questions when a voice from the back of the room called out: "Why don't you smack her." As the life drained out of me, I attempted to continue as if I had not heard someone suggest I should be punched.

When hit with something that throws you off stride, be prepared to think of yourself as a shock absorber. Take a second or two to feel the shock of the objectionable comment so you can decide how you want to handle it. Onstage, you may opt to let it roll off your back so you don't become too emotional or distracted. Resist the temptation to respond in the moment, as a better strategy is to deal with the offender offstage. And you can take comfort in the knowledge that you don't have to stand there and take threatening, belittling, or sexist comments alone. A number of organizations monitor egregious behavior and call out the perpetrators.

Name It. Change It. is a nonprofit working to end sexist and misogynist media coverage of women candidates (www.nameitchangeit.org). An organization founded by Jane Fonda, Gloria Steinem, and Robin Morgan called the Women's Media Center is committed to making women more visible and powerful in the media by nurturing and supporting women spokespeople (www.womensmediacenter.com). The New Agenda is a website run by activists who have vowed "to draw a line in the sand against sexism and misogyny and to advance key goals for women" (www.thenew agenda.net).

The most frequently downloaded study by the American Psychological Association (APA) is titled the "Sexualization of Girls."[16] The report looks at how media images of sexual readiness, objectification, and narrowly defined standards of beauty impact girls. SPARK, a grassroots group, is engaging girls as part of the solution in protecting them from sexual exploitation (www.sparksummit.com). Girls are getting tools to be catalysts for change as activists, organizers, policy influencers, and media makers. At a SPARK Summit, actress Geena Davis led the audience in a pledge to take sexy back, saying that when more women and men pull together to make change, the gender imbalance in society will end.[17] The Girl Scouts are also responding to the growing evidence about how many girls suffer from negative body image and low self-worth with programs to help girls and tweens accept and be proud of themselves.[18]

Develop the Bench

Sport aficionados love their stats, and Coach Pat Summitt is extremely proud of her basketball team's unmatched win/lose record at the University of Tennessee. Yet, there is another set of numbers she likes to tout: "One hundred percent of the players who have remained at Tennessee for four years have received their degrees."[19] Summitt also takes great personal satisfaction in the number of former players and staff members who have chosen to follow in her footsteps by becoming coaches themselves.

In the world of political consultants, Jill Alper is considered a "candidate whisperer" for her role in advising presidential candidates and chief executives such as Governor Jennifer Granholm. Alper says that "the presence of women on a team doesn't necessarily guarantee anything, but their absence is a factor."[20] That sentiment was echoed by former White House press secretary Dana Perino, who worked for George W. Bush. Perino says there were no women in the room when the decision was being made to choose Sarah Palin as John McCain's running mate: "It was a group of men who decided that the women who supported Hillary Clinton would automatically support Palin."[21]

Most top-level political campaigns are run and staffed predominantly by men. Sometimes the guys don't know what's what when it comes to prepping women. I have to chuckle about the male campaign manager who wanted to order the candidate's makeup online. Then there was the fellow who refused to schedule time for a candidate's hair to be highlighted and styled prior to shooting the TV spots. Thousands of dollars were being invested in commercials, but the candidate couldn't have time to fix her hair?

If gender differences matter at the beauty counter, they have even more impact when it comes to substantive issues. An area where women need more representation is speech writing. There are a few good women writing for some very big names, but we need more. Sarah Hurwitz has penned major addresses for President Obama. Lissa Muscatine is a longtime speechwriter for Hillary Clinton. President Reagan's eloquence often flowed from Peggy Noonan's keypad. It's not that women are better writers; rather, they bring their life experience and pick up on different nuances. Former US representative Debbie Halvorson needed women voters to beat back a challenge for her seat in Illinois. An appealing story that didn't get told often enough was how, as a single mom, Halvorson sat alone at night at the kitchen table with a stack of bills. In a tight economy, many women would have related to Halvorson's story of trying to find the ends so they could meet.

Former White House speechwriter Vinca LaFleur says there may be fewer high-profile women speechwriters because women don't tend to be big self-promoters. This may be an argument for encouraging more women to enter the field. Inherently, the speechwriter's job requires keeping one's ego in check because you are writing for someone else. As LaFleur says: "At the end of the day the speech is theirs....It is the speaker's reputation that is on the line, not yours." As a speechwriter you must also be a diplomat, in that you must be ready to make the best case for your ideas and then be ready to let go if your argument is not the most persuasive. "But, you can't be a patsy or a pushover." LaFleur says she became a better speechwriter when she started to do more public speaking herself. "It helps you understand everything so much better when you have felt that clench in the throat yourself." [22]

Do It for Yourself

Helping other women goes hand in hand with helping yourself. Here's how.

Take Yourself Seriously

With a name like *Mankiller,* you would think people would take Wilma very seriously, especially since she's a chief. This wasn't always the case for Chief Wilma Mankiller, who was the first woman to lead the Cherokee Nation. The chief recounted a conversation with a young man who picked her up at the airport when she visited "a named Eastern college" for a speech. He wanted to know how he should address her since, he said, *chief* was a male title. His suggestions were "chief-ess" or perhaps "chief-ette"? Wilma slowly responded that he could call her "Ms-Chief" (*mischief*). Then the student pressed her about the origin of her name. *Mankiller* was the title given to the sentry who was responsible for village security, but Wilma told the student that *Mankiller* was a nickname, and she had earned it.[23]

The young man probably didn't mean any disrespect, but having to demonstrate credentials over and over is exasperating. Now that I'm in my forties, it was genuinely amusing when a sixtyish man walked into a crisis communications training, took one look at me, and asked, "So, you are the one who is in charge of this?" Looking him directly in the eye with a smile, I said, "Yep, you're stuck with me." Ten years ago, the comment would have unleashed my insecurities. It takes willpower not to cringe and skulk away. This is a good time to adopt the champion stance and take a deep breath. Then decide how you want to handle the implication that you couldn't possibly know what you are talking about.

Women at the podium have made great strides, but we haven't yet leveled the playing field. If you want others to take you seriously, you must first treat yourself with respect. In *Esquire* magazine, Tina Fey shared the advice she gave to high school girls during a commencement address.

> If you find yourself two years from now at spring break, don't lift your shirt up. And if you do, have your own camera. The foolishness is that there's some disgusting middleman. They're your boobs. At least have the sense to film it yourself and get the money from it.
>
> That's what baffles me about *Girls Gone Wild*. We could sell this ourselves! Talk about giving away the store. First of all, don't do it. But if you're going to do it, keep your hands on the money, for God's sakes. You don't need a middleman. It's your boobs.[24]

There is a level of seriousness to Fey's advice that should not be discounted. If you want an audience to believe that you are worth listening to, then you need to believe it. Ann Lewis was the guiding hand that helped elect Barbara Mikulski to the US Senate in 1986. Mikulski was the first Democratic woman elected to that body in her own right and is now the longest-serving woman senator. Lewis, a former White House communications director and adviser to Hillary Clinton's presidential campaign, says it is important for women to stop measuring themselves against perfection and to start measuring themselves against the competition. She says, look around the room, and you will see you are competent and capable. "Once you are in the room, recognize that you belong there. You don't have to take a test every day. If you are there, you belong there."[25]

Ask for Help

"What would Margaret do?" is a question US senator Susan Collins frequently asks herself as she goes about her legislative work in the halls of Washington. Collins met the legendary Senator Margaret Chase Smith on a high school trip to the nation's Capitol and returned home believing there wasn't anything a woman couldn't do. The time the senator spent with Collins inspired the student to make her own successful bid for Congress. Mainers didn't need to be convinced that Collins and sister Senator

Olympia Snowe could handle the job of representing them. The all-female delegation has been serving the citizens of Maine for a decade.

Asking for help can mean hiring help. Don't hesitate to make an investment in your personal and professional growth. A speech coach can zero in on delivery techniques to speed your improvement. Speechwriters can add polish, depth, and humor to the big-occasion address. A live, in-studio appearance is a great time for a media trainer to craft sound bites, nudge your on-camera skills to the next level, and provide suggestions on what to wear. Vocal coaches and speech therapists will improve the quality of your sound with exercises that address stuttering, low volume, and pitch issues.

Professional consultants should work with you and the other members of your communications team. Don't try to go it alone. When you are starting out, guidance helps you develop good habits and boost confidence. For women who've reached a pinnacle of success, the corner office can be a lonely place. Pollster Celinda Lake says it is essential to develop and nurture a team as you climb the ladder of success so you do not find yourself surrounded only by yes-people.[26] Lake says leadership can be isolating, and you need to have good protectors, people who are looking out for your best interests so you are not constantly looking over your shoulder.

Be a Buddy

"What would Elizabeth say?" One can imagine Susan B. Anthony pondering that question as she embarked on yet another speaking event. Never was there a more dynamic duo or odder couple than Anthony and Elizabeth Cady Stanton. Filmmaker Ken Burns's *Not for Ourselves Alone* tells the story of the enduring partnership between the tall, slim bespectacled Anthony, who never married, and the pint-sized but plump Stanton, who married and had seven children. At home with her brood, Stanton wrote the "Declaration of Sentiments" presented at the first Women's Rights Convention in Seneca Falls: "We hold these truths to be self-evident that all men and women are created equal...." She also authored countless pamphlets, articles, and many of the words Anthony delivered as she crisscrossed the country. By her own calculation, Anthony estimated "she had delivered 75 to 100 speeches a year for forty-five years, not counting thirty years of addresses to Congress and the New York State Legislature."[27] Awareness of their individual strengths made the pair a formidable team. As Anna Howard Shaw put it in her book *The Story of a Pioneer.* "[Miss Anthony] often said that Mrs. Stanton was the brains of the association; while she was just its hands and feet; but in truth the two women worked marvelously together."[28] Together they were the driving force behind the women's rights movement for fifty years.

When Thelma and Louise set out on their road adventure, they were hoping to escape the dreariness of their lives with a little fun on a girls' weekend away. When the getaway spiraled out of control with law enforcement in pursuit, they decided together to escape the system that was loaded against them. They were forced to run for their lives, yet they drew strength from their friendship and growing self-reliance. Similarly, no one wants to crash and burn onstage. Sometimes it is the simplest things that will ensure a colleague doesn't flounder. Be the one to tell your office mate that she has lipstick on her teeth or that her skirt isn't flattering (but don't tell her the latter on the day of the presentation, when it's too late to do anything about it.) Listen with patience as she practices the remarks one more time or be a coach and run her through a mock news interview.

Batman had Robin, and Oprah has her sidekick, Gayle King. One of the most successful collaborations in the history of television is the duo that has produced the *Oprah Winfrey Show, Oprah Magazine,* and Oprah's new cable network. The many achievements of the best friends and business associates in an industry that isn't always kind to women have been undercut by a swirl of gossip about their relationship. It's troubling but not surprising that they have had to disavow rumors. The pair represents a model of leadership that doesn't fit into the traditional masculine definition of power. In addition to their media savvy, they share an affinity for designer footwear.

Seek Out Opportunities

On a presidential mission to Poland while serving as the secretary of labor, Elizabeth Dole was prepared to give toasts at the evening dinners. While her counterparts stumbled for words, Dole spoke about how moved she was by the Polish people's struggle to throw off the yoke of communism. She compared the hardships the Poles had endured for freedom with the struggle of the American people two hundred years ago. She quoted Thomas Paine: "Those who expect to reap the blessings of freedom must undergo the fatigue of supporting it."[29] It was reported that people were crying when she was finished.

Think about creating opportunities for yourself in the near and long term at professional and nonprofessional gatherings. Be willing to take a chance by daring to ask the first question after a panel discussion. Have a question written down and step up to the microphone when the moderator opens the floor. It's good way to practice with low risk in front of a large audience. Volunteer to be the person who facilitates the breakout session at a conference. Present a brief thank-you along with the gift to the boss at an office party.

Public speaking doesn't only happen on the job; opportunities for practice abound at social gatherings. A friend's baby shower is a speaking opportunity. The next meeting of a book club is a chance to prepare a ninety-second summary of your impression of the author's intention. You could say the prayer at Thanksgiving dinner. The pressure you would face in a business or professional situation doesn't exist under these circumstances, so you can be yourself without worrying about a performance evaluation. These events can also help you overcome the drive for perfection. It's okay to make a mistake in front of the book club members. They will simply be impressed that you are organized. At the baby shower, you don't need your negotiator's poker face. Your friend will be surprised and delighted by a heartwarming speech of congratulations.

Pat Yourself on the Back

At the end of her workout videos, Cindy Crawford turns to the camera and says: "Pat yourself on the back and be glad you're done." After sixty minutes of squats and crunches, a little self-aggrandizement is in order. The same is true after you leave the stage. Don't be so quick to say, "I blew it," or endlessly nitpick the minutia of the presentation. Put a stop to the mind-set of *Well, if I did something, it couldn't have been that good or significant.*

An important aspect of patting yourself on the back is accepting praise when it is given. It shows respect to the person who offers it and sends a signal to other women who are watching. CEO Bloomfield says she has learned to accept praise in stages. "When I was younger, my reaction to compliments was to turn them into a joke like, I'm just glad I didn't fall off the stage.... When I got a little older, I would go overboard in giving credit to everyone else involved, which was an overreaction to seeing people who never shared credit. But now I've learned to acknowledge approval more gracefully."[30]

The ability to give yourself credit when it is due is especially critical if you find yourself in the unfortunate situation where accomplishments go unnoticed. It can be extremely demotivating to work for a boss who doesn't acknowledge your contributions. There isn't much you can do about the bad leadership except to resolve to work around it. Make sure to be your own self-validator. But still ask colleagues for feedback, join a networking group, and keep your eyes open for someone else who could be your mentor.

From her years in Washington politics, Ann Lewis has seen the genders handle praise very differently. When men receive public accreditation, they go back to their office and spend half their time on the phone telling their friends how well they did. When women do something significant, they go back to the desk and ask themselves, What can I do next? Lewis says women need to be a little more like Tarzan. When Tarzan successfully fought off the lion in the jungle, he pounded his chest and roared. Women need to do a little more chest pounding.

FINDING INSPIRATION

In November 2007, Hillary Clinton returned to her alma mater, Wellesley College, to launch Hillblazers—college students who would mobilize for her campaign. Forty years earlier, Clinton had been selected by her classmates to deliver the first-ever student commencement address at the school. Upon her return as a US senator and presidential candidate, she paid tribute to the school by saying, "In so many ways, this all-women's college prepared me to compete in the all-boys club of presidential politics."[31] She also shared that after her first month of classes as a freshman, she didn't think she could cut it at Wellesley. Her worst fears about traveling east to college from the Midwest were confirmed when she met her worldly-wise classmates who spoke multiple languages. When her French teacher told her, "Mademoiselle, your talents lie elsewhere," she called home ready to pack her bags. But her mother, who had never had the opportunity to attend college, would hear nothing of her quitting.

Throughout the lengthy and often heated campaign, perseverance was a theme Clinton revisited by speaking of the endurance exhibited by the pioneers in the fight for the women's vote. She described the suffragists as emblematic of the many Americans who rise to face challenges and remain faithful to the values of opportunity and equality for all. At the Democratic National Convention, Clinton ended her historic bid with what many commentators considered her best speech, so far. In that address, she honored the spirit of those who have persevered by acknowledging that it took many people united behind her candidacy to put eighteen million cracks in the glass ceiling.

> I'm a United States Senator because in 1848 a group of courageous women and a few brave men gathered in Seneca Falls, New York, many traveling for days and nights, to participate in the first convention on women's rights in our history. And so dawned a struggle for the right to vote that would last 72 years, handed down by mother to daughter to granddaughter—and a few sons and grandsons along the way.
>
> These women and men looked into their daughters' eyes, imagined a fairer and freer world, and found the strength to fight. To rally and picket. To endure ridicule and harassment. To brave violence and jail.
>
> And after so many decades—88 years ago on this very day—the Nineteenth Amendment guaranteeing women the right to vote would be forever enshrined in our Constitution. My mother was born before women could vote. But in this election, my daughter got to vote for her mother for president.
>
> This is the story of America. Of women and men who defy the odds and never give up.[32]

Don't allow a setback or stumble to prevent you from keeping at it. Think of yourself as Dorothy and her companions as they journeyed down the yellow brick road. Upon arriving in Emerald City, they were initially hesitant to seek an audience with the almighty Wizard of Oz. They didn't feel worthy until Toto pulled back a curtain to reveal that the wizard wasn't a wizard at all. The great Oz was a man with a noisy contraption. With the wizard unmasked, Dorothy's entourage realized that each already had what they had sought all long. The Lion was courageous, the Tin Man had a warm heart, the Scarecrow had a brain, and the ruby-red slippers were all Dorothy needed to go home. They didn't need validation from a wizard in the form of a ribbon, medal, or diploma. And neither do you need a magical wand or witch's broom to become well-spoken.

STANDING OVATION POINT: WELL-SPOKEN WOMEN HAVE NO LIMITS

Since her days as an undergraduate at Wellesley, Hillary Clinton has believed that "politics is about making the impossible—possible."[33] As secretary of state, Hillary Clinton has made the progress of women the heart of US foreign policy. Speaking at the United Nations Commission on the Status of Women in March 2010, Clinton stated that "the world cannot make lasting progress if women and girls in the twenty-first century are denied their rights and left behind."[34] The speech was heard by hundreds of women and a smattering of men as the seats at the UN headquarters that typically are occupied by navy pinstripes were filled with women in brightly colored power suits and vividly patterned traditional dresses and head wraps. Clinton used the occasion to mark the anniversary of the speech on women's rights she had given fifteen years earlier in China.

> In 1995, in one voice, the world declared human rights are women's rights and women's rights are human rights. And for many, those words have translated into concrete actions. But, for others they remain a distant aspiration. Change on a global scale cannot and does not happen overnight. It takes time, patience, and persistence. And as hard as we have

worked these past fifteen years, we have more work to do. So today, let us renew our commitment to finishing the job. And let us intensify our efforts because it is both the right thing to do and it is the smart thing as well. We must declare with one voice that women's progress is human progress, and human progress is women's progress, once and for all.[35]

The remarks did not create much media buzz, even though they were spoken in New York City, the nation's media center. There weren't any big headlines, nor were they the subject of cable news chatter. There was no mention of the event on the evening newscasts. But for those gathered in the auditorium, the speech had a resounding impact. The assemblage of diplomats, UN officials, and representatives from women's organizations around the world paid tribute to the woman who has brought voice to the cause of women for decades. When the speech was concluded, the room broke into applause. Once again, Clinton had earned a standing ovation.

Applause Principles: The Well-Spoken Sisterhood

- Set a positive tone by graciously accepting praise and complimenting the accomplishments of other women in the room.
- Don't get tricked into thinking that the goal is to be one of the boys. You win when you bring your best self.
- Be proactive in reaching out to the women around you. Don't allow competitiveness to leave you stranded. There is strength in solidarity.
- Seek guidance from mentors and professionals. Invest time, resources, and energy in skill development and personal growth.
- Give yourself a high-five when you deliver a rock 'em, sock 'em performance.

EPILOGUE

Hopefully you agree that well-spoken women are awesome and now feel inspired to try something you might not have done before. This book has been about capturing the essence of well-spoken women, from Tina Fey to Ann Richards and Maya Angelou to Melinda Gates, to help you improve your speaking ability. The intent has been to define the characteristics and practices of accomplished presenters to provide you with a practical guide to speaking success. As the case studies have revealed, a well-spoken woman is not simply a charismatic personality, although charisma plays a part. Rather, she dedicates herself to the task of developing a real connection with an audience by bringing her best self to the stage. The concept of the well-spoken woman's Power Persona introduced in chapter 1 is the guide to your journey of improvement.

WELL-SPOKEN POWER PERSONA

The Power Persona is the totality of a signature style, a synchronized message, and self-assuredness. The Persona is a concept of such paramount importance that you will benefit from meeting three additional amazing women who further illuminate that Persona. Dr. Jane Goodall is a conservationist who has brought the world's attention to the plight of the great apes. Dr. Goodall may be soft-spoken, but her signature style speaks volumes. Elizabeth Warren is a media-savvy financial expert who doesn't pull any punches in her advocacy against unscrupulous banking practices. On TV she delivers memorable sound bites that demystify the complexities of economics. Humanitarian Eleanor Roosevelt shared the life lesson that courage is easier than fear. Overcoming stage fright enabled the First Lady to champion the concerns of everyday Americans.

Dr. Jane Goodall: A Singular Individual

Spend an hour listening to Jane Goodall, and it feels like ten minutes have gone by. It is hard to resist the world's most famous primatologist when she returns an audience's welcome applause with the greeting she loves best. It is the one you will hear if you travel with her to the Gombe National Park in Tanzania—the call of the chimpanzee: "Who-ooo, who-oo, who-oo, who-oo, Who-oo, Who-oo, WHOO, WHOO, WHOO, WHOEEH, WHOEEH, WHOEEH, Hello!"[1] Goodall emits a big sound that captures the audience by surprise because it emanates from deep within a tiny frame. The petite scientist nails the full range of the ape's cry from the low resonance of the "who-ooo" to the high-pitched screech of the "WHOEEH." But, what else would you expect from someone who has learned and lived the language of the chimpanzee?

At the age of twenty-three, Goodall traveled alone to East Africa to pursue her passion of studying animals. There was no money for college, so her mother suggested she try to get a job as a secretary on the continent. Anthropologist Louis Leakey gave her a shot at following her dreams when she showed up on his doorstep. After fifty years of research, Goodall says she left the forest to inspire young people to become conservationists. As the researcher travels constantly to talk about the loss of wild places and the lack of clean water and air, she radiates the quiet, reassuring calm of a Zen master. In her soft yet crisp British accent, she explains how her latest endeavor, Roots and Shoots, is mobilizing the next generation to lay down the roots of a strong foundation to solve looming environmental problems. She believes that young people are like fragile shoots with the strength to break through concrete to reach sunlight.

When Goodall speaks about the public awareness campaign, she reinforces her message with simple props that convey her playfulness and seriousness. A fluffy monkey toy adorns the lecterns from which she speaks. In her pockets she carries mementos such as a piece of limestone from the prison on Robbins Island where Nelson Mandela was held captive. The rock reminds her of the resiliency of the human spirit. To close her presentation, she rings a tiny bell. The bell was made from metal salvaged from a defused land mine that was removed from the killing fields in Cambodia.

The bell represents the crumbling of Pol Pot's evil regime. Goodall concludes by expressing her faith in the indomitable spirit of humans to find solutions and in nature's resiliency and ability to bounce back.

Elizabeth Warren: Message Maven

In May 2010, *Time* magazine named Elizabeth Warren along with two other women the "New Sheriffs of Wall Street" for their "willingness to break ranks and challenge the status quo" as they tell "Wall Street how to clean up its act." Warren, who serves as the special adviser to the Consumer Financial Protection Bureau (CFPB), was singled out for her efforts to protect investors and consumers against what she calls the "tricks and traps" that banks hide in credit card agreements and mortgages. According to Warren, the titans of Wall Street have created an "ever more dangerous" economy that has resulted in an unheard number of Americans facing ruin.[2]

A former Harvard professor specializing in bankruptcy and consumer law, Warren is an unlikely media sensation with her closely cropped blonde hair and sensible turtlenecks. But her laserlike focus on championing the middle class is so powerfully appealing that it led Jon Stewart to good-naturedly tease during a *Daily Show* interview that the way she says things makes him want to "make out" with her even though her husband is waiting backstage. Warren wears her concern for the stability of the economy on her sleeve as she explains that the American middle class has been "hacked at, chipped at, and pulled on for the past thirty years."[3] Born in Oklahoma, Warren says she has worried about money since the time she was a child. In an interview in *Newsweek*, she recalled that "[w]hen she was sick, her mother would weigh her temperature against the amount the family owed the doctor before deciding whether to take her in."[4] It was a debate scholarship that enabled her to attend college, and she then graduated from Rutgers Law School.

The professor discovered her true calling was not in academia but as an advocate during a taping of the *Dr. Phil Show*. In response to a question about a family that was considering putting a second mortgage on their house, she advised against the idea because it would put them at risk for foreclosure. After the program taping concluded, she thought to herself:

I've been doing scholarly work for more than 20 years, and I may have just done more good in the last 90 seconds than I ever accomplished with anything I wrote.... I began to think that instead of writing one more thing to impress other academics or to reassure myself that I'm a serious scholar, I should [focus] on the question of change, of real impact, of how to be helpful.[5]

Not everyone cheered when Warren's selection to head the CFPB was announced. Verbal barbs were hurled at her, claiming she was unnecessarily biased against Wall Street and would create rules and regulations that would tighten credit and reduce profits. Those who disagree with her vision of protecting the consumer from fraud and abuse should take note. Warren is the rare policy expert who can provide in media sound-bite time a cogent description of the boom-and-bust cycle of the banking system dating back to the time of the Revolutionary War. Her ability to speak plainly and passionately on Dr. Phil's show and before congressional oversight panels bodes well for consumers who seek a financial watchdog.

Eleanor Roosevelt: Freedom Is Exhilarating

Eleanor Roosevelt was a niece of President Theodore Roosevelt; she married a distant cousin, Franklin, who later became president himself. Although born to a life of wealth and privilege, Eleanor had little self-confidence. In fact, she struggled for decades to find her groove. Orphaned at the age of ten by the passing of her alcoholic father and beautiful society mother, who had expressed disappointment in Eleanor's looks, she was raised by a strict Victorian grandmother. Roosevelt described herself as an extraordinarily timid child crippled by the fear of everything, including public speaking. A reluctant debutante, Roosevelt loved to read and would have preferred to attend college rather than the society balls that were de rigueur for the daughters of New York's upper class.

Even after her marriage and the birth of her children, Eleanor considered herself unworthy and felt homely. In her book *You Learn by Living*, she shared an episode from a Washington dinner party that summed up her feelings of inferiority. Husband Franklin was serving as the assistant secretary of the navy, a position that required active participation in the busy social scene. At events, people were drawn to Franklin's charms while Eleanor often stood to the side, tongue-tied and self-conscious. On one particularly miserable evening, she concluded that no one would notice if she left. Arriving at the front door of her home, she didn't have a key to get in. Rather than return to the party, she waited outside in the cold for three hours, sitting on the doormat in her evening dress.

Roosevelt was gradually propelled into public life as her husband's profile rose, and she wrote that she ultimately overcame her fears by doing what she didn't think was possible.

> In doing it you not only free yourself from some shackling fear but you stretch your mental muscles and gain the freedom that comes with achievement. Every time you meet a crisis and live through it, you make it simple for the next time.[6]

The ordeal and anguish of public speaking was tackled step-by-step. Her anxiety manifested in "a bad habit of laughing when there was nothing to laugh at."[7] With the help of an aide and vocal coaches, she learned to control her pitch and bit by bit gained confidence. Roosevelt wrote that it took great effort, but she gradually learned that

> [c]ourage is more exhilarating than fear and in the long run it is easier. We do not have to become heroes overnight. Just one step at a time, meeting each thing that comes up, seeing it is not as dreadful as it appeared, discovering we have the strength to stare it down.[8]

Roosevelt employed the belief that "no one can make you feel inferior without your consent."[9]

During the Great Depression, Roosevelt traveled across America to see firsthand the impact and devastation wrought on families. At the time, this type of trip was unheard of for a First Lady, and some considered it unladylike and a betrayal of her class. But Roosevelt wanted to meet unemployed coal miners, factory workers, and destitute farmers so she could report back on the conditions she witnessed to the president. After Franklin died, Eleanor accepted President Truman's invitation to serve as the lone woman member of the delegation to the newly created United Nations. As the chair of the human rights commission, she helped draft the Universal Declaration of Human Rights to ensure the fair and humane treatment of people by their governments.

Biographer Blanche Wiesen Cook wrote: "ER's gifts as a speaker were ultimately the result of her great love for people. Because she cared about the audience, she knew that it mattered to make eye contact directly with everybody in the room."[10] Once she had slain the dragon of fear, Roosevelt grew to be an admired figure respected worldwide for her humanitarian efforts. The woman who didn't like to talk held regular press conferences as First Lady. She stipulated that male reporters were banned from covering the events so that news organizations would need to hire women reporters. Of the thousands and thousands of letters that poured in until the end of her life, some of the most rewarding must have been the ones written by women seeking her guidance on public speaking.

Well-spoken women Jane Goodall, Elizabeth Warren, and Eleanor Roosevelt have demonstrated the right stuff when it comes to speaking out for those without a voice. Propelled by drive and conviction, these women took risks to enlighten the public about the plight of all who inhabit the planet. The naysayers and critics could not sidetrack them from their focus on matters of principle. Such well-spoken women show us the way.

RISING VOICES

Who are the well-spoken voices of the future? Where will they come from? Will they earn graduate degrees, run for office, direct large organizations? The social-media world is providing new venues for women's voices to have influence. Sheryl Sandberg wants to be your "friend" as she holds court in a fabulous red sheath dress for a *Vogue* photo shoot and finesses questions at techie conferences in Silicon Valley. Sandberg, who was hired away from Google to take Facebook to the next level, says her business is "all about people."[11] Without a shred of cyber-geekness, the energetic and approachable Sandberg is taking the lead in addressing the privacy concerns surrounding the largest social-networking site in the cosmos.

Poised beyond her twenty-two years, Katie Spotz calmly explained to Diane Sawyer that crossing the Atlantic Ocean alone in a rowboat taught her to be "patient, open, and accepting of the forces beyond your control."[12] The world's youngest rower to complete the solo voyage raised money for The Blue Planet Run Foundation, a nonprofit whose goal is to bring clean drinking water to the one billion people who lack it. Shortly after the trip, which took 70 days to cross 2,800 miles of open seas from South America to Africa, Spotz was already contemplating her next adventure.

What is next for Chelsea Clinton, Meghan McCain, Bristol Palin, Barbara and Jenna Bush, and Malia and Sasha Obama? The Obama girls may need to graduate from high school before they contribute to a political dynasty. In South Carolina, Nikki Haley shook up the old boys' network when, at the age of thirty-eight, she was elected the state's first woman governor. There were only a handful of women serving in Congress when Ellen Malcolm founded a political organization with the funny name of EMILY'S List twenty-five years ago. In 2010, when Malcolm turned the reins of power over to new leadership, a record number of women were serving. Stephanie Schriock now heads the fund-raising powerhouse committed to electing progressive women.

A new generation of activists has supplemented the banners and picket signs of the suffragists with blogs and tweets to mobilize young women across the political spectrum. Jessica Valenti founded the website Feministing.com in 2004 "to better connect feminists online and off." Across the partisan divide, Karin Agness's Network of Enlightened Women is, as one member shared, "an organization of intellectual women that went to a shooting range last week, is hosting a traditional tea party next week, and will host a Health Care Roundtable next month." Another online voice who also speaks the old-fashioned way is Morgane Richardson, founder of Refuse the Silence: Women of Color in Academia Speak Out. Richardson advocates on behalf of women of color who are navigating the issues of race, class, and gender on college campuses.

These Generation X and Y women are a small sample of the emerging voices that will continue to shape the business, cultural, and political landscape as the boomers retire. These women and their families are playing a role in determining what lies ahead for all of us. The generation Y'ers have the added distinction of having grown up with access to cell phones, instant messaging, and the Internet, and as a result they are likely to be nimble users of new technologies. This familiarity with the virtual world provides them with more channels to speak out in service to their communities, causes, and country.

As the digital age of communications continues to expand, so, too, will the diversity and numbers of women presenters. The richness of their life experiences will enrich our public dialogue with valuable insights and innovative ideas. As more women seize new opportunities, they can contribute while knowing that they have been well served by the well-spoken women who came before them.

THE WELL-SPOKEN WOMEN UP CLOSE AND PERSONAL

Ann Richards

Born:	September 1, 1933, Lakeview, Texas
Died:	September 13, 2006, esophageal cancer
Birth Name:	Dorothy Ann Willis
Education:	BA, Baylor University
Family:	Divorced, four children
Hardest Job:	Public schoolteacher, Fulmore Junior High, Austin, Texas
Accomplishment:	Created the "New Texas," opening state government to more women and minorities than any previous governor
Legacy:	Ann Richards School for Young Women Leaders
Speech Collection:	Ann W. Richards Papers at the University of Texas at Austin

Indra Nooyi

Born:	October 18, 1955, Chennai, India
Birth Name:	Indra Krishnamurthy
Education:	BA, Madras Christian College
	MA, Indian Institute of Management, Calcutta
	MA, Yale School of Management
Family:	Married, two daughters
Formative Training:	Studied Chicago Bulls videos to learn about teamwork
Interest:	Expert on New York Yankees statistics

Recognition: 2010 #1 on *Fortune*'s List of 50 Most Powerful Women, #6 on *Forbes*'s List of 100 World's Most Powerful Women

Barbara Jordan

Born: February 21, 1936, Houston, Texas

Died: January 17, 1996, complications of leukemia and multiple sclerosis

Birth Name: Barbara Charline Jordan

Education: BA, Texas Southern University
JD, Boston University School of Law

Family: Youngest of three sisters

Recognition: Presidential Medal of Freedom, Barbara Jordan Statue at the University of Texas at Austin

Legacy: Barbara Jordan Freedom Foundation, Barbara Jordan High School for Careers

Speech Collection: *Barbara Jordan: Speaking the Truth with Eloquent Thunder*, edited by Max Sherman (Austin: University of Texas Press, 2007)

Pat Summitt

Born: June 14, 1952, Clarksville, Tennessee

Birth Name: Patricia Sue Head

Education: BA, University of Tennessee–Martin

Family: Divorced, one son

Nickname: Bone

Childhood: As a baby was raised in a two-room log cabin

Accomplishments: 1975 Olympic silver medalist, coached US women to Olympic gold in 1984, eight NCAA championships, seven times NCAA Coach of the Year, Naismith Coach of the Century, 2000 Basketball Hall of Fame inductee

Legacy: Created cradle of coaches, with nearly one-third of all players becoming coaches from youth leagues to the pros

Melinda Gates

Born:	August 15, 1964, Dallas, Texas
Birth Name:	Melinda Ann French
Education:	BA, Duke University
	MBA, Duke University
Family:	Married, three children
Household Ban:	iPhones® and iPads®
Interest:	Distance runner
Recognition:	*Time* magazine Person of the Year along with husband for "giving away more money than anyone ever has"
Legacy:	Bill and Melinda Gates Foundation

Elizabeth Dole

Born:	July 29, 1936, Salisbury, North Carolina
Birth Name:	Mary Elizabeth Hanford
Education:	Duke University
	MA, Harvard School of Education
	JD, Harvard Law School
	University of Oxford
Family:	Married, stepdaughter
Nicknames:	Steel Magnolia and Sugar Lips
Career:	First woman to serve as the president of the American Red Cross since it was founded by Clara Barton in 1881
Recognition:	1995 Raoul Wallenburg Award for Humanitarian Service, 1994 League of Women Voters Leadership Award, Churchwoman of the Year by Religious Heritage of America, North Carolinian of the Year

Maya Angelou

Born:	April 4, 1928, Saint Louis, Missouri
Birth Name:	Marguerite Ann Johnson
Education:	High school graduate

	Self-taught Arabic, Fanti, French, Italian, Spanish
Family:	Divorced, one son
Recognition:	Presidential Medal of Freedom, Presidential Medal of Arts, Reynolds Professor of American Studies at Wake Forest University, thirty honorary degrees
Accomplishments:	Thirty-one books, including a cookbook; three Grammy Awards for spoken-word albums; nominated for a Pulitzer Prize for the film *Georgia, Georgia*
Papers:	The Schomberg Center for Research in Black Culture

Suze Orman

Born:	June 5, 1951, Chicago, Illinois
Birth Name:	Susan Lynn Orman
Education:	BA, University of Illinois at Urbana-Champaign
Family:	Partner Kathy Travis
Early Job:	Waited tables until she was in her thirties
Recognition:	2010 *Forbes*'s "World's 100 Most Powerful Women," 2009, *Time* magazine "The World's Most Influential People," seven Gracie Allen Awards for cable show, two Emmys for PBS specials
Accomplishments:	Single most successful fund-raiser in the history of PBS, authored six *New York Times* bestsellers, host of MSNBC cable show and QVC's *Financial Freedom Hour*

Madeleine Albright

Born:	May 15, 1937, Prague, Czechoslovakia
Birth Name:	Maria Jana Korbelova
Education:	BA, Wellesley College
	MA, PhD, Columbia University
Family:	Divorced, three daughters
Early Job:	Babysat for twenty-five cents an hour
Early Ambition:	Journalist, copy girl at the *Denver Post*
Career Path:	Chief legislative assistant to Senator Edmund Muskie,

member National Security Council, president of the Center for National Policy, US Representative to United Nations, secretary of state, chair of the Albright Stonebridge Group, chair of Albright Capital Management LLC

Legacy: The Madeleine Korbel Albright Institute for Global Affairs at Wellesley College

Hillary Clinton

Born: October 26, 1947, Chicago, Illinois

Birth Name: Hillary Diane Rodham

Education: BA, Wellesley College
JD, Yale Law School

Family: Married, one daughter

Early Job: Gutted salmon in Alaskan factory

Political History: Young Republican who campaigned for Barry Goldwater

Career Path: Wellesley College valedictorian, attorney, child advocate, First Lady of Arkansas, First Lady of United States, US senator, presidential candidate, secretary of state

Appendix 2

AMERICA'S WELL-SPOKEN WOMEN: A SPEECH TIMELINE

The words of women have power and make history. Yet the women who've used words to defend, heal, instruct, champion, and energize have not always been given the recognition they deserve. The speech collections that include women tend to focus on a narrow list of the most famous. An example is the compilation by former presidential speechwriter and columnist for the *New York Times* William Safire. He described his one-thousand-page volume of speeches as "history's outstanding instances of oratorical eloquence." The book contained two hundred speeches, a mere thirteen of which were given by women. Five years later, when the "instant classic" was revised and expanded, the percentage of women decreased!

The Well-Spoken Women's Timeline helps set the record straight and will serve as a useful reference to inspiring moments and significant achievements. The collection reminds us of the resolve to be heard, even when doing so was an act of extreme bravery. In colonial America, Mary Dyer's insistence on articulating her Quaker faith led to her execution by hanging. A contemporary of Dyer's named Anne Hutchinson was also persecuted for preaching her faith. Hutchinson was a Bible study leader and a member of the Massachusetts Bay Colony until she was tried in a legal court for teaching men in public. Banished from the colony, Hutchinson and her family were later killed in an Indian raid.

A gap of more than 150 years exists between those deaths and the first Women's Rights Convention held in Seneca Falls, New York, in 1848. From that point on, women en masse took to the stage and the streets with gusto. During the late nineteenth century, thousands organized on the state and federal levels for equal rights and social and labor reforms, sometimes facing angry, abusive audiences. The hatchet-wielding Carrie Nation was prepared for the resistance she encountered with her anti-alcohol campaign. The temperance movement leader used the hatchet to smash liquor barrels and paid her legal fines with money earned from lecturing. She also sold tiny hatchet lapel pins.

American's first black woman millionaire was a crusading mogul. Madam C. J. Walker, who developed, manufactured, and marketed a hair tonic for African American women, gave back to her community through economic empowerment programs and antilynching campaigns. Mary Parker Follett was one of the first recognized experts to speak on management theory and labor relations. Throughout the twentieth century, women spoke out on environmental conservation, international affairs, scientific discoveries, workplace issues, and civil rights. It has been forty years since Phyllis Schlafly emerged to disparage Gloria Steinem and the second wave of the women's movement. Honored with the Congressional Medal of Freedom, movie star Audrey Hepburn was the forerunner celebrity humanitarian to Mia Farrow and Angelina Jolie. Each of the featured women in this timeline opens a window on a unique perspective on the topics, questions, and challenges that have shaped our lives.

WELL-SPOKEN WOMEN THEN AND NOW

1637	Anne Hutchinson, prayer meeting leader
Massachusetts Bay Colony	Condemned for asserting leadership in the Boston Church
June 1, 1660	Mary Dyer, Quaker preacher
Boston, Massachusetts	Hung for refusing to renounce her faith
March 1802	Deborah Sampson, Revolutionary War soldier
Boston, Massachusetts	"Address, Delivered with Applause"

July 4, 1828 New Harmony, Indiana	Frances Wright, social reformer Independence Day address on patriotism
September 21, 1832 Boston, Massachusetts	Frances M. Stewart, education advocate First public lecture by African American woman. Stewart never spoke publicly again.
May 16, 1838 Philadelphia, Pennsylvania	Angelina E. Grimke, abolitionist "What Has the North to Do with Slavery?"
July 19–20, 1848 Seneca Falls, New York	Lucretia Mott, Women's Rights Convention organizer Opening and closing remarks
May 29, 1851 Akron, Ohio	Sojourner Truth, former slave Women's Rights Convention, "Ain't I a Woman?"
1853 South Butler, New York	Antoinette Brown Blackwell, first ordained minister Participated in religious services at the age of nine
February 8, 1858 Orange, New Jersey	Lucy Stone, first full-time lecturer on suffrage "Taxation without Representation"
1864 Washington, DC	Anna Dickinson, twenty-one-year-old antislavery activist First woman to address US Congress. President Abraham Lincoln is in the audience.

February 16, 1871 Washington, DC	Victoria Woodhull, first woman presidential candidate "Constitutional Equality"
1872–1873 New York	Susan B. Anthony, first woman honored on US currency Speaks in twenty-nine Post Office Districts after her arrest for voting
1882 Saratoga, New York	Clara Barton, American Red Cross founder American Social Science Association, "History of War"
January 18, 1892 Washington, DC	Elizabeth Cady Stanton, writer and political strategist US Congress Judiciary Committee, "Solitude of Self"
1893 Chicago, Illinois	Anna Howard Shaw, physician and minister "The Fate of Republics"
January 1900 Chicago, Illinois	Ida B. Wells-Barnett, journalist and daughter of slaves "Lynch Law in America"
January 16, 1906 Washington, DC	Belva Lockwood, attorney First woman to argue before the US Supreme Court; wins $5 million settle- ment for the Cherokee Nation
February 23, 1906 Chicago, Illinois	Jane Addams, first American woman to receive Nobel Peace Prize Pays tribute to first US president, George Washington

October 10, 1906 Washington, DC	Mary Church Terrell, social justice activist "What It Means to Be Colored in Capital of US"
June 1911 Eureka Springs, Arkansas	Carrie Nation, antialcohol crusader Collapses on stage and later dies
June 13, 1911 Stockholm, Sweden	Carrie Chapman Catt, fought for Nineteenth Amendment "Is Woman Suffrage Progressing?"
August 15, 1912 Charleston, West Virginia	Mother Jones, labor activist "Appeal to the Cause of Miners in the Paint Creek"
March 13, 1913 Washington, DC	Inez Miholland, suffrage orator and attorney Dresses as Joan of Arc and, riding white horse, leads massive suffrage parade
April 1917 Washington, DC	Rep. Jeanette Rankin, first woman elected to Congress Brief speech in vote against World War I
July 9, 1917 New York, New York	Emma Goldman, queen of the anarchists "Address to the Jury," trial for antiwar activities
August 1917 Philadelphia, Pennsylvania	Madam C. J. Walker, entrepreneur "Woman's Duty to Woman" keynote at Beauty Culturists Union convention
May 14, 1921 Vassar College, New York	Marie Currie, physicist and chemist "On the Discovery of Radium"

November 18, 1921 Park Theater, New York	Margaret Sanger, founder American Birth Control League "The Morality of Birth Control"
June 30, 1925 Cedar Point, Ohio	Helen Keller, first deaf-blind person to earn BA degree Lion's Club International, campaign against blindness
January 1933 London, England	Mary Parker Follett, management guru Speaks on management theory at London School of Economics
June 30, 1933 Chicago, Illinois	Mary McLeod Bethune, civil rights activist "A Century of Progress of Negro Women"
December 9, 1948 New York, New York	Eleanor Roosevelt, United Nations delegate "Adoption of Declaration of Human Rights"
June 1, 1950 Washington, DC	Margaret Chase Smith, US senator "Declaration of Conscience"
February 2, 1953 New York, New York	Elizabeth Gurley Flynn, labor leader Statement at the Smith Act Trial to refute allegations of advocating govern- ment overthrow
April 21, 1954 Columbus, Ohio	Rachel Carson, marine biologist and environmentalist "Exceeding Beauty of the Earth"

1964 San Francisco, California	Betty Friedan, feminist and author "The Crisis in Women's Identity"
April 1966 Sacramento, California	Dolores Huerta, National Farm Workers Association founder Rallied for worker's rights
April 1968 Memphis, Tennessee	Coretta Scott King, civil rights activist Marched on Memphis following husband's assassination
November 12, 1969 Oakland, California	Angela Davis, Black Panther activist Protests against racial inequality and Vietnam War
August 10, 1970 Washington, DC	Shirley Chisholm, US Representative "For the Equal Rights Amendment"
September 23, 1971 Cambridge, Massachusetts	Gloria Steinem, feminist "Why Harvard Law School Needs Women More Than Women Need It"
February 1972 Washington, DC	Phyllis Schlafly, founder Eagle Forum Launches the Stop E.R.A. campaign
July 25, 1974 Washington, DC	Barbara Jordan, US Representative Presents case for impeachment of President Nixon
November 18, 1977 Houston, Texas	Bella Abzug, US Representative Presides over National Women's Conference

January 1980 Long Beach, California	Beverly LaHaye, Concerned Women for America founder American Pro-Family Conference for Christian Right
September 6, 1983 New York, New York	Jeanne Kirkpatrick, US ambassador to the United Nations Condemns Soviet Union aggression.
December 26, 1983 Kobe, Japan	Samantha Smith, eleven-year-old "Ambassador of Peace" "Look Around and See Only Friends"
July 19, 1984 San Francisco, California	Geraldine Ferraro, US Representative Accepts vice-presidential nomination
February 1986 Cambridge, Massachusetts	Mary Kay Ash, cosmetics mogul Addresses Harvard University students
1988 New York, New York	Audrey Hepburn, Goodwill Ambassador Launches UNICEF tour
July 19, 1988 Atlanta, Georgia	Ann Richards, Texas State Treasurer Democratic National Convention keynoter
October 11, 1991 Washington, DC	Anita Hill, professor Testimony at Clarence Thomas sexual harassment hearing
August 1992 Waterville Valley, New Hampshire	Orit Gadiesh, Bain & Co. vice chair "True North: Pride at Bain & Co."

August 19, 1992 Houston, Texas	Mary Fisher, activist "A Whisper of AIDs"
September 25, 1992 Washington, DC	Bernadine Healy, National Institutes of Health director "Diversity in the Scientific and Techno- logical Workforce"
January 19, 1993 Washington, DC	Maya Angelou Presidential inauguration poem, "On the Pulse of Morning"
April 2, 1993 Sweet Briar, Virginia	Wilma Mankiller, Cherokee Nation chief "Rebuilding the Cherokee Nation"
December 8, 1992 Stockholm, Sweden	Toni Morrison, Nobel Prize in Literature recipient Nobel lecture
May 25, 1995 Washington, DC	Kathleen Sullivan, astronaut "Challenges to the Marine Eco-System"
September 5, 1995 Beijing, China	Hillary Clinton, First Lady UN Fourth World Conference on Women
September 1995 Washington, DC	Elizabeth Birch, Human Rights Campaign Addresses Christian Coalition on gay rights
August 14, 1996 San Diego, California	Elizabeth Dole, former cabinet member Republican National Convention

July 14, 1997 Prague, Czech Republic	Madeleine Albright, secretary of state Address to the People of Prague
March 23, 1998 Geneva, Switzerland	Sister Helen Prejean, anti–death penalty activist "Hands Off Cain"
April 12, 2000 West Point, New York	Charlene Barshefsky, US trade representative "The Case of China's WTO Accession"
April 2001 Colorado	Ingrid Newkirk, PETA cofounder "Animal Rights"
January 7, 2005 Las Vegas, Nevada	Carly Fiorina, Hewlett-Packard CEO Keynote at Consumer Electronics Show
March 9, 2006 Washington, DC	Sandra Day O'Connor, retired Supreme Court justice Defends judicial independence against conservative attacks
January 4, 2007 US Capitol	Nancy Pelosi, US Representative Sworn in as first woman Speaker of the House.
March 7, 2007 Washington, DC	Condoleezza Rice, secretary of state International Women's Day, Women of Courage
October 12, 2007 Cambridge, Massachusetts	Drew Faust, Harvard University's first woman president Installation address

January 8, 2008 Manchester, New Hampshire	Hillary Clinton, first woman to win presidential primary Election night victory speech
March 24, 2008 New York, New York	Indra Nooyi, PepsiCo CEO Keynote at Catalyst Awards
September 3, 2008 Minneapolis, Minnesota	Sarah Palin, governor of Alaska Accepts vice-presidential nomination
June 9, 2009 New York, New York	Muriel Siebert, first woman to own a seat on New York Stock Exchange American Museum of Finance honors women of Wall Street
May 26, 2010 Norwalk, Connecticut	Ursula Burns, Xerox CEO First African American woman Fortune 500 CEO; keynote on technology's shifting role in business

Appendix 3

FREQUENTLY ASKED QUESTIONS

Q. I want to become well-spoken. How do I begin?

The starting point for improving your communications skills is an honest assessment of your speaking strengths and weaknesses. Use the three main components of speaking style—the three Vs of communication: vocal, visual, and verbal—to identify the techniques and practices that you have mastered as well as the areas that need work. Rate yourself on each of the elements listed below that comprise voice quality, visual style, and verbal content preparation.

	Weak	Fair	Good	Excellent
Voice Quality				
Inflection				
Conversational Pace				
Volume Control				
Resonance				
Use of Pause				
Controlled Breathing				
Visual Style				
Eye Contact				
Champion Stance				
Hand Gestures				
Upper-Body Animation				
Facial Expression				
Professional Wardrobe				
Visual Aids				

Verbal Content Prep			
Audience Research			
Event Profile			
Message Development			
Colorful Narrative			
Strong Open and Close			
Well-Designed Text or Notes			

Once you have finished rating each of the skill sets, you will have a clearer picture of what aspects of your speaking style need the most work. If several areas are relatively weak, don't try to correct them all at the same time. Focus on improving one skill or technique at a time so that you do not become overwhelmed by trying to do too much. A one-step-at-a-time approach will ensure steady progress.

Q. I'm a midcareer professional. Is it too late to start?

American folk artist Grandma Moses didn't start painting until she was seventy-six years old. It is never too late to learn a new talent or brush up on skills that may be rusty. Start by doing the self-assessment of the techniques and practices described above. Then consider: What will it take to motivate you to work on skill improvement? Is there an event coming up that could be an opportunity to shine, if you are well prepared? What resources are at your disposal? Do you have communications support staff?

If you are an experienced presenter looking to ratchet up your skills, then you may benefit from professional coaching. As you seek to move into a higher-profile position or take on larger responsibilities, don't allow inadequate skills to impede your progress. All of the Well-Spoken Women sought the assistance of experts to hone their skills. Ask a colleague to refer a speech coach or media trainer. There may be classes available at a local university or adult extension program. Toastmasters workshops are another good option.

The best way to accurately assess how you currently come across is by videotaping yourself in front of an audience. With the live audience, you get a sense of your ability to interact and respond in the moment. If that is not possible, then tape yourself rehearsing a presentation. Seek feedback from a respected colleague, mentor, or coach.

Q. Do I have to radically change my appearance to be taken seriously?

No. At some point everyone has felt too something—awkward, inexperienced, nerdy, pale, soft-spoken, young, different—to fit in. Wardrobe choices don't provide the complete answer, although you can wear glasses to look older or conservative clothes to blend in. A neutral, professional appearance may help you feel more secure. Ultimately, a presenter feels comfortable in her own skin when she is jazzed up about what she is going to say and has put the requisite effort into preparing the content.

Given the reality that audiences focus on a woman's appearance more intently than a man's, it is smart to ensure your look doesn't stand in the way of being viewed credibly. Remember the advice to quickly turn and look at yourself in the mirror before walking out the door. If something distracts attention away from your face, remove it. I worked with a candidate running for state attorney general who insisted on wearing a peace-sign necklace while campaigning. Was it the reason she lost the race? No. Was it the best accessory for televised forums where government corruption and drug laws were the topics of discussion? No.

A colleague shared a story about testifying with a co-worker before a congressional committee that was considering significant reform legislation that would directly affect the industry she represented. After the hearing was concluded, the co-worker was approached by several people who told her: "You did great, you did great. It went really well." To which she responded: "Well, that's good, but how did I look?" When appearance is a secondary issue, the chances are your message was heard loud and clear.

Q. I've heard that women shouldn't use self-deprecating humor because it undermines credibility. Is that the case?

Comedian Joan Rivers, the queen of self-deprecating humor, has entertained audiences for forty years. As a pioneer in show business, Rivers was willing to talk about plastic surgery, abortion, her love life—nothing was out of bounds. There are downsides to making a joke at your own expense. The foulmouthed approach used by Rivers would likely get you fired. It can also cause the people who are predisposed to question your abilities to do just that. Ask yourself: Do you really want to emphasize a shortcoming?

At the beginning of her convention address, Ann Richards provided a classic example of how self-deprecating humor can be used to connect with the audience.

> You know tonight I feel a little like I did when I played basketball in the eighth grade. I thought I looked real cute in my uniform until I heard a boy yell from the bleachers, make that basket, bird legs. And my greatest fear is that same guy is somewhere out there in the audience tonight, and he's going to cut me down to size.

The key determinant for deciding whether to use self-deprecating humor or any humor is this: Does it drive home a bigger point? Self-deprecating humor shouldn't be used as a means to extract a pity party or to fish for compliments. Richards's basketball story was a lighthearted way for her to convey that she thinks that the speech is a big deal, she is a little nervous, and she hopes the audience will be on her side. She draws the audience in by telling them she is just like them.

Q. I'm nervous about doing a virtual presentation. How can I make the new technology work for me?

Online communications is becoming commonplace, with many organizations opting to supplement meetings and conferences with webinars, videoconferences, and podcasts. Talking to remote audiences presents special challenges, as the technology can create a feeling of isolation and the lack of response can be deafening. While the format may be foreign, there is no mystery to what it takes to be effective. With competent IT support staff, you can focus on engaging the audience with an animated delivery style and a relevant message.

Make sure all participants are prepared with an agenda and the appropriate equipment that they know how to use. Avoid using a cell phone or speaker phone because the audio quality is usually weak. Speak into a headset or landline phone. It is imperative that you do a test run beforehand to work out any kinks. If the technology malfunctions during the presentation, be ready with a plan B. Is it possible to continue the meeting with a conference call? Can you follow up via e-mail?

Use the on-camera delivery techniques outlined in chapter 8 for how to sit, where to look, and what to wear. Talking to an online camera is the same as talking to a camera in a television studio. Use good vocal inflection and upper-body animation. Have a glass of room-temperature water handy to keep your vocal cords hydrated. Remove any objects in the background that may be distracting such as pictures, posters, and general clutter. Turn off cell phones or other devices that could create noisy distractions.

Q. How do I prepare for a panel discussion?

Panel discussions are popular and can be a good forum for showcasing expertise without having to devote a tremendous amount of time to preparation. Most panels run from an hour to ninety minutes and include a moderator with four or five panelists. Generally, you are asked to speak between five and ten minutes and then take a few questions. The moderator's job is to keep the trains running on time by giving a compelling introduction of the topic and personalized introductions for each panelist. Send the moderator your one- or two-paragraph biography in advance.

Recognize that you can't say everything there is to be said about a subject in five minutes, so plan to elaborate on one or two points. On panels with multiple presenters, be ready to ditch your full talk and give a shortened version when others run over their allotted time. Volunteer to speak first; then you get to frame the debate without worrying about running out of time. Don't be alarmed if another speaker steals your best material. Feel free to revisit the point by saying: "I want to reinforce what a previous speaker mentioned because it is so important...." During the question period, allow the other panelists to respond before you chime in again. Don't feel as if you have to respond to every question, particularly if you have nothing new to add.

Do pay attention to what is being said and avoid looking bored by staring off into space or texting messages. Eye contact should be with the audience while you are talking, not on the moderator. When responding to a question, look at the questioner. Most panels are seated, so don't slouch in the chair. Use the champion seated stance outlined in chapter 4.

Q. How can I maximize a chance encounter with someone I would like to impress? What's the best way to respond when you are unexpectedly asked to deliver a brief summary of a work project?

In situations when you have little or no time to make a big impression, the solution is a combination of the preplanned spontaneity discussed in chapter 6 and the message map from chapter 5. Avoid being caught tongue-tied in a chance encounter or flat-footed at a staff meeting by being ready with a message map. What pet projects or causes do you want to talk about? Develop a map for them. What subjects at work do you know you will be expected to address at some point? Start developing a map now, and you will be prepared when you have no notice.

The message map structure can be used to draft an "elevator speech" (two minutes in length) on any topic. Perhaps you would like to raise money for a charitable organization. With the problem, solution, call to action, and benefit structure, you can eloquently and efficiently turn an impromptu meeting into a fund-raising opportunity. Do a survey of the work projects currently on your desk. Develop maps for each topic and keep them on your computer so they are easily accessible and can be updated as needed.

Q. How can I develop my speech-writing talents?

The only way to become a speechwriter is to do it. And the only way to get good at it is to do a lot of it. Look for opportunities to get experience. One field where they abound is politics. Astonishingly, most candidates running in congressional House races do not have a good stump speech on paper. The candidate may have it in her head, but if it were written down, she would be able to improve the content and delivery more quickly. Taking on this type of assignment could be the most difficult job you will not get paid to do—at least, not at first. But this payless task will provide you with invaluable lessons.

It goes without saying that you will need a thick skin, even if you are working gratis. Keep criticism in perspective by recognizing it often comes from people who don't know the first thing about good speech writing. Be curious and open-minded. Read lots of speeches. Watch the Oscars for the acceptance speeches as well as the president's State of the Union address. When you hear a funny story or an inspiring quote, jot it down and put new life into it by recycling it.

In time you will develop your own writing style just as speakers develop a signature speaking style. Maya Angelou described the experience of writing the poem for President Clinton's inauguration ceremony as all consuming, saying: "I have a sensation that a nation is looking over my shoulder." After weeks of reading the words of scholars and listening to advice, she carried out her writing routine of sequestering herself in a hotel room with a thesaurus, bottle of sherry, playing cards, and numerous yellow legal pads. The result—in longhand—was the much-heralded "On the Pulse of Morning."

Q. I am an introvert. How can I work up the courage to speak at an office meeting?

The experts say extroverts "speak to think" while introverts "think to speak." An extrovert will start talking before she knows what she wants to say. As a result, it often takes her a while to make a point, whereas an introvert will think carefully about what she wants to say before she opens her mouth. The latter approach is excellent preparation for presentations and reduces the likelihood of a gaffe.

Introverts need to give themselves extra time to mull over what they will say before a presentation. With plenty of time to organize thoughts and practice aloud, you can keep your stress level in check. You'll also need additional time after the presentation to decompress. The act of speaking is much more draining for introverts, as more time is required to analyze what transpired and how the audience reacted. Learn to manage modesty by preparing to share something about your background, expertise, and accomplishments. As uncomfortable as it may feel, the presentation is as much about you as it is about your ideas.

Q. I have the opportunity to introduce a notable figure in my field. How can I do a stellar job?

It can be nerve-racking to prepare and deliver an introduction for someone you admire and respect. What do you leave in? What do you take out? How personal should it be? At all costs, avoid relying on clichés: "Our guest today is a speaker who needs no introduction." A long-winded recitation of the speaker's résumé and biographical background will drain the life out of the room.

A well-executed introduction sets the stage for the presenter, who will be grateful that you made an extra effort. Craft the introduction around four critical questions: What is the speaker's topic? How is the topic relevant to the audience? Why is the speaker qualified to deliver the topic? What is your relationship to the speaker? By addressing these questions, you motivate the audience to listen and reinforce the speaker's credentials.

Secretary of State Condoleezza Rice spoke of the "certain kinship" she shares with Madeleine Albright at the ceremony to unveil Albright's official portrait. Rice said if she had remained a music major, she might have ended up "playing at Nordstrom or a piano bar." It was Albright's father who "opened up a world to me that I never would have known" when she enrolled in his international politics course.[1]

If you haven't met the speaker, search the Internet. Take a minute to chat with her—what are her hobbies and passions? Ask colleagues for suggestions—perhaps they can share a humorous anecdote. Your research will ensure that the introduction conveys sincerity and authenticity. If you are unsure about the correct pronunciation of the speaker's name, ask in advance. It is amateurish to do it while you are making the introduction.

Q. What are some additional resources for viewing speeches by well-spoken women?

It is likely you can watch the women you admire online. The convention speeches by Ann Richards, Barbara Jordan, Sarah Palin, Elizabeth Dole, and Hillary Clinton are all available. YouTube.com is an excellent source for interviews and short talks with women in business, the nonprofit sector, and government.

A website that features "riveting talks by remarkable people" is TED.com. The presenters at TED conferences have twenty minutes to share their "ideas worth spreading" on technology, global issues, entertainment, science, and a host of other themes. Melinda Gates, Amy Tan, Eve Ensler, Anna Deavere Smith, Temple Grandin, and Doris Kearns Goodwin are among the many featured women.

The Iowa State University Carrie Chapman Catt Center for Women and Politics (http://www.las.iastate.edu/cattcenter/) has an online archive of women's political communication. It contains a virtual collection of political speech texts and a videotape collection of political campaign commercials.

ACKNOWLEDGMENTS

Lucy Stone, who was the first and for many years the only woman in America to campaign full-time for women's rights, inspired this book. Nothing could stop "Locomotive Lucy." When doused with cold water midspeech, Stone picked up her shawl and finished the talk. When spattered with egg, she challenged the listeners to rid their minds of her spoken truths as easily as she wiped away the sticky mess. When confronted with skepticism and anger, she disarmed her detractors with a well-reasoned argument and good humor. Stone's courageous determination to devote her life to "speak for the women" makes her the well-spoken woman's woman.

The insight and advice of kind and talented people sustained this effort. There is no one happier that it is finished than my husband, Paul Hagen, who provided tons of editing suggestions. His unconditional emotional support was there even when he had other demands on his time, which was nearly every day for two years. My friend Sacha Millstone is a special person with the ability to believe in you more than you believe in yourself and the willingness to tirelessly tell you so. Sacha is the ultimate connector who links people with ideas to those who can get the job done. My sister, Lisa Hanson, is a reality touchstone. There aren't many who will repeatedly give you a diplomatic but honest response to the question "Is this stupid, or what?"

Barbara Lee is an extraordinary woman who has devoted herself to lifting up all women through her support for the arts and her commitment to social justice. Barbara and I have a shared passion for electing the first woman president. Gloria Steinem has so much to teach us all. I am grateful for her generosity, and the mere thought of her committing outrageous acts and fomenting everyday rebellion brings a smile. Ann Richards liked to say, "You dance with the one that brung 'ya," and Jane Danowitz of the Women's Campaign Fund provided me with an early home in the women's community in Washington, DC.

Kersti Frigell is a Boulder, Colorado-based artist who created the well-spoken women portraits and illustrations in this book, including the cover. Nearly thirty drawings were produced on a tight deadline, all while Kersti reassured me that it was "no problem" to send the latest request right away. My thanks to the team at Prometheus Books for their belief in the relevance of the subject matter. Literary agent Gail Ross at the Ross Yoon Agency took on a first-time author, even when we were told a book about the presentation styles of famous men would sell better. Some of the most rewarding training experiences in my career have come through my association with Michael Sheehan Associates. My thanks to Michael and to Joanna Caplan, Deb McGraw, and Sara McLaren for all of our shared adventures.

One of the most enjoyable aspects of writing the book was the opportunity to "interview" really cool women who shared their perspectives from behind and in front of the stage curtain: Suze Orman, Tammy Baldwin, Shirley Bloomfield, Debbie Coffey, Vinca LaFleur, Isabelle Goetz, Jill Alper, Amy Weiss, Celinda Lake, and Ann Lewis.

Many thanks to the friends and colleagues who pointed me in the right direction and who gave pointed, much appreciated feedback: Kathy Beusterien, Allida Black, Matt Burgess, Julie Burton, Amy Conroy, Pearse Edwards, Becky Fleischauer, Amy Greene, Page Harrington, Adrienne Kimmell, Mac McCorkle, Bill Murat, Ruya Norton, Lenny Santiago, Barbara Shaw, Traci Siegel, Joan Wages, and Nord Wennerstrom. And, thanks to Elizabeth Johnson and Erin Williams for assisting with research and data collection.

NOTES

INTRODUCTION

1. Sari Bashi and Maryana Iskander, "Why Legal Education Is Failing Women," *Yale Journal of Law and Feminism* 18 (2006): 389.

CHAPTER 1: THE WELL-SPOKEN WOMAN PERSONA

1. Suze Orman, interview with the author, December 30, 2010.

2. Ann Richards and Peter Knobler, *Straight from the Heart: My Life in Politics and Other Places* (New York: Simon & Schuster, 1989), p. 26.

3. Ibid., p. 62.

4. Leslie Stahl, interview by Walter Scott, *Parade Magazine*, October 10, 2010, http://www.parade.com/celebrity/personality-parade/2010/10/10/lesley-stahl-60-minutes.html.

5. Bart Barnes, "Dorothy I. Height, Founding Matriarch of U.S. Civil Rights Movement, Dies at 98," *Washington Post*, April 21, 2010, http://www.washingtonpost.com/wp-dyn/content/article/2010/04/20/AR2010042001287.html.

6. Holly Gleason, "Dolly Parton: Here I Come Again," *Saturday Evening Post*, October 1, 1989.

7. Dolly Parton, interview by Bob Edwards, *Morning Edition*, NPR, September 24, 2002.

8. Mike Shropshire and Frank Schaefer, *The Thorny Rose of Texas: An Intimate Portrait of Governor Ann Richards* (Secaucus, NJ: Carol Publishing Group, 1994), p. 225.

9. Ann Oldenburg, "Lady Gaga Explains Her VMA Raw Meat Dress," *USA Today*, September 13, 2010, http://www.usatoday.com/communities/entertainment/post/2010/09/lady-gaga-explains-her-vma-raw-meat-dress/1/.

10. Shropshire and Schaefer, *The Thorny Rose of Texas*, p. 213.

11. Richards and Knobler, *Straight from the Heart*, p. 23.

12. Ann Richards, "The Keynote Address," speech, Democratic National

Convention, Atlanta, GA, July 19, 1988, http://www.nytimes.com/1988/07/19/us/text-richards.html.

13. Ann Richards, "Welcoming Remarks," speech, Women's Campaign Research Fund Conference, Austin, TX, September 27, 1991.

14. Liz Carpenter, "How to Write a Speech," *Texas Monthly*, July 2003, http://www.texasmonthly.com/preview/2003-07-01/howto4/.

15. Ann Richards, interview by Morley Safer, *60 Minutes*, CBS, October 27, 1991.

16. Margaret Chase Smith, "Declaration of Conscience," speech, US Senate Floor, Washington, DC, June 1, 1950, http://www.mcslibrary.org/program/library/declaration.htm.

17. Margaret Chase Smith, story produced by Joe Richman and Samara Freemark, *All Things Considered*, NPR, October 16, 2008.

18. Jay Conger and Nancy Rothbard, "Orit Gadiesh: Pride at Bain & Co. (B)," supplement, *Harvard Business Review*, no. 494047-PDF-ENG, September 9, 1993.

19. Molly Ivins, "Remembering Ann Richards," *Truthdig*, September 15, 2006, http://www.truthdig.com/report/item/20060915_molly_ivins_remembering_ann_richards/.

20. Ann Richards, "Commencement Address," speech, Mount Holyoke College, South Hadley, MA, May 28, 1995, http://www.mtholyoke.edu/offices/comm/csj/950605/richards.html.

21. Evan Thomas, "Transition: Ann Richards," *Newsweek*, September 25, 2006, http://www.newsweek.com/2006/09/24/transition-ann-richards-73.html.

CHAPTER 2: THE CONFIDENCE CONUNDRUM

1. Thomas Jefferson, letter to Samuel Kercheval, September 5, 1816, in *The Jeffersonian Cyclopedia*, ed. John P. Foley (New York and London: Funk & Wagnalls, 1900), entry 7284.

2. Tina Fey, "Acceptance Speech for Mark Twain Prize," Kennedy Center, Washington, DC, November 15, 2010, http://video.pbs.org/video/1645426185/.

3. Tina Fey, interview by Walter Scott, *Parade Magazine*, November 28, 2010.

4. Indra Nooyi, "Commencement Address," speech, Columbia University Business School, New York, May 15, 2005.

5. Ann Curry, interview by Jimmy Fallon, *Late Night with Jimmy Fallon*, NBC, May 27, 2010.

6. Sudipto Dey, "I Am Proud to Call US My Home," *Economic Times*, May 20, 2005, http://articles.economictimes.indiatimes.com/2005-05-20/news/2749 4483_1_pepsico-president-indra-k-nooyi-finger/.

7. "Indra Nooyi at the Asia Society (with Vishakha Desai)," YouTube video, 1:10, from Asia Society President's Forum Interview, filmed April 14, 2009, posted by "asiasociety," July 15, 2009, http://www.youtube.com/watch?v=NJW9 IhH2g8w/.

8. Indra Nooyi, "Keynote on Women in Business," speech, Catalyst Awards Conference, New York, April 9, 2008.

9. Patricia Scileppi Kennedy and Gloria Hartmann O'Shields, *We Shall Be Heard: Women Speakers in America, 1828–Present* (Dubuque, IA: Kendall/Hunt, 1993), p. 45.

10. Robin S. Doak. *Dolores Huerta: Labor Leader and Civil Rights Activist* (Minneapolis: Compass Point Books, 2008), p. 86.

11. Michael McCarthy, "Erin Andrews Interview: I Need to Find My Smile Again," *USA Today*, March 29, 2010, http://www.usatoday.com/sports/columnist/mccarthy/2010-03-29-andrews-interview_N.htm.

12. Samantha Smith, letter to Yuri Andropov, December 1982, http://www.samanthasmith.info/samantha's_letter1.htm.

13. Shirley Chisholm, "Presidential Campaign Announcement," speech, Concord Baptist Church, Brooklyn, NY, January 27, 1972.

14. Paul Kane, "Pelosi Makes History and Enemies as an Effective House Speaker," *Washington Post*, May 2, 2010, http://www.washingtonpost.com/wp-dyn/content/article/2010/05/02/AR2010050202769_pf.html.

15. Manuel Foig-Franzia, "Credit Crisis Cassandra," *Washington Post*, May 26, 2009, http://www.washingtonpost.com/wp-dyn/content/article/2009/05/25/AR2009052502108.html.

16. "Brooksley Born Honored with JFK Profile in Courage Award," video, 09:07, NECN.com, May 18, 2009, http://www.necn.com/searchNECN/search/v/39581252/brooksley-born-honored-with-jfk-profile-in-courage-award.htm.

17. "Conversation with Indra Nooyi SOM 80," YouTube video, 37:01, from Yale School of Management Leaders Forum Lecture Series, posted by "Yale-University," May 3, 2010, http://www.youtube.com/watch?v=-msw7mJPF6A/.

CHAPTER 3: THE VOICE

1. Caroline Kennedy, "Tribute to Ted Kennedy," speech, Edward Kennedy Memorial Service, Boston, August 28, 2009.

2. Kathleen Hall Jamieson, *Beyond the Double Bind: Women and Leadership* (New York: Oxford University Press, 1995), p. 81.

3. Andrea Moore Kerr, *Lucy Stone: Speaking Out for Equality* (New Brunswick, NJ: Rutgers University Press, 1992), p 44.

4. David M. Halbfinger, "Gillibrand Gets the Gavel on Big Stage," *New York Times*, July 13, 2009, http://www.nytimes.com/2009/07/14/nyregion/14 gillibrand.html.

5. Michelle Cottle, "Senator Surprise," *Newsweek*, January 23, 2011, http://www.newsweek.com/2011/01/23/senator-surprise.html.

6. Albert Mehrabian, *Silent Messages: Implicit Communication of Emotions and Attitudes* (Belmont, CA: Wadsworth, 1971).

7. Ibid., pp. 56, 50.

8. Mary Beth Rogers, *Barbara Jordan: American Hero* (New York: Bantam Books, 1998), p. 41.

9. Eva Ramos, "Interview with Barbara Jordan, 1992," YouTube video, 6:16, posted by "sawndiddle," April 25, 2008, http://www.youtube.com/watch?v=EBqDprWP8p8/.

10. Mary Beth Rogers, *Barbara Jordan: American Hero* (New York: Bantam Books, 1998), p. 61.

11. Barbara Jordan, "Statement on the Articles of Impeachment," speech, US House Judiciary Committee, Washington, DC, July 25, 1974, http://www.americanrhetoric.com/speeches/barbarajordanjudiciarystatement.htm.

12. Emily Brontë, "High Waving Heather 'neath Stormy Blasts Bending," in *The Complete Poems of Emily Brontë*, ed. Clement King Shorter and William Robertson Nicoll (London: Hodder & Stoughton, 1908).

13. Barbara Jordan, "The Keynote Address," speech, Democratic National Convention, New York, July 12, 1976, http://www.americanrhetoric.com/speeches/barbarajordan1976dnc.html.

CHAPTER 4: STAND UP STRAIGHT

1. Michelle Obama, "International Olympic Committee Address," speech, Copenhagen, Denmark, October 2, 2009.

2. Robin Givhan, "First Lady's Olympian Effort Falls Short: But Her Impassioned Appeal Earns Plaudits," *Washington Post*, October 3, 2009, http://www.washingtonpost.com/wp-dyn/content/article/2009/10/02/AR2009100205214.html.

3. Ed Henry, "Michelle Obama Steals the Show in Copenhagen," CNN.com, October 2, 2009, http://articles.cnn.com/2009-10-02/politics/michelle.obama.olympics_1_ioc-members-michelle-obama-olympic-flame?_s=PM:POLITICS.

4. Pat Summitt and Sally Jenkins, *Reach for the Summit: The Definite Dozen System for Succeeding at Whatever You Do* (New York: Broadway Books, 1998), pp. 12–13.

5. Ibid., p. 68.

6. Ibid., p. 109.

7. Ibid., p. 223.

8. Ibid., p. 24.

CHAPTER 5: MINDING THE MESSAGE

1. Patricia Sellers, "Melinda Gates Goes Public," CNNMoney.com, January 7, 2008, http://money.cnn.com/2008/01/04/news/newsmakers/gates.fortune/index.htm.

2. Tony Hayward, press conference, Deepwater Horizon oil spill, Port Fourchon, LA, May 31, 2010.

3. National Oceanic and Atmospheric Administration, National Climatic Data Center, "Greenhouse Gases: Frequently Asked Questions," updated February 23, 2010, http://www.ncdc.noaa.gov/oa/climate/gases.html.

4. Perry Bacon Jr., "Language Lessons for Democrats, from the Political Brain of Drew Westen," *Washington Post*, May 18, 2010, http://www.washingtonpost.com/wp-dyn/content/article/2010/05/17/AR2010051703823.html.

5. Steve Lohr and Stephanie Strom, "No Longer in Shadow, Melinda Gates Puts Her Mark on Foundation," *New York Times*, July 6, 2006, http://www.nytimes.com/2006/07/06/us/06gates.html.

6. Alan Houston Monroe, *Principles and Types of Speech*, 4th ed. (Chicago: Scott Foresman, 1955), p. 307.

7. Frank I. Luntz, *Words that Work: It's Not What You Say, It's What People Hear* (New York: Hyperion, 2007), p. 167.

8. Dan Morse, "At Komen Race, Breast Cancer Fundraisers Wear the Cause Proudly," *Washington Post*, June 6, 2010, http://www.washingtonpost.com/wp-dyn/content/article/2010/06/05/AR2010060502953.html.

9. Melinda and Bill Gates, "Why We Are Impatient Optimists," speech, Sidney Harman Hall, Washington, DC, October 27, 2009, http://www.gatesfoundation.org/livingproofproject/Pages/impatient-optimists-speech.aspx.

CHAPTER 6: PREPLANNED SPONTANEITY

1. John F. Dickerson and Nancy Gibbs, "Campaign 2000: Elizabeth Unplugged," *Time*, May 17, 1999, http://www.time.com/time/magazine/article/0,9171,990969,00.html.

2. Robert J. Dole and Elizabeth Hanford Dole (with Richard Norton Smith and Kerry Tymchuk), *Unlimited Partners: Our American Story* (New York: Simon & Schuster, 1996), p. 91.

3. Ibid., p. 51.

4. Ibid., p. 90.

5. Kerry A. Goodenow, "Elizabeth H. Dole," *Harvard Crimson*, May 27, 2010, http://www.thecrimson.com/article/2010/5/27/dole-harvard-government/.

6. Molly Meijer Wertheimer and Nichola D. Gutgold, *Elizabeth Hanford Dole: Speaking from the Heart* (Westport, CT: Praeger, 2004), p. 20.

7. David A. Peoples, *Presentation Plus: David Peoples' Proven Techniques*, 2nd ed. (New York John Wiley and Sons, 1992), p. 124.

8. Elisabeth Bumiller, "We Have Met the Enemy and He Is PowerPoint," *New York Times*, April 26, 2010, http://www.nytimes.com/2010/04/27/world/27powerpoint.html.

9. Ibid.

CHAPTER 7: WELL-WRITTEN IS WELL-SPOKEN

1. "Dr. Angelou Honored by Oprah Winfrey and Denzel Washington," 7:08, filmed 1992, video 13 of 16, http://mayaangelou.com/media/video/.

2. Academy of Achievment, "Maya Angelou Interview," January 22, 1997, page 5 of 9, http://www.achievement.org/autodoc/page/ang0int-5/.

3. Bob Minzesheimer, "Maya Angelou Celebrates Her 80 Years of Pain and Joy," *USA Today*, March 26, 2008, http://www.usatoday.com/life/books/news/2008-03-26-maya-angelou_N.htm.

4. Alicia Keys, "Alicia Keys Inducts Prince," speech, Rock and Roll Hall of Fame Museum, Cleveland, OH, March 15, 2004, http://rockhall.com/inductees/prince/transcript/alicia-keys-inducts-prince/.

5. Maya Angelou, "Remarks at the Funeral Service for Coretta Scott King," speech, New Birth Missionary Baptist Church, Lithonia, GA, February 7, 2006, http://www.americanrhetoric.com/speeches/mayaangeloueulogyforcorettaking.htm.

6. "Caroline Phillips: Hurdy-Gurdy for Beginners," TED video, 5:41, from TEDGlobal 2010 conference, filmed July 2010, posted September 2010, http://www.ted.com/talks/lang/eng/caroline_phillips_hurdy_gurdy_for_beginners.html.

7. "Robin Chase on Zipcar and Her Next Big Idea," TED video, 13:43, from TED 2007 conference, filmed March 2007, posted January 2008, http://www.ted.com/talks/robin_chase_on_zipcar_and_her_next_big_idea.html.

8. Laura Bush, "Remarks at White House Correspondents Dinner," speech, Washington, DC, April 30, 2005.

9. "Maya Angelou (2 of 5)," YouTube video, 8:23, from interview by Armstrong Williams from *On Point*, posted by "arightside," September 2, 2008, http://www.youtube.com/watch?v=yXKxZpRytrM&feature=related/.

10. "Dr. Angelou Receives a 2008 Gracie Grand Award," 5:42, filmed May 28, 2008, video 8 of 16, http://mayaangelou.com/media/video/.

11. "Sylvia Earle's TED Prize Wish to Protect Our Oceans," TED video, 18:16, from TED2009 conference, filmed February 2009, posted February 2009, http://www.ted.com/talks/sylvia_earle_s_ted_prize_wish_to_protect_our_oceans.html.

12. Mary McLeod Bethune, "The Sacrifices and Achievements of African American Women over the Past 100 Years," speech, Chicago Women's Federation, Chicago, June 1933.

13. Sarah Brady, "Gun Violence in America," speech, Democratic National Convention, Chicago, August 26, 1996.

14. Susan B. Anthony, "The Constitutional Argument," speech, Monroe and Ontario Counties, NY, June 1873, http://gos.sbc.edu/a/anthony.html.

15. Barbara Mikulski, "Floor Speech on Lily Ledbetter," Washington, DC, June 18, 2008, http://democrats.senate.gov/checklistforchange/images/Floor%20Transcript/Senator%20Barbara%20Mikulski.pdf.

16. Carly Fiorina, "Commencement Address," speech, North Carolina Agricultural and Technical State University, Greensboro, NC, May 7, 2005, http://www.businessweek.com/technology/content/may2005/tc2005059_6954.htm.

17. Mary Fisher, "A Whisper of AIDS," speech, Republican National Convention, Houston, TX, August 19, 1992, http://www.americanrhetoric.com/speeches/maryfisher1992rnc.html.

18. Carrie Chapman Catt, "Speech before Congress," Washington, DC, January 1, 1917, http://womenshistory.about.com/od/cattcarriec/a/cong_1917_speec.htm.

19. J. K. Rowling, "The Fringe Benefits of Failure and the Importance of Imagination," speech, Harvard University, Cambridge, MA, June 5, 2008, http://harvardmagazine.com/2008/06/the-fringe-benefits-failure-the-importance-imagination/.

20. "Speech by Meryl Streep Given at National Women's History Museum's 'Our Nation's Daughters' Gala," Washington, DC, September 21, 2010, http://www.nwhm.org/html/about/press/featured_press/MerylsSpeech.pdf.

21. Academy of Achievement, "Maya Angelou Interview," January 22, 1997, page 2 of 9, http://www.achievement.org/autodoc/page/ang0int-2.

CHAPTER 8: CONQUERING THE CAMERA

1. Suze Orman, interview with the author, December 30, 2010.

2. Isabelle Goetz (owner Isabelle Okyo Salon), in discussion with the author, November 3, 2010.

CHAPTER 9: THE ART OF DIPLOMACY

1. Tammy Baldwin, interview with the author, July 12, 2010.

2. Madeleine Albright, interview by Oprah Winfrey, *The Oprah Winfrey Show*, January 2001.

3. Madeleine Albright, interview by Ed Bradley, "Madam Secretary," *60 Minutes*, CBS, February 9, 1997.

4. Madeleine Albright, *Madam Secretary: A Memoir* (New York: Hyperion, 2003), p. 69.

5. James Bennet, "Standoff with Iraq: The White House; Bad Vibes from the Heartland Launch Fleet of Finger Pointers," *New York Times*, February 19, 1998, http://www.nytimes.com/1998/02/19/world/standoff-with-iraq-white-house-bad-vibes-heartland-launch-fleet-finger-pointers.html.

6. Roxanne Rivera, "Building Towers, Razing Sexism," *New York Times*, September 19, 2010, http://www.nytimes.com/2010/09/19/jobs/19pre.html.

7. Stephanie Schriock, "EMILY'S List Majority Council Meeting," speech, Washington, DC, April 29, 2010.

8. Dana Milbank, "Nancy Pelosi the Liberal House Speaker Is Heckled by Liberals," *Washington Post*, June 9, 2010, http://www.washingtonpost.com/wp-dyn/content/article/2010/06/08/AR2010060804327.html?hpid=opinionsbox1/.

9. "Sen. Kay Hagan Blasted by Outraged Parent," YouTube video, 2:00, from interview by Bill O'Neil, WXII 12 News, Kernersville, NC, filmed August 18, 2010, posted by "WXIItv," August 18, 2010, http://www.youtube.com/watch?v=NW5PE4OxW0o/.

10. Albright, *Madam Secretary*, p. 205.

11. Ibid., p. 240.

12. Madeleine Albright, interview by Ed Bradley.

13. Steven Harmon, "Fallout from Whitman Voting Controversy May Be Lasting," *Oakland Tribune*, September 30, 2009.

14. "Elizabeth Edwards on Facing Life's Adversities," interview by Michele Norris, NPR, May 7, 2009, http://www.npr.org/templates/story/story.php?storyId=103895496/.

15. Roxanne Roberts and Amy Argetsinger, "Meghan McCain Plays Hooky from Book Tour, Gets Caught via Her Own Tweet," *Washington Post*, September 24, 2010, http://voices.washingtonpost.com/reliable-source/2010/09/rs_meghan_mccain.html.

16. Madeleine Albright with Elaine Shocas, Vivienne Becker, and Bill Woodward, *Read My Pins: Stories from a Diplomat's Jewel Box* (New York: HarperCollins, 2009), p. 20.

CHAPTER 10: THE WELL-SPOKEN SISTERHOOD IN FLATTERING PANTS

1. Ana Brashares, *The Sisterhood of the Traveling Pants* (New York: Dell Laurel-Leaf, 2005).

2. Liz Halloran, "Framing Health Care Debate as Battle of Sexes," NPR, October 22, 2009, http://www.npr.org/templates/story/story.php?storyId =114011389/.

3. Hillary Rodham Clinton, "Remarks to the United Nations Fourth World Conference on Women Plenary Session," speech, Beijing, China, September 5, 1995, http://clinton3.nara.gov/WH/EOP/First_Lady/html/China/plenary .html.

4. Ibid.

5. Hillary Rodham Clinton, *Living History* (New York: Simon & Schuster, 2003), p. 303.

6. Ibid., p. 305.

7. Ibid., p. 306.

8. Hillary Rodham Clinton, "Remarks Upon Receipt of the Roosevelt Institute's Four Freedoms Award at the Roosevelt Institute's Four Freedoms Medals Gala Dinner," speech, Roosevelt Institute's Four Freedoms Medals Gala Dinner, New York, September 11, 2009, http://www.state.gov/secretary/rm/2009a/ 09/129164.htm.

9. Barack Obama, Democratic Presidential Primary Debate, Manchester, NH, January 5, 2008, http://www.presidency.ucsb.edu/ws/index.php?pid=76224 #axzz1Oqcd5H67/.

10. Maria Parra-Sandoval, question to Hillary Clinton, Presidential Primary Debate, November 15, 2007, http://www.presidency.ucsb.edu/ws/index.php ?pid=76041#axzz1Oqcd5H67/.

11. Ann Richards and Peter Knobler, *Straight from the Heart: My Life in Politics and Other Places* (New York: Simon & Schuster, 1989), p. 178.

12. Ibid.

13. Rachel E. Stassen-Berger, "Margaret Anderson Kelliher: From Farm to Summit Avenue?" *Star-Tribune*, April 18, 2010, http://www.startribune.com/ politics/91274434.html.

14. Sandra Day O'Connor, interview by David Letterman, *Late Show*, CBS, June 23, 2009.

15. Joan Biskupic, "Ginsburg 'Lonely' without O'Connor," *USA Today*,

January 25, 2007, http://www.usatoday.com/news/washington/2007-01-25 -ginsburg-court_x.htm.

16. American Psychological Association, "Sexualization of Girls" (Washington, DC: American Psychological Association, 2007). Available at http:// www.apa .org/pi/women/programs/girls/report.aspx.

17. Geena Davis, "Introduction to the Sexualization Protest: Action, Resistance, Knowledge (SPARK) Summit," video, Hunter College, New York, October 22, 2010, http://www.sparksummit.com/2010/12/01/in-case-you-missed-the -opening-ceremonies/.

18. Girl Scouts of the United States of America, "Body Image," 2011, http://www.girlscouts.org/research/facts_findings/body_image.asp.

19. Pat Summitt and Sally Jenkins, *Reach for the Summit: The Definite Dozen System for Succeeding at Whatever You Do* (New York: Broadway Books, 1998), p. 31.

20. Jill Alper, interview by the author, November 18, 2010.

21. Dana Perino, "Panel Discussion on the Media," speech, NoLimits.org conference, Washington, DC, November 6, 2009.

22. Vinca LaFleur, interview with the author, November 3, 2010.

23. Wilma Mankiller, "Rebuilding the Cherokee Nation," speech, Sweet Briar College, VA, April 2, 1993, http://gos.sbc.edu/m/mankiller.html.

24. A. J. Jacobs, "The Real Tina Fey," *Esquire*, April 13, 2010, http:// www.esquire.com/features/tina-fey-funny-quotes-040710/.

25. Ann Lewis, interview with the author, December 8, 2010.

26. Celinda Lake, interview with the author, December 21, 2010.

27. Lynn Sherr, *Failure Is Impossible: Susan B. Anthony in Her Own Words* (New York: Times Books, 1995), p. 132.

28. Anna Howard Shaw with Elizabeth Jordan, *The Story of a Pioneer* (New York: Harper & Brothers, 1915), p. 240. Published 2008 by Project Gutenberg, ebook #354, available at http://www.gutenberg.org/ebooks/354/.

29. Molly Meijer Wertheimer and Nichola D. Gutgold, *Elizabeth Hanford Dole: Speaking from the Heart* (Westport, CT: Praeger, 2004), p. 62.

30. Shirley Bloomfield, interview with the author, December 23, 2010.

31. Hillary Clinton, "Remarks on Student Activism at Wellesley College," speech, Wellesley College, Wellesley, MA, November 1, 2007, http://www .presidency.ucsb.edu/ws/index.php?pid=77072#axzz1Oqcd5H67/.

32. Hillary Clinton, "Address at the Democratic National Convention in Denver: 'United We Can Build a Better America,'" speech, Denver, CO, August 26, 2008, http://www.presidency.ucsb.edu/ws/index.php?pid=78527#axzz1Oqcd5H67/.

33. Clinton, "Remarks on Student Activism at Wellesley College."

34. Hillary Clinton, "Women's Progress Is Human Progress," speech, United Nations, New York, March 12, 2010.

35. Ibid.

EPILOGUE

1. "Jane Goodall: Reason for Hope," YouTube video, 59:23, from speech at Joan B. Croc Institute for Peace and Justice, University of San Diego, filmed April 17, 2008, posted by "UCtelevision, May 9, 2008, http://www.youtube.com/watch?v=s3FEWKdIvcA/.

2. Michael Scherer, "The New Sheriffs of Wall Street," *Time*, May 13, 2010, http://www.time.com/time/nation/article/0,8599,1988953,00.html.

3. Elizabeth Warren, interview by Jon Stewart, *The Daily Show*, January 26, 2010, http://www.thedailyshow.com/watch/tue-january-26-2010/elizabeth-warren/.

4. Daniel McGinn, "The Debt Crusader," *Newsweek*, April 20, 2009, http://www.newsweek.com/2009/04/10/the-debt-crusader.html.

5. Ibid.

6. Eleanor Roosevelt, *You Learn by Living: Eleven Keys for a More Fulfilling Life* (Louisville, KY: Westminster John Knox Press, 1960), p. 38.

7. Blanche Wiesen Cook, *Eleanor Roosevelt: Volume One, 1884–1933* (New York: Viking, 1992), p. 340.

8. Roosevelt, *You Learn by Living*, p. 41

9. Eleanor Roosevelt (attributed), BrainyQuote, http://www.brainyquote.com/quotes/authors/e/eleanor_roosevelt_2.html.

10. Wiesen Cook, *Eleanor Roosevelt Volume One*, p. 340.

11. Sheryl Sandberg, "It's All about People," speech, Interactive Advertising Bureau (IAB) MIXX Conference, October 15, 2010.

12. Katie Spotz, interview by Diane Sawyer, *ABC News*, March 18, 2010.

APPENDIX 3: FREQUENTLY ASKED QUESTIONS

1. Condoleezza Rice, "Remarks at the Unveiling of the Portrait of Madeleine Albright," speech, Washington, DC, April 14, 2008.

INDEX

Pages in **bold** indicate charts, tables, and boxed materials.